THERE IS NO DEATH

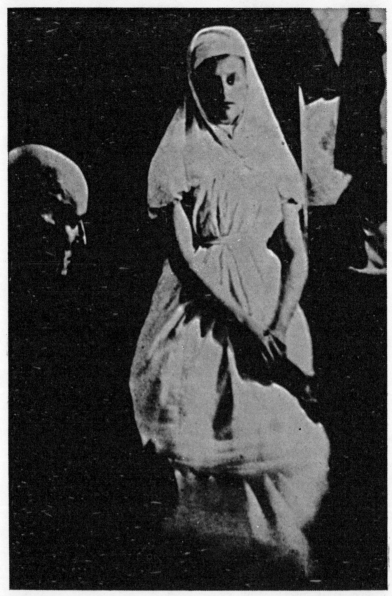

The most famous materialization of all time—the phantom form of 'Katie King', photographed by Sir William Crookes while investigating the mediumship of Florence Cook.

THERE IS NO DEATH

My Eyewitness Experiences
With the Great Mediums

By

FLORENCE MARRYAT

CAUSEWAY BOOKS
NEW YORK, NEW YORK 10016

53626

Published by Causeway Books

95 Madison Avenue New York, N.Y. 10016

Copyright © 1973 by Causeway Books

Library of Congress Catalog Card No.: 72-97381

ISBN: 0-88356-011-9

Printed in the United States of America

INTRODUCTION TO THE CAUSEWAY EDITION

Death is not the end!

That is the message of this remarkable book, which describes the incredible phenomena of Spiritualism in its golden age of the nineteenth century. Written over eighty years ago, it is still as fresh and wonderful as when it first appeared.

The woman who wrote this sensational book not only knew all the great mediums of her time, but was also gifted with rare psychic powers herself. She relates how she materialized the spirit of a murdered man in a blaze of light.

She personally attended the séances of Florence Cook, the marvelous medium who was investigated by the famous scientist Sir William Crookes. She knew Mrs. Guppy Volckman, and here tells how this medium, one of the heaviest women in London, was levitated over the heads of the sitters at a séance. Here are personal experiences with Lottie Fowler (who was consulted by royal physicians at the time of a dangerous illness of the Prince of Wales, later King Edward VII), with the great William Eglinton, Mrs. Eva Hatch, Bessie Fitzgerald, and many other renowned sensitives.

Florence Marryat (1837?–1899) was also one of the great women novelists of the nineteenth century. She was the youngest daughter of distinguished author Frederick Marryat who wrote the immortal sea stories *Peter Simple, Mr. Midshipman Easy,* and *Masterman Ready.* Florence Marryat was often referred to as "Mrs. Ross Church", following her first marriage at the age of sixteen to Captain Ross Church of the Madras Staff Corps. They were divorced after 47 years, and she then married Colonel Francis Lean of the Royal Marines.

Modern enthusiasts for Women's Liberation might like to reflect on the achievements of this emancipated woman novelist nearly a hundred years before the permissive society. Florence Marryat raised eight children and wrote books in her spare time. She edited the journal *London Society,* she collaborated in writing stage plays, and toured the provinces, acting with

her own company. She travelled throughout England and the
U.S. on lecture tours. She wrote over a hundred short stories,
numerous essays, poems, and recitations. She also published
nearly eighty novels, many of which were immensely popular.

She wrote three books on Spiritualism, of which the present
is the most famous; it was reprinted many times over the years.

It is full of stories which would be incredible were they not
from a respected and reputable writer, describing first-hand
experiences. She was a Catholic, and after her first introduction
to Spiritualism could not accept the opposition of the church
to the subject. She insisted on permission to attend séances. She
devoted herself to publicising the cause of Spiritualism.

Her book first appeared in 1891. It caused an instant sensation, and years afterwards she continued to receive many letters
every day, requesting more information or advice. Hundreds
of educated people—men of letters, scientists, and clergymen—
were brought to the study of Spiritualism by this courageous
book.

The message of the book is that individuality survives death,
which is only the beginning of a further chapter in human
evolution. The authoress claimed personal experience of the
reality of individual survival, and here narrates first-hand
accounts of the materialization of spirit forms, as well as convincing messages from individuals who had passed over.

The book is absolutely sincere. It has been a great consolation to thousands of readers who needed reassurance that death
is not the end, and that one's loved ones continue to evolve in
a mysterious spiritual existence independent of the physical
body. It offers a more convincing view of the afterlife than the
old-fashioned ideas of instant Heaven or Hell.

The question of survival and evolution of the soul is one of
the oldest questions of mankind, and an essential feature of
the religions of the world. Even though modern spiritualist
mediums are perhaps not so sensational in their evidences as

during the great days of the nineteenth century, there is evidence in plenty for those who are unprejudiced seekers. The Spiritualist movement has continued to grow and spread throughout the world, and is striving to perfect the sensitivity of its mediums and the quality of their evidence.

This book has always been a classic of its kind, and the present reissue after many years will raise fascinating and absorbing topics for a new generation of readers unfamiliar with the great past history of Spiritualism. It should bring new hope and inspiration in a materialistic world.

MICHAEL LORD

There is
nothing to fear
in death, death is as Natural as Life itself..embrace it

CONTENTS

CAUSEWAY: A bridge from here to there

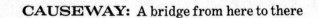

THERE IS NO DEATH

CHAPTER I

FAMILY GHOSTS

IT has been strongly impressed upon me for some years past to write an account of the wonderful experiences I have passed through in my investigation of the science of Spiritualism. In doing so I intend to confine myself to recording facts. I will describe the scenes I have witnessed with my own eyes, and repeat the words I have heard with my own ears, leaving the deduction to be drawn from them wholly to my readers. I have no ambition to start a theory nor to promulgate a doctrine; above all things I have no desire to provoke an argument. I have had more than enough of arguments, philosophical, scientific, religious, and purely aggressive, to last a lifetime; and were I called upon for my definition of the rest promised to the weary, I should reply—a place where every man may hold his own opinion, and no one is permitted to dispute it.

But though I am about to record a great many incidents that are so marvellous as to be almost incredible, I do not expect to be disbelieved, except by such as are capable of deception themselves. They—conscious of their own infirmity—invariably believe that other people must be telling lies. Byron wrote, "He is a fool who denies that which he cannot disprove"; and though Carlyle gives us the comforting assurance that the population of Great Britain consists "chiefly of fools", I pin my faith upon receiving credence from the few who are not so.

Why should I be disbelieved? When the late Lady Brassey published the "Cruise of the *Sunbeam*," and Sir Samuel and

Lady Baker related their experiences in Central Africa, and Livingstone wrote his account of the wonders he met with whilst engaged in the investigation of the source of the Nile, and Henry Stanley followed up the story and added thereto, did they anticipate the public turning up its nose at their narrations, and declaring it did not believe a word they had written? Yet their readers had to accept the fact they offered for credence, on their authority alone. Very few of them had even *heard* of the places described before; scarcely one in a thousand could, either from personal experience or acquired knowledge, attest the truth of the description. What was there—for the benefit of the general public—to *prove* that the *Sunbeam* had sailed round the world, or that Sir Samuel Baker had met with the rare beasts, birds, and flowers he wrote of, or that Livingstone and Stanley met and spoke with those curious, unknown tribes that never saw white men till they set eyes on them? Yet had any one of those writers affirmed that in his wanderings he had encountered a gold field of undoubted excellence, thousands of fortune-seekers would have left their native land on his word alone, and rushed to secure some of the glittering treasure.

Why? Because the authors of those books were persons well known in society, who had a reputation for veracity to maintain, and who would have been quickly found out had they dared to deceive. I claim the same grounds for obtaining belief. I have a well-known name and a public reputation, a tolerable brain, and two sharp eyes. What I have witnessed, others, with equal assiduity and perseverance, may witness for themselves. It would demand a voyage round the world to see all that the owners of the *Sunbeam* saw. It would demand time and trouble and money to see what I have seen, and to some people, perhaps, it would not be worth the outlay. But if I have journeyed into the Debateable Land (which so few really believe in, and most are terribly afraid of), and come forward now to tell what I have seen there, the world has no more right to disbelieve me than it had to disbelieve Lady Brassey. Because the general public has not penetrated Central Africa is no reason that Livingstone did not do so; because the general public has not seen (and does not care to see) what I have seen, is no argument against the truth of what I write. To those who *do* believe in the possibility of communion with disembodied spirits, my story will be interesting perhaps, on account of its dealing throughout in a remarkable degree with the vexed question of identity and recognition. To the materialistic portion of creation who may credit me with not being a bigger fool than the remainder of the thirty-eight millions of Great Britain, it may prove a new source of speculation and research. And for those of my fellow-creatures who possess no curiosity, nor imagination, nor desire to prove for themselves what they cannot accept on the testimony of others, I never had, and never shall have, anything in common. They are the sort of people who ask you with a pleasing smile if Irving wrote "The Charge of the Light Brigade," and say they like Byron's "Sardanapalus" very well, but it is not so funny as "Our Boys."

Now, before going to work in right earnest, I do not think it is generally known that my father, the late Captain Marryat, was not only a believer in ghosts, but himself a ghost-seer. I am delighted to be able to record this fact as an introduction to my own experiences. Perhaps the ease with which such manifestations have come to me is a gift which I inherit from him, anyway I am glad he shared the belief and the power of spiritual sight with me. If there were no other reason to make me bold to repeat what I have witnessed, the circumstance would give me courage. My father was not like his intimate friends, Charles Dickens, Lord Lytton, and many other men of genius, highly strung, nervous, and imaginative. I do not believe my father had any "nerves," and I think he had very little imagination. Almost all his works are founded on his personal experiences.

His *forte* lay in a humorous description of what he had seen. He possessed a marvellous power of putting his recollections into graphic and forcible language, and the very reason that his books are almost as popular to-day as when they were written, is because they are true histories of their time. There is scarcely a line of fiction in them. His body was as powerful and muscular as his brain. His courage was indomitable—his moral courage as well as his physical (as many people remember to their cost to this day), and his hardness of belief on many subjects is no secret. What I am about to relate therefore did not happen to some excitable, nervous, sickly sentimentalist, and I repeat that I am proud to have inherited his constitutional tendencies, and quite willing to stand judgment after him.

I have heard that my father had a number of stories to relate of supernatural (as they are usually termed) incidents that had occurred to him, but I will content myself with relating such as were proved to be (at the least) very remarkable coincidences. In my work, "The Life and Letters of Captain Marryat," I relate an anecdote of him that was entered in his private "log," and found amongst his papers. He had a younger brother, Samuel, to whom he was very much attached, and who died unexpectedly in England whilst my father, in command of H.M.S. *Larne*, was engaged in the first Burmese war. His men broke out with scurvy and he was ordered to take his vessel over to Pulu Pinang for a few weeks in order to get the sailors fresh fruit and vegetables. As my father was lying in his berth one night, anchored off the island, with the brilliant tropical moonlight making everything as bright as day, he saw the door of his cabin open, and his brother Samuel entered and walked quietly up to his side. He looked just the same as when they had parted, and uttered in a perfectly distinct voice, "Fred! I have come to tell you that I am dead." When the figure entered the cabin my father jumped up in his berth, thinking it was some one coming to rob him, and when he saw who it was and heard it speak, he leaped out of bed with the intention of detaining it, but it was gone. So vivid was the impression made upon him by the apparition that he drew out his log at once and wrote down all particulars concerning it, with the hour and day of its appearance. On reaching England after the war was over, the first dispatches put into his hand were to announce the death of his brother, who had passed away at the very hour when he had seen him in the cabin.

But the story that interests me most is one of an incident which occurred to my father during my lifetime, and which we have always called "The Brown Lady of Rainham." I am aware that this narrative has reached the public through other sources, and I have made it the foundation of a Christmas story myself. But it is too well authenticated to be omitted here. The last fifteen years of my father's life were passed on his own estate of Langham, in Norfolk, and amongst his county friends were Sir Charles and Lady Townshend of Rainham Hall. At the time I speak of, the title and property had lately changed hands, and the new baronet had re-papered, painted, and furnished the Hall throughout, and come down with his wife and a large party of friends to take possession. But to their annoyance, soon after their arrival, rumours arose that the house was haunted, and their guests began, one and all (like those in the parable), to make excuses to go home again. Sir Charles and Lady Townshend might have sung, "Friend after friend departs," with due effect, but it would have had none on the general exodus that took place from Rainham. And it was all on account of a Brown Lady, whose portrait hung in one of the bedrooms, and in which she was represented as wearing a brown satin dress with yellow trimmings, and a ruff around her throat—a very harmless, innocent-looking young woman. But they all declared they had seen her walking about the house—some in the corridor, some in their bedrooms, others in the lower premises, and

neither guests nor servants would remain in the Hall. The
baronet was naturally very much annoyed about it, and
confided his trouble to my father, and my father was indig-
nant at the trick he believed had been played upon him. There
was a great deal of smuggling and poaching in Norfolk at
that period, as he knew well, being a magistrate of the
county, and he felt sure that some of these depredators were
trying to frighten the Townshends away from the Hall again.
The last baronet had been a solitary sort of being, and lead a
retired life, and my father imagined some of the tenantry had
their own reasons for not liking the introduction of revelries
and "high jinks" at Rainham. So he asked his friends to let
him stay with them and sleep in the haunted chamber, and
he felt sure he could rid them of the nuisance. They accepted
his offer, and he took possession of the room in which the
portrait of the apparition hung, and in which she had been
often seen, and slept each night with a loaded revolver under
his pillow. For two days, however, he saw nothing, and the
third was to be the limit of his stay. On the third night,
however, two young men (nephews of the baronet) knocked
at his door as he was undressing to go to bed, and asked him
to step over to their room (which was at the other end of the
corridor), and give them his opinion on a new gun just arrived from London. My father was in his shirt and trousers,
but as the hour was late, and everybody had retired to rest
except themselves, he prepared to accompany them as he was.
As they were leaving the room, he caught up his revolver, "in
case we meet the Brown Lady," he said, laughing. When the
inspection of the gun was over, the young men in the same
spirit declared they would accompany my father back again,
"in case you meet the Brown Lady," they repeated, laughing
also. The three gentlemen therefore returned in company.

The corridor was long and dark, for the lights had been
extinguished, but as they reached the middle of it, they saw
the glimmer of a lamp coming towards them from the other

end. "One of the ladies going to visit the nurseries," whispered the young Townshends to my father Now the bedroom doors in that corridor faced each other, and each room had a double door with a space between, as is the case in many old-fashioned country houses. My father (as I have said) was in a shirt and trousers only, and his native modesty made him feel uncomfortable, so he slipped within one of the *outer* doors (his friends following his example), in order to conceal himself until the lady should have passed by. I have heard him describe how he watched her approaching nearer and nearer, through the chink of the door, until, as she was close enough for him to distinguish the colours and style of her costume, he recognized the figure as the facsimile of the portrait of "The Brown Lady." He had his finger on the trigger of his revolver, and was about to demand it to stop and give the reason for its presence there, when the figure halted of its own accord before the door behind which he stood, and holding the lighted lamp she carried to her features, grinned in a malicious and diabolical manner at him. This act so infuriated my father, who was anything but lamb-like in disposition, that he sprang into the corridor with a bound, and discharged the revolver right in her face. The figure instantly disappeared—the figure at which for the space of several minutes *three* men had been looking together—and the bullet passed through the outer door of the room on the opposite side of the corridor, and lodged in the panel of the inner one. My father never attempted again to interfere with "The Brown Lady of Rainham," and I have heard that she haunts the premises to this day. That she did so at that time, however, there is no shadow of doubt.

Before the question of Spiritualism, however, arose in modern times, I had had my own little private experiences on the subject. From an early age I was accustomed to see, and to be very much alarmed at seeing, certain forms that appeared to me at night. One in particular, I remember, was that of a very short or deformed old woman, who was very constant to me. She used to stand on tiptoe to look at me as I lay in bed, and however dark the room might be, I could always see every article in it, as if illuminated, whilst she remained there.

I was in the habit of communicating these visions to my mother and sisters (my father had passed from us by that time), and always got well ridiculed for my pains. "Another of Flo's optical illusions," they would cry, until I really came to think that the appearances I saw were due to some defect in my eye-sight. I have heard my first husband say, that when he married me he thought he should never rest for an entire night in his bed, so often did I wake him with the description of some man or woman I had seen in the room. I recall these figures distinctly. They were always dressed in white, from which circumstance I imagined that they were natives who had stolen in to rob us, until, from repeated observation, I discovered they only formed part of another and more enlarged series of my "optical illusions." All this time I was very much afraid of seeing what I termed "ghosts." No love of occult science led me to investigate the cause of my alarm. I only wished never to see the "illusions" again, and was too frightened to remain by myself lest they should appear to me.

When I had been married for about two years, the head-quarters of my husband's regiment, the 12th Madras Native Infantry, was ordered to Rangoon, whilst the left wing, commanded by a Major Cooper, was sent to assist in the bombardment of Canton. Major Cooper had only been married a short time, and by rights his wife had no claim to sail with the head-quarters for Burmah, but as she had no friends in Madras, and was moreover expecting her confine-ment, our colonel permitted her to do so, and she accompan-ied us to Rangoon, settling herself in a house not far from our own. One morning, early in July, I was startled by receiving a hurried scrawl from her, containing only these words,

"Come! come! come!" I set off at once, thinking she had been taken ill, but on my arrival I found Mrs. Cooper sitting up in bed with only her usual servants about her. 'What is the matter?" I exclaimed. "Mark is dead," she answered me; "he sat in that chair" (pointing to one by the bedside) "all last night. I noticed every detail of his face and figure. He was in undress, and he never raised his eyes, but sat with the peak of his forage cap pulled down over his face. But I could see the back of his head and his hair, and I know it was he. I spoke to him but he did not answer me, and I am *sure* he is dead."

Naturally, I imagined this vision to have been dictated solely by fear and the state of her health. I laughed at her for a simpleton, and told her it was nothing but fancy, and reminded her that by the last accounts received from the seat of war, Major Cooper was perfectly well and anticipating a speedy reunion with her. Laugh as I would, however, I could not laugh her out of her belief, and seeing how low-spirited she was, I offered to pass the night with her. It was a very nice night indeed. As soon as ever we had retired to bed, although a lamp burned in the room, Mrs. Cooper declared that her husband was sitting in the same chair as the night before, and accused me of deception when I declared that I saw nothing at all. I sat up in bed and strained my eyes, but I could discern nothing but an empty arm-chair, and told her so. She persisted that Major Cooper sat there, and described his personal appearance and actions. I got out of bed and sat in the chair, when she cried out, "Don't, don't! *You are sitting right on him!*" It was evident that the apparition was as real to her as if it had been flesh and blood. I jumped up again fast enough, not feeling very comfortable myself, and lay by her side for the remainder of the night, listening to her asseverations that Major Cooper was either dying or dead. She would not part with me, and on the third night I had to endure the same ordeal as on the second. After the third night the apparition ceased to appear to her, and I was permitted to return home. But before I did so, Mrs. Cooper showed me her pocket-book, in which she had written down against the 8th, 9th, and 10th of July this sentence: "Mark sat by my bedside all night."

The time passed on, and no bad news arrived from China, but the mails had been intercepted and postal communication suspended. Occasionally, however, we received letters by a sailing vessel. At last came September, and on the third of that month Mrs. Cooper's baby was born and died. She was naturally in great distress about it, and I was doubly horrified when I was called from her bedside to receive the news of her husband's death, which had taken place from a sudden attack of fever at Macao. We did not intend to let Mrs. Cooper hear of this until she was convalescent, but as soon as I re-entered her room, she broached the subject.

"Are there any letters from China?" she asked. (Now this question was remarkable in itself, because the mails having been cut off, there was no particular date when letters might be expected to arrive from the seat of war.) Fearing she would insist upon hearing the news, I temporized and answered her, "We have received none." "But there is a letter for me," she continued; "a letter with the intelligence of Mark's death. It is useless denying it. I know he is dead. He died on the 10th of July." And on reference to the official memorandum, this was found to be true. Major Cooper had been taken ill on the first day he had appeared to his wife, and died on the third. And this incident was the more remarkable, because they were neither of them young nor sentimental people, neither had they lived long enough together to form any very strong sympathy or accord between them. But as I have related it, so it occurred.

CHAPTER II

MY FIRST SÉANCE

I HAD returned from India and spent several years in England before the subject of Modern Spiritualism was brought under my immediate notice. Cursorily I had heard it mentioned by some people as a dreadfully wicked thing, diabolical to the last degree, by others as a most amusing pastime for evening parties, or when one wanted to get some "fun out of the table." But neither description charmed me, nor tempted me to pursue the occupation. I had already lost too many friends. Spiritualism (so it seemed to me) must either be humbug or a very solemn thing, and I neither wished to trifle with it or to be trifled with by it. And after twenty years' continued experience I hold the same opinion. I have proved Spiritualism *not* to be humbug, therefore I regard it in a sacred light. For, *from whatever cause* it may proceed, it opens a vast area for thought to any speculative mind, and it is a matter of constant surprise to me to see the indifference with which the world regards it. That it *exists* is an undeniable fact. Men of science have acknowledged it, and the churches cannot deny it. The only question appears to be, "*What* is it, and *whence* does the power proceed?" If (as many clever people assert) from ourselves, then must these bodies and minds of ours possess faculties hitherto undreamed of, and which we have allowed to lie culpably fallow. If our bodies contain magnetic forces sufficient to raise substantial and apparently living forms from the bare earth, which our eyes are clairvoyant enough to see, and which can articulate words which our ears are clairaudient enough to hear—if, in addition to this, our minds can read each other's inmost thoughts, can see what is passing at a distance, and foretell what will happen in the future, then are our human powers greater than we have ever imagined, and we ought to do a great deal more with them than we do. And even regarding Spiritualism from *that* point of view, I cannot understand the lack of interest displayed in the discovery, to turn these marvellous powers of the human mind to greater account.

To discuss it, however, from the usual meaning given to the word, namely as a means of communication with the departed, leaves me as puzzled as before. All Christians acknowledge they have spirits independent of their bodies, and that when their bodies die, their spirits will continue to live on. Wherein, then, lies the terror of the idea that these liberated spirits will have the privilege of roaming the universe as they will? And if they argue the *impossibility* of their return, they deny the records which form the only basis of their religion. No greater proof can be brought forward of the truth of Spiritualism than the truth of the Bible, which teems and bristles with accounts of it from beginning to end.

Putting the churches and the Bible, however, on one side, the History of Nations proves it to be possible. There is not a people on the face of the globe that has not its (so-called) superstitions, nor a family hardly, which has not experienced some proofs of spiritual communion with earth. Where learning and science have thrust all belief out of sight, it is only natural that the man who does not believe in a God nor a Hereafter should not credit the existence of spirits, nor the possibility of communicating with them. But the lower we go in the scale of society, the more simple and childlike the mind, the more readily does such a faith gain credence, and the more stories you will hear to justify belief. It is just the same with religion, which is hid from the wise and prudent, and revealed to babes.

If I am met here with the objection that the term "Spiritualism" has been at times mixed up with so much that is evil as to become an offence, I have no better answer to make than by turning to the irrefragable testimony of the Past and Present to prove that in all ages and of all religions, there have been corrupt and demoralized exponents whose vices have threatened to pull down the fabric they lived to raise. Christianity itself would have been overthrown before now, had we been unable to separate its doctrine from its practice.

I held these views in the month of February, 1873, when I made one of a party of friends assembled at the house of Miss Elizabeth Philip, in Gloucester Crescent, and was introduced to Mr. Henry Dunphy of the *Morning Post*, both of them since gone to join the great majority. Mr. Dunphy soon got astride his favourite hobby of Spiritualism, and gave me an interesting account of some of the *séances* he had attended. I had heard so many clever men and women discuss the subject before, that I had begun to believe on their authority that there must be "something in it," but I held the opinion that sittings in the dark must afford so much liberty for deception, that I would engage in none where I was not permitted the use of my eyesight.

I expressed myself somewhat after this fashion to Mr. Dunphy. He replied, "Then the time has arrived for you to investigate Spiritualism, for I can introduce you to a medium who will show you the faces of the dead." This proposal exactly met my wishes, and I gladly accepted it. Annie Thomas (Mrs. Pender Cudlip), the novelist, who is an intimate friend of mine, was staying with me at the time and became as eager as I was to investigate the phenomena. We took the address Mr. Dunphy gave us of Mrs. Holmes, the American medium, then visiting London, and lodging in Old Quebec Street, Portman Square, but we refused his introduction preferring to go *incognito*. Accordingly, the next evening, when she held a public *séance*, we presented ourselves at Mrs. Holmes' door; and having first removed our wedding-rings and tried to look as virginal as possible, sent up our names as Miss Taylor and Miss Turner. I am perfectly aware that this medium was said afterwards to be untrustworthy. So may a servant who was perfectly honest, whilst in my service, leave me for a situation where she is detected in theft. That does not alter the fact that she stole nothing from me. I do not think I know *a single medium* of whom I have not (at some time or other) heard the same thing, and I do not think I know a single woman whom I have not also, at some time or other, heard scandalized by her own sex, however pure and chaste she may imagine the world holds her. The question affects me in neither case. I value my acquaintances for what they are *to me*, not for what they may be to others; and I have placed trust in my media from what I individually have seen and heard, and proved to be genuine in their presence, and not from what others may imagine they have found out about them. It is no detriment to my witness that the media I sat with cheated somebody else, either before or after. My business was only to take care that *I* was not cheated, and I have never, in Spiritualism, accepted anything at the hands of others that I could not prove for myself.

Mrs. Holmes did not receive us very graciously on the present occasion. We were strangers to her—probably sceptics, and she eyed us rather coldly. It was a bitter night, and the snow lay so thick upon the ground that we had some difficulty in procuring a hansom to take us from Bayswater to Old Quebec Street. No other visitors arrived, and after a little while Mrs. Holmes offered to return our money (ten shillings), as she said if she did sit with us, there would probably be no manifestations on account of the inclemency of the weather. (Often since then I have proved her assertion to be true, and found that any extreme of heat or cold is liable to make a *séance* a dead failure.)

But Annie Thomas had to return to her home in Torquay on the following day, and so we begged the medium to try at least to show us some thing, as we were very curious on the subject. I am not quite sure what I expected or hoped for on this occasion. I was full of curiosity and anticipation, but I am sure that I never thought I should see any face which I could recognize as having been on earth. We waited till nine o'clock in hopes that a circle would be formed, but as no one else came, Mrs. Holmes consented to sit with us alone, warning us, however, several times, to prepare for a disappointment. The lights were therefore extinguished, and we sat for the usual preliminary dark *séance*, which was good, perhaps, but has nothing to do with a narrative of facts, proved to be so. When it concluded, the gas was re-lit and we sat for "Spirit Faces."

There were two small rooms connected by folding doors. Annie Thomas and I were asked to go into the back room—to lock the door communicating with the landings, and secure it with our own seal, stamped upon a piece of tape stretched across the opening—to examine the window and bar the shutter inside—to search the room thoroughly in fact to see that no one was concealed in it—and we did all this as a matter of business. When we had satisfied ourselves that no one could enter from the back, Mr. and Mrs. Holmes, Annie Thomas, and I, were seated on four chairs in the front room, arranged in a row before the folding doors, which were opened, and a square of black calico fastened across the aperture from one wall to the other. In this piece of calico was cut a square hole about the size of an ordinary window, at which we were told the spirit faces (if any) would appear. There was no singing, nor noise of any sort made to drown the sounds of preparation, and we could have heard even a rustle in the next room. Mr. and Mrs. Holmes talked to us of their various experiences, until, we were almost tired of waiting, when something white and indistinct, like a cloud of tobacco smoke, or a bundle of gossamer, appeared and disappeared again.

"They are coming! I *am* glad!" said Mrs. Holmes. "I didn't think we should get anything to-night"—and my friend and I were immediately on the tiptoe of expectation. The white

mass advanced and retreated several times, and finally settled
before the aperture and opened in the middle, when a
female face was distinctly to be seen above the black calico.
What was our amazement to recognize the features of Mrs.
Thomas, Annie Thomas's mother. Here I should tell my
readers that Annie's father, who was a lieutenant in the Royal
Navy and captain of the coastguard at Morston in Norfolk,
had been a near neighbour and great friend of my father,
Captain Marryat, and their children had associated like
brothers and sisters. I had therefore known Mrs. Thomas well,
and recognized her at once, as, of course, did her daughter.
The witness of two people is considered sufficient in law. It
ought to be accepted by society. Poor Annie was very much
affected, and talked to her mother in the most incoherent
manner. The spirit did not appear able to answer in words,
but she bowed her head or shook it, according as she wished to
say "yes" or "no." I could not help feeling awed at the
appearance of the dear old lady, but the only thing that
puzzled me was the cap she wore, which was made of white
net, quilled closely round her face, and unlike any I had ever
seen her wear in life. I whispered this to Annie, and she replied
at once, "It is the cap she was buried in," which settled the
question. Mrs. Thomas had possessed a very pleasant but very
uncommon looking face, with bright black eyes, and a complexion of pink and white like that of a child. It was some
time before Annie could be persuaded to let her mother go,
but the next face that presented itself astonished her quite as
much, for she recognized it as that of Captain Gordon, a
gentleman whom she had known intimately and for a
length of time. I had never seen Captain Gordon in the flesh,
but I had heard of him, and knew he had died from a sudden
accident. All I saw was the head of a good-looking, fair,
young man, and not feeling any personal interest in his
appearance, I occupied the time during which my friend
conversed with him about olden days, by minutely examining

the working of the muscles of his throat, which undeniably stretched when his head moved. As I was doing so, he leaned forward, and I saw a dark stain, which looked like a clot of blood, on his fair hair, on the left side of the forehead.

"Annie! what did Captain Gordon die of?" I asked. "He fell from a railway carriage," she replied, "and struck his head upon the line." I then pointed out to her the blood upon his hair. Several other faces appeared, which we could not recognize. At last came one of a gentleman, apparently moulded like a bust in plaster of Paris. He had a kind of smoking cap upon the head, curly hair, and a beard, but from being perfectly colourless, he looked so unlike nature, that I could not trace a resemblance to any friend of mine, though he kept on bowing in my direction, to indicate that I knew, or had known him. I examined this face again and again in vain. Nothing in it struck me as familiar, until the mouth broke into a grave, amused smile at my perplexity. In a moment I recognized it as that of my dear old friend, John Powles, whose history I shall relate *in extenso* further on. I exclaimed "Powles," and sprang towards it, but with my hasty action the figure disappeared. I was terribly vexed at my imprudence, for this was the friend of all others I desired to see, and sat there, hoping and praying the spirit would return, but it did not. Annie Thomas's mother and friend both came back several times; indeed, Annie recalled Captain Gordon so often, that on his last appearance the power was so exhausted, his face looked like a faded sketch in water-colours, but "Powles" had vanished altogether. The last face we saw that night was that of a little girl, and only her eyes and nose were visible, the rest of her head and face being enveloped in some white flimsy material like muslin. Mrs. Holmes asked her for whom she came, and she intimated that it was for me. I said she must be mistaken, and that I had known no one in life like her. The medium questioned her very closely, and tried to put her "out of court," as it were. Still, the child persisted that she came for me. Mrs. Holmes said to me, "Cannot you remember *anyone* of that age connected with you in the spirit world? No cousin, nor niece, nor sister, nor the child of a friend?" I tried to remember, but I could not, and answered, "No! no child of that age." She then addressed the little spirit. "You have made a mistake. There is no one here who knows you. You had better move on." So the child did move on, but very slowly and reluctantly. I could read her disappointment in her eyes, and after she had disappeared, she peeped round the corner again and looked at me, longingly. This was "Florence," my dear *lost* child (as I then called her) who had left me as a little infant of ten days old, and whom I could not at first recognize as a young girl of ten years. Her identity, however, has been proved to me since, beyond all doubt, as will be seen in the chapter which relates my reunion with her, and is headed "My Spirit Child." Thus ended the first *séance* at which I ever assisted, and it made a powerful impression upon my mind. Mrs. Holmes, in bidding us good night, said, "You two ladies must be very powerful mediums. I never held so successful a *séance* with strangers in my life before." This news elated us—we were eager to pursue our investigations, and were enchanted to think we could have *séances* at home, and as soon as Annie Thomas took up her residence in London, we agreed to hold regular meetings for the purpose. This was the *séance* that made me a student of the psychological phenomena, which the men of the nineteenth century term Spiritualism. Had it turned out a failure, I might now have been as most men are. *Quien sabe?* As it was, it incited me to go on and on, until I have seen and heard things which at that moment would have seemed utterly impossible to me. And I would not have missed the experience I have passed through for all the good this world could offer me.

CHAPTER III

CURIOUS COINCIDENCES

BEFORE I proceed to write down the results of my private and premeditated investigations, I am reminded to say a word respecting the permission I received for the pursuit of Spiritualism. As soon as I expressed my curiosity on the subject, I was met on all sides with the objection that, as I am a Catholic, I could not possibly have anything to do with the matter, and it is a fact that the Church strictly forbids all meddling with necromancy, or communion with the departed. Necromancy is a terrible word, is it not? especially to such people as do not understand its meaning, and only associate it with the dead of night and charmed circles, and seething cauldrons, and the arch fiend, in *propria persona*, with two horns and a tail. Yet it seems strange to me that the Catholic Church, whose very doctrine is overlaid with Spiritualism, and who makes it a matter of belief that the Saints hear and help us in our prayers and the daily actions of our lives, and recommends our kissing the ground every morning at the feet of our guardian angel, should consider it unlawful for us to communicate with our departed relatives. I cannot see the difference in iniquity between speaking to John Powles, who was and is a dear and trusted friend of mine, and Saint Peter of Alcantara, who is an old man whom I never saw in this life. They were both men, both mortal, and are both spirits. Again, surely my mother, who was a pious woman all her life, and is now in the other world, would be just as likely to take an interest in my welfare, and to try and promote the prospect of our future meeting, as Saint Veronica Guiliani, who is my patron. Yet were I to spend half my time in prayer before Saint Veronica's altar, asking her help and guidance, I should be doing right (according to the Church), but if I did the same thing at my mother's grave, or spoke to her at a *séance*, I should be doing wrong. These distinctions without a difference were hard nuts to crack, and I was bound to settle the matter with my conscience before I went on with my investigations.

It is a fact that I have met quite as many Catholics as Protestants (especially of the higher classes) amongst the investigators of Spiritualism, and I have not been surprised at it, for who could better understand and appreciate the beauty of communications from the spirit world than members of that Church which instructs us to believe in the communion of saints, as an ever-present, though invisible mystery. Whether my Catholic acquaintances had received permission to attend *séances* or not, was no concern of mine, but I took good care to procure it for myself, and I record it here, because rumours have constantly reached me of people having said behind my back that I can be "no Catholic" because I am a spiritualist.

My director at that time was Father Dalgairn, of the Oratory at Brompton, and it was to him I took my difficulty. I was a very constant press writer and reviewer, and to be unable to attend and report on spiritualistic meetings would have seriously militated against my professional interests. I represented this to the Father, and (although under protest) I received his permission to pursue the research in the cause of science. He did more than ease my conscience. He became interested in what I had to tell him on the subject, and we had many conversations concerning it. He also lent me from his own library the lives of such saints as had heard voices and seen visions, of those in fact who (like myself) had been the victims of "Optical Illusions." Amongst these I found the case of Saint Anne-Catherine of Emmerich, so like my own, that I began to think that I too might turn out to be a saint in disguise. It has not come to pass yet, but there is no knowing what may happen.

She used to see the spirits floating beside her as she walked to mass, and heard them asking her to pray for them as they pointed to "les taches sur leurs robes." The musical instruments used to play without hands in her presence, and voices from invisible throats sound in her ears, as they have done in mine. I have only inserted this clause, however, for the satisfaction of those Catholic acquaintances with whom I have sat at *séances*, and who will probably be the first to exclaim against the publication of *our* joint experiences. I trust they will acknowledge, after reading it, that I am not worse than themselves, though I may be a little bolder in avowing my opinions.

Before I began this chapter, I had an argument with that friend of mine called Self (who has but too often worsted me in the Battle of Life), as to whether I should say anything about table-rapping or tilting. The very fact of so common an article of furniture as a table, as an agent of communication with the unseen world, has excited so much ridicule and opens so wide a field for chicanery, that I thought it would be wiser to drop the subject, and confine myself to those phases of the science or art, or religion, or whatever the reader may like to call it, that can be explained or described on paper. The philosophers of the nineteenth century have invented so many names for the cause that makes a table turn round—tilt—or rap—that I feel quite unable (not being a philosopher) to cope with them. It is "magnetic force" or "psychic force,"—it is "unconscious cerebration" or "brain-reading"—and it is exceedingly difficult to tell the outside world of the private reasons that convince individuals that the answers they receive are *not* emanations from their own brains. I shall not attempt to refute their reasonings from their own standpoint. I see the difficulties in the way, so much so that I have persistently refused for many years past to sit at the table with strangers, for it is only a lengthened study of the matter that can possibly convince a person of its truth. I cannot, however, see the extreme folly myself of holding communication (under the circumstances) through the raps or tilts of a table, or any other object. These tiny indications of an influence ulterior to our own are not necessarily confined to a table. I have received them through a cardboard box, a gentleman's hat, a footstool, the strings of a guitar, and on the back of my chair, even on the pillow of my bed. And which, amongst the philosophers I have alluded to, could suggest a simpler mode of communication?

I have put the question to clever men thus: "Suppose yourself, after having been able to write and talk to me, suddenly deprived of the powers of speech and touch, and made invisible, so that we could not understand each other by signs, what better means than by taps or tilts on any article, when the right word or letter is named, could you think of by which to communicate with me?"

And my clever men have never been able to propose an easier or more sensible plan, and if anybody can suggest one, I should very much like to hear of it. The following incidents all took place through the much-ridiculed tipping of the table, but managed to knock some sense out of it nevertheless. On looking over the note book which I faithfully kept when we first held *séances* at home, I find many tests of identity which took place through my own mediumship, and which could not possibly have been the effects of thought-reading. I devote this chapter to their relation. I hope it will be observed with what admirable caution I have headed it. I have a few drops of Scotch blood in me by the mother's side, and I think they must have aided me here. "Curious coincidences."

It was not until the month of June, 1873, that we formed a home circle, and commenced regularly to sit together. We became so interested in the pursuit, that we used to sit every evening, and sometimes till three and four o'clock in the morning, greatly to our detriment, both mental and physical. We seldom sat alone, being generally joined by two or three friends from outside, and the results were sometimes very startling, as we were a strong circle. The memoranda of these sittings, sometimes with one party and sometimes with another, extend over a period of years, but I shall restrict myself to relating a few incidents that were verified by subsequent events.

The means by which we communicated with the influences around us was the usual one. We sat round the table and laid our hands upon it, and I (or anyone who might be selected for the purpose) spelled over the alphabet, and raps or tilts occurred when the desired letter was reached. This in reality is not so tedious a process as it may appear, and once used to it, one may get through a vast amount of conversation in an hour by this means. A medium is soon able to guess the word intended to be spelt, for there are not so many after all in use in general conversation.

Some one had come to our table on several occasions, giving the name of "Valerie," but refusing to say any more, so we thought she was an idle or frivolous spirit, and had been in the habit of driving her away. One evening, on the 1st of July, however, our circle was augmented by Mr. Henry Stacke, when "Valerie" was immediately spelled out, and the following conversation ensued. Mr. Stacke said to me, "Who is this?" and I replied carelessly, "O! she's a little devil! She never has anything to say." The table rocked violently at this, and the taps spelled out.

"Je ne suis pas diable."

"Hullo! Valerie, so you can talk now! For whom do you come?"

"Monsieur Stacke."

"Where did you meet him?"

"On the Continent."

"Whereabouts?"

"Between Dijon and Mâcon."

"How did you meet him?"

"In a railway carriage."

"What were you doing there?"

Here she relapsed into French, and said,

"Ce m'est impossible de dire."

At this juncture Mr. Stacke observed that he had never been in a train between Dijon and Mâcon but once in his life, and if the spirit was with him then, she must remember what was the matter with their fellow-passenger.

"Mais oui, oui—il etait fou," she replied, which proved to be perfectly correct. Mr. Stacke also remembered that two ladies in the same carriage had been terribly frightened, and he had assisted them to get into another. "Valerie" continued, "Priez pour moi."

"Pourquoi, Valerie?"

"Parceque j'ai beaucoup péché."

There was an influence who frequented our society at that time and called himself "Charlie."

He stated that his full name had been "Stephen Charles Bernard Abbot,"—that he had been a monk of great literary attainments—that he had embraced the monastic life in the reign of Queen Mary, and apostatized for political reasons in that of Elizabeth, and been "earth bound" in consequence ever since.

"Charlie" asked us to sing one night, and we struck up the very vulgar refrain of "Champagne Charlie," to which he greatly objected, asking for something more serious.

I began, "Ye banks and braes o' bonnie Doon."

"Why, that's as bad as the other," said Charlie. "It was a ribald and obscene song in the reign of Elizabeth. The drunken roysterers used to sing it in the street as they rolled home at night."

"You must be mistaken, Charlie! It's a well-known Scotch air."

"It's no more Scotch than I am," he replied. "The Scotch say they invented everything. It's a tune of the time of Elizabeth. Ask Brinley Richards."

Having the pleasure of the acquaintance of that gentleman, who was the great authority on the origin of National

Ballads, I applied to him for the information, and received an answer to say that "Charlie" was right, but that Mr. Richards had not been aware of the fact himself until he had searched some old MSS. in the British Museum for the purpose of ascertaining the truth.

I was giving a sitting once to an officer from Aldershot, a cousin of my own, who was quite prepared to ridicule every thing that took place. After having teased me into giving him a *séance*, he began by cheating himself, and then accused me of cheating him, and altogether tired out my patience. At last I proposed a test, though with little hope of success.

"Let us ask John Powles to go down to Aldershot," I said, "and bring us word what your brother officers are doing."

"O, yes! by Jove! Capital idea! Here! you fellow Powles, cut off to the camp, will you, and go to the barracks of the 84th, and let us know what Major R—— is doing." The message came back in about three minutes. "Major R—— has just come in from duty," spelt out Powles. "He is sitting on the side of his bed, changing his uniform trousers for a pair of grey tweed."

"I'm sure that's wrong," said my cousin, "because the men are never called out at this time of the day."

It was then four o'clock, as we had been careful to ascertain. My cousin returned to camp the same evening, and the next day I received a note from him to say, "That fellow Powles is a brick. It was quite right. R—— was unexpectedly ordered to turn out his company yesterday afternoon, and he returned to barracks and changed his things for the grey tweed suit exactly at four o'clock."

But I have always found my friend Powles (when he *will* condescend to do anything for strangers, which is seldom) remarkably correct in detailing the thoughts and actions of absentees, sometimes on the other side of the globe.

I went one afternoon to pay an ordinary social call on a lady named Mrs. W——, and found her engaged in an earnest conversation on Spiritualism with a stout woman and a commonplace man—two material looking individuals as ever I saw, and who appeared all the more so under a sultry August sun. As soon as Mrs. W—— saw me, she exclaimed, "Oh! here is Mrs. Ross-Church. She will tell you all about the spirits. Do, Mrs. Ross-Church, sit down at the table and let us have a *séance*."

A *séance* on a burning, blazing afternoon in August, with two stolid and uninteresting, and worse still, *uninterested* looking strangers, who appeared to think Mrs. W—— had a "bee in her bonnet." I protested—I reasoned—I pleaded—all in vain. My hostess continued to urge, and society places the guest at the mercy of her hostess. So, in an evil temper, I pulled off my gloves, and placed my hands indifferently on the table. The following words were at once rapped out—

"I am Edward G——. Did you ever pay Johnson the seventeen pounds twelve you received for my saddlery?"

The gentleman opposite to me turned all sorts of colours, and began to stammer out a reply, whilst his wife looked very confused. I asked the influence, "Who are you?" It replied, "*He* knows! His late colonel! Why hasn't Johnson received that money?" This is what I call an "awkward" coincidence, and I have had many such occur through me—some that have driven acquaintances away from the table, vowing vengeance against me, and racking their brains to discover *who* had told me of their secret peccadilloes. The gentleman in question (whose name even I do not remember) confessed that the identity and main points of the message were true, but he did *not* confide to us whether Johnson had ever received that seventeen pounds twelve.

I had a beautiful English greyhound, called "Clytie," a gift from Annie Thomas to me, and this dog was given to straying from my house in Colville Road, Bayswater, which runs parallel to Portobello Road, a rather objectionable quarter, composed of inferior shops, one of which, a fried fish shop, was an intolerable nuisance, and used to fill the air around with its rich perfume. On one occasion "Clytie" stayed away from home so much longer than usual, that I was afraid she was lost in good earnest, and posted bills offering a reward for her. "Charlie" came to the table that evening and said, "Don't offer a reward for the dog. Send for her."

"Where am I to send?" I asked.

"She is tied up at the fried fish shop in Portobello Road. Send the cook to see."

I told the servant in question that I had heard the greyhound was detained at the fish shop, and sent her to inquire. She returned with "Clytie." Her account was, that on making inquiries, the man in the shop had been very insolent to her, and she had raised her voice in reply; that she had then heard and recognized the sharp, peculiar bark of the greyhound from an upper storey, and, running up before the man could prevent her, she had found "Clytie" tied to a bedstead with a piece of rope, and had called in a policeman to enable her to take the dog away. I have often heard the assertion that Spiritualism is of no practical good, and, doubtless, it was never intended to be so, but this incident was, at least, an exception to the rule.

When abroad, on one occasion, I was asked by a Catholic Abbé to sit with him. He had never seen any manifestations before, and he did not believe in them, but he was curious on the subject. I knew nothing of him further than that he was a priest, and a Jesuit, and a great friend of my sister's, at whose house I was staying. He spoke English, and the conversation was carried on in that language. He had told me beforehand that if he could receive a perfectly private test, that he should never doubt the truth of the manifestations again. I left him, therefore to conduct the investigation entirely by himself, I acting only as the medium between him and the influence. As soon as the table moved he put his question direct, without asking who was there to answer it.

"Where is my chasuble?"

Now a priest's chasuble, *I* should have said, must be either hanging in the sacristy or packed away at home, or been sent away to be altered or mended. But the answer was wide of all my speculations.

"At the bottom of the Red Sea."

The priest started, but continued—

Who put it there?"

"Elias Dodo."

"What was his object in doing so?"

"He found the parcel a burthen, and did not expect any reward for delivering it."

The Abbé really looked as if he had encountered the devil. He wiped the perspiration from his forehead, and put one more question.

"Of what was my chasuble made?"

"Your sister's wedding dress."

The priest then explained to me that his sister had made him a chasuble out of her wedding dress—one of the forms of returning thanks in the Church, but that after a while it became old fashioned, and the Bishop, going his rounds, ordered him to get another. He did not like to throw away his sister's gift, so he decided to send the old chasuble to a priest in India, where they are very poor, and not so particular as to fashion. He confided the packet to a man called Elias Dodo, a sufficiently singular name, but neither he nor the priest he sent it to had ever heard anything more of the chasuble, or the man who promised to deliver it.

A young artist of the name of Courtney was a visitor at my house. He asked me to sit with him alone, when the table began rapping out a number of consonants—a farrago of nonsense, it appeared to me, and I stopped and said so. But Mr. Courtney, who appeared much interested, begged me to proceed. When the communication was finished, he said to me, "This is the most wonderful thing I have ever heard. My father has been at the table talking to me in Welsh. He has told me our family motto, and all about my birth-place and relations in Wales." I said, "I never heard you were a Welshman." "Yes! I am," he replied, "my real name is Powell. I have only adopted the name of Courtney for professional purposes."

This was all news to me, but had it not been, *I cannot speak Welsh.*

I could multiply such cases by the dozen, but that I fear to tire my readers, added to which the majority of them were of so strictly private a nature that it would be impossible to put them into print. This is perhaps the greatest drawback that one encounters in trying to prove the truth of Spiritualism. The best tests we receive are when the very secrets of our hearts, which we have not confided to our nearest friends, are revealed to us. I could relate (had I the permission of the persons most interested) the particulars of a well-known law suit, in which the requisite evidence, and names and addresses of witnesses, were all given through my mediumship, and were the cause of the case being gained by the side that came to me for "information." Some of the coincidences I have related in this chapter might, however, be ascribed by the sceptical to the mysterious and unknown power of brain reading, whatever that may be, and however it may come, apart from mediumship, but how is one to account for the facts I shall tell you in my next chapter?

CHAPTER IV

EMBODIED SPIRITS

I was having a sitting one day in my own house with a lady friend, named Miss Clark, when a female spirit came to the table and spelt out the name "Tiny."

"Who are you?" I asked, "and for whom do you come?"

"I am a friend of Major M——" (mentioning the full name), "and I want your help."

"Are you any relation to Major M——?"

"I am the mother of his child."

"What do you wish me to do for you?"

"Tell him he must go down to Portsmouth and look after my daughter. He has not seen her for years. The old woman is dead, and the man is a drunkard. She is falling into evil courses. He must save her from them."

"What is your real name?"

"I will not give it. There is no need. He always called me 'Tiny'."

"How old is your daughter?"

"Nineteen! Her name is Emily! I want her to be married. Tell him to promise her a wedding trousseau. It may induce her to marry."

The influence divulged a great deal more on the subject which I cannot write down here. It was an account of one of those cruel acts of seduction by which a young girl had been led into trouble in order to gratify a man's selfish lust, and astonished both Miss Clark and myself, who had never heard of such a person as "Tiny" before. It was too delicate a matter for me to broach to Major M—— (who was a married man, and an intimate friend of mine), but the spirit came so many times and implored me so earnestly to save her daughter, that at last I ventured to repeat the communication to him. He was rather taken aback, but confessed it was true, and that the child, being left to his care, had been given over to the charge of some common people at Portsmouth, and he had not inquired after it for some time past. Neither had he ever heard of the death of the mother, who had subsequently married, and had a family. He instituted inquiries, however, at once, and found the statement to be quite true, and that the girl Emily, being left with no better protection than that of the drunken old man, had actually gone astray, and not long after she was had up at the police court for stabbing a soldier in a public-house—a fit ending for the unfortunate offspring of a man's selfish passions. But the strangest part of the story to the unitiated will lie in the fact that the woman whose spirit thus manifested itself to two utter strangers, who knew neither her history nor her name, was at the time *alive*, and living with her husband and family as Major M—— took pains to ascertain.

And now I have something to say on the subject of communicating with the spirits of persons still in the flesh. This will doubtless appear the most incomprehensible and fanatical assertion of all, that we wear our earthly garb so loosely, that the spirits of people still living in this world can leave the body and manifest themselves either visibly or orally to others in their normal condition. And yet it is a fact that spirits have so visited myself (as in the case I have just recorded), and given me information of which I had not the slightest previous idea. The matter has been explained to me after this fashion—that it is not really the spirit of the living person who communicates, but the spirit, or "control," that is nearest to him: in effect what the Church calls his "guardian angel," and that this guardian angel, who knows his inmost thoughts and desires better even than he knows them himself, is equally capable of speaking in his name. This idea of the matter may shift the marvel from one pair of shoulders to another, but it does not do away with it. If I can receive information of events before they occur (as I will prove that I have), I present a nut for the consideration of the public jaw, which even the scientists will find difficult to crack. It was at one time my annual custom to take my children to the sea-side, and one summer, being anxious to ascertain how far the table could be made to act without the aid of "unconscious cerebration," I arranged with my friends, Mr. Helmore and Mrs. Colnaghi, who had been in the habit of sitting with us at home, that *we* should continue to sit at the sea-side on Tuesday evenings as theretofore, and *they* should sit in London on the Thursdays, when I would try to send them messages through "Charlie," the spirit I have already mentioned as being constantly with us.

The first Tuesday my message was, "Ask them how they are getting on without us," which was faithfully delivered at their table on the following Thursday. The return message from them which "Charlie" spelled out for us on the second Tuesday, was: "Tell her London is a desert without her," to which I emphatically, if not elegantly, answered, "Fiddle-de-dee!" A few days afterwards I received a letter from Mr. Helmore, in which he said, "I am afraid 'Charlie' is already tired of playing at postman, for to all our questions about you last Thursday, he would only rap out, 'Fiddle-de-dee'."

The circumstance to which this little episode is but an introduction happened a few days later. Mr. Colnaghi and Mr. Helmore, sitting together as usual on Thursday evening, were discussing the possibility of summoning the spirits of *living persons* to the table, when "Charlie" rapped three times to intimate they could.

"Will you fetch some one for us, Charlie?"

"Yes."

"Whom will you bring?"

"Mrs. Ross-Church."

"How long will it take you to do so?"

"Fifteen minutes."

It was in the middle of the night when I must have been fast asleep, and the two young men told me afterwards that they waited the results of their experiment with much trepidation, wondering (I suppose) if I should be conveyed bodily into their presence and box their ears well for their impertinence. Exactly fifteen minutes afterwards, however, the table was violently shaken and the words were spelt out. "I am Mrs. Ross-Church. How *dared* you send for me?" They were very penitent (or they said they were), but they described my manner as most arbitrary, and said I went on repeating, "Let me go back! Let me go back! There is a great danger hanging over my children! I must go back to my children!" (And here I would remark *par parenthese*, and in contradiction of the guardian angel theory, that I have always found that whilst the spirits of the departed come and go as they feel inclined, the spirits of the living invariably *beg* to be sent back again or permitted to go, as if they were chained by the will of the medium.) On this occasion I was so positive that I made a great impression on my two friends, and the next day Mr. Helmore sent me a cautiously worded letter to find out if all was well with us at Charmouth, but without disclosing the reason for his curiosity.

The *facts* are that on the morning of *Friday*, the day *after* the *séance* in London, my seven children and two nurses were all sitting in a small lodging-house room, when my brother-in-law, Dr. Henry Norris, came in from ball practice with the volunteers, and whilst exhibiting his rifle to my son, accidentally discharged it in the midst of them, the ball passing through the wall within two inches of my eldest daughter's head. When I wrote the account of this to Mr. Helmore, he told me of my visit to London and the words I had spelt out on the occasion. But how did I know of the occurrence the *night before* it took place? And if I—being asleep and unconscious—did *not* know of it, "Charlie" must have done so.

My ærial visits to my friends, however, whilst my body was in quite another place, have been made still more palpable than this. Once, when living in the Regent's Park, I passed a very terrible and painful night. Grief and fear kept me awake most of the time, and the morning found me exhausted with the emotion I had gone through. About eleven o'clock there walked in, to my surprise, Mrs. Fitzgerald (better known as a medium under her maiden name of Bessie Williams), who lived in the Goldhawk Road, Shepherd's Bush. "I couldn't help coming to you," she commenced, "for I shall not be easy until I know how you are after the terrible scene you have passed through." I stared at her. "Whom have you seen?" I asked. "Who has told you of it?" "Yourself," she replied. "I was waked up this morning between two and three o'clock by the sound of sobbing and crying in the front garden. I got out of bed and opened the window, and then I saw you standing on the grass plat in your night-dress and crying bitterly. I asked you what was the matter, and you told me so and so, and so and so." And here followed a detailed account of all that had happened in my own house on the other side of London, with the *very words* that had been used, and every action that had happened. I had seen no one and spoken to no one between the occurrence and the time Mrs. Fitzgerald called upon me. If her story was untrue, *who* had so minutely informed her of a circumstance which it was to the interest of all concerned to keep to themselves?

When I first joined Mr. d'Oyley Carte's "Patience" Company in the provinces, to play the part of "Lady Jane," I understood I was to have four days' rehearsal. However, the lady whom I succeeded, hearing I had arrived, took herself off, and the manager requested I would appear the same night of my arrival. This was rather an ordeal to an artist who had never sung on the operatic stage before, and who was not note perfect. However, as a matter of obligation, I consented to do my best, but I was very nervous. At the end of the second act, during the balloting scene, Lady Jane has to appear suddenly on the stage, with the word "Away!" I forget at this distance of time whether I made a mistake in pitching the note a third higher or lower. I know it was not out of harmony, but it was sufficiently wrong to send the chorus astray, and bring my heart up into my mouth. It never occurred after the first night, but I never stood at the wings again waiting for that particular entrance but I "girded my loins together," as it were, with a kind of dread lest I should repeat the error. After a while I perceived a good deal of whispering about me in the company, and I asked poor

Federici (who played the colonel) the reason of it, particularly as he had previously asked me to stand as far from him as I could upon the stage, as I magnetized him so strongly that he couldn't sing if I was near him. "Well! do you know," he said to me in answer, "that a very strange thing occurs occasionally with reference to you, Miss Marryat. While you are standing on the stage sometimes, you appear seated in the stalls. Several people have seen it beside myself. I assure you it is true."

"But *when* do you see me?" I inquired with amazement.

"It's always at the same time," he answered, "just before you run on at the end of the second act. Of course it's only an appearance, but it's very queer." I told him then of the strange feelings of distrust of myself I experienced each night at that very moment, when my spirit seems to have preceded myself upon the stage.

I had a friend many years ago in India, who (like many other friends) had permitted time and separation to come between us, and alienate us from each other. I had not seen him nor heard from him for eleven years, and to all appearance our friendship was at an end. One evening the medium I have alluded to above, Mrs. Fitzgerald, who was a personal friend of mine, was at my house, and after dinner she put her feet up on the sofa—a very unusual thing for her—and closed her eyes. She and I were quite alone in the drawing-room, and after a little while I whispered softly, "Bessie, are you asleep?" The answer came from her control "Dewdrop," a wonderfully sharp Red Indian girl. "No! she's in a trance. There's somebody coming to speak to you! I don't want him to come. He'll make the medium ill. But it's no use. I see him creeping round the corner now."

"But why should it make her ill?" I argued, believing we were about to hold an ordinary *séance*.

"Because he's a *live* one, he hasn't passed over yet," replied Dewdrop, "and live ones always make my medium feel sick.

But it's no use. I can't keep him out. He may as well come. But don't let him stay long."

"Who is he, Dewdrop?" I demanded curiously.

"*I* don't know! Guess *you* will! He's an old friend of yours, and his name is George." Whereupon Bessie Fitzgerald laid back on the sofa cushions, and Dewdrop ceased to speak. It was some time before there was any result. The medium tossed and turned, and wiped the perspiration from her forehead, and pushed back her hair, and beat up the cushions and threw herself back upon them with a sigh, and went through all the pantomime of a man trying to court sleep in a hot climate. Presently she opened her eyes and glanced languidly around her. Her unmistakable actions and the name "George" (which was that of my friend, then resident in India) had naturally aroused my suspicions as to the identity of the influence, and when Bessie opened her eyes, I asked softly, "George, is that you?" At the sound of my voice the medium started violently and sprung into a sitting posture, and then, looking all round the room in a scared manner, she exclaimed, "Where am I? Who brought me here?" Then catching sight of me, she continued, "Mrs. Ross-Church!— Florence! Is this *your* room? O! let me go! *Do* let me go!"

This was not complimentary, to say the least of it, from a friend whom I had not met for eleven years, but now that I had got him I had no intention of letting him go, until I was convinced of his identity. But the terror of the spirit at finding himself in a strange place seemed so real and uncontrollable that I had the greatest difficulty in persuading him to stay, even for a few minutes. He kept on reiterating, "Who brought me here? I did not wish to come. Do let me go back. I am so very cold" (shivering convulsively), "so very, *very* cold."

"Answer me a few questions," I said, "and then you shall go. Do you know who I am?"

"Yes, yes, you are Florence."

"And what is your name?" He gave it at full length. "And do you care for me still?"

"Very much. But let me go."

"In a minute. Why do you never write to me?"

"There are reasons. I am not a free agent. It is better as it is."

"I don't think so. I miss your letters very much. Shall I ever hear from you again?"

"Yes!"

"And see you?"

"Yes; but not yet. Let me go now. I don't wish to stay. You are making me very unhappy."

If I could describe the fearful manner in which, during this conversation, he glanced every moment at the door, like a man who is afraid of being discovered in a guilty action, it would carry with it to my readers, as it did to me, the most convincing proof that the medium's body was animated by a totally different influence from her own. I kept the spirit under control until I had fully convinced myself that he knew everything about our former friendship and his own present surroundings; and then I let him fly back to India, and wondered if he would wake up the next morning and imagine he had been labouring under nightmare.

These experiences with the spirits of the living are certainly amongst the most curious I have obtained. On more than one occasion, when I have been unable to extract the truth of a matter from my acquaintances I have sat down alone, as soon as I believed them to be asleep, and summoned their spirits to the table and compelled them to speak out. Little have they imagined sometimes how I came to know things which they had scrupulously tried to hide from me. I have heard that the power to summons the spirits of the living is not given to all media, but I have always possessed it. I can do so when they are awake as well as when they are asleep, though it is not so easy. A gentleman once *dared* me to do this with him, and I only conceal his name because I made him look ridiculous. I waited till I knew he was engaged at a dinner-party, and then about nine o'clcok in the evening I sat down and summoned him to come to me. It was some little time before he obeyed, and when he did come, he was eminently sulky. I got a piece of paper and pencil, and from his dictation I wrote down the number and names of the guests at the dinner-table, also the dishes of which he had partaken, and then in pity for his earnest entreaties I let him go again. "You are making me ridiculous," he said, "everyone is laughing at me."

"But why? What are you doing?" I urged.

"I am standing by the mantel-piece, and I have fallen fast asleep," he answered. The next morning he came pell-mell into my presence.

"What did you do to me last night?" he demanded. "I was at the Watts Phillips, and after dinner I went fast asleep with my head upon my hand, standing by the mantel-piece, and they were all trying to wake me and couldn't. Have you been playing any of your tricks upon me?"

"I only made you do what you declared I couldn't," I replied. "How did you like the white soup and the turbot, and the sweetbreads, etc., etc."

He opened his eyes at my nefariously obtained knowledge, and still more when I produced the paper written from his dictation. This is not a usual custom of mine—it would not be interesting enough to pursue as a custom—but I am a dangerous person to *dare* to do anything.

The old friend whose spirit visited me through Mrs. Fitzgerald had lost a sister to whom he was very tenderly attached before he made my acquaintance, and I knew little of her beyond her name. One evening, not many months after the interview with him which I have recorded, a spirit came to me, giving the name of my friend's sister, with this message, "My brother has returned to England, and would like to know your address. Write to him to the Club,

Leamington, and tell him where to find you." I replied, "Your brother has not written to me, nor inquired after me for the last eleven years. He has lost all interest in me, and I cannot be the first to write to him, unless I am sure that he wishes it."

"He has *not* lost all interest in you," said the spirit; "he thinks of you constantly, and I hear him pray for you. He wishes to hear from you."

"That may be true," I replied, "but I cannot accept it on your authority. If your brother really wishes to renew our acquaintance, let him write and tell me so."

"He does not know your address, and I cannot get near enough to him to influence him."

"Then things must remain as they are," I replied somewhat testily. "I am a public person. He can find out my address, if he chooses to do so."

The spirit seemed to reflect for a moment; then she rapped out, "Wait, and I will fetch my brother. He shall come here himself and tell you what he thinks about it." In a short time there was a different movement of the table, and the name of my old friend was given. After we had exchanged a few words, and I had told him I required a test of his identity, he asked me to get a pencil and paper, and write from his dictation. I did as he requested, and he dictated the following sentence, "Long time, indeed, has passed since the days you call to mind, but time, however long, does not efface the past. It has never made me cease to think of and pray for you as I felt you, too, did think of and pray for me. Write to the address my sister gave you. I want to hear from you."

Notwithstanding the perspicuity and apparent genuineness of this message, it was some time before I could make up my mind to follow the directions it gave me. My pride stood in the way to prevent it. *Ten days afterwards*, however, having received several more visits from the sister, I did as she desired me, and sent a note to her brother to the Leamington

Club. The answer came by return of post, and contained (amongst others) *the identical words* he had told me to write down. Will Mr. Stuart Cumberland, or any other clever man, explain to me *what* or *who* it was that had visited me ten days beforehand, and dictated words which could hardly have been in my correspondent's brain before he received my letter? I am ready to accept any reasonable explanation of the matter from the scientists, philosophers, chemists, or arguists of the world, and I am open to conviction, when my sense convinces me, that their reasoning is true. But my present belief is, that not a single man or woman will be found able to account on any ordinary grounds for such an extraordinary instance of "unconscious cerebration."

Being subject to "optical illusions," I naturally had several with regard to my spirit child, "Florence," and she always came to me clothed in a white dress. One night, however, when I was living alone in the Regent's Park, I saw "Florence" (as I imagined) standing in the centre of the room, dressed in a green riding habit slashed with orange colour, with a cavalier hat of grey felt on her head, ornamented with a long green feather and a gold buckle. She stood with her back to me, but I could see her profile as she looked over her shoulder, with the skirt of her habit in her hand. This being a most extraordinary attire in which to see "Florence," I felt curious on the subject, and the next day I questioned her about it.

"Florence!" I said, "why did you come to me last night in a green riding habit?"

"I did not come to you last night, mother! It was my sister Eva."

"Good heavens!" I exclaimed, "is anything wrong with her?"

"No! she is quite well."

"How could she come to me then?"

"She did not come in reality, but her thoughts were much with you, and so you saw her spirit clairvoyantly."

My daughter Eva, who was on the stage, was at that time

fulfilling a stock engagement in Glasgow, and very much employed. I had not heard from her for a fortnight, which was a most unusual occurrence, and I had begun to feel uneasy. This vision made me more so, and I wrote at once to ask her if all was as it should be. Her answer was to this effect: "I am so sorry I have had no time to write to you this week, but I have been so awfully busy. We play 'The Colleen Bawn' here next week, and I have had to get my dress ready for 'Anne Chute.' It's so effective. I wish you could see it. *A green habit slashed with orange, and a grey felt hat with a long green feather and big gold buckle.* I tried it on the other night, and it looked to nice, etc., etc."

Well, my darling girl had had her wish, and I *had* seen it.

CHAPTER V

OPTICAL ILLUSIONS

As I have alluded to what my family termed my "optical illusions," I think it as well to describe a few of them, which appeared by the context to be something more than a mere temporary disturbance of my visual organs. I will pass over such as might be traced, truly or otherwise, to physical causes, and confine myself to those which were subsequently proved to be the reflection of something that unknown to me, had gone before. In 1875 I was much engaged in giving dramatic readings in different parts of the country, and I visited Dublin for the first time in my life, for that purpose, and put up at the largest and best-frequented hotel there. Through the hospitality of the residents and the duties of my professional business, I was engaged both day and night, and when I *did* get to bed, I had every disposition to sleep, as the saying is, like a "top." But there was something in the hotel that would not let me do so. I had a charming bedroom, cheerful, bright and pretty, and replete with every comfort, and I would retire to rest "dead beat," and fall off to sleep at once, to be waked perhaps half a dozen times a night by that inexplicable something (or nothing) that rouses me whenever I am about to enjoy an "optical illusion," and to see figures, sometimes one, sometimes two or three, sometimes a whole group standing by my bedside and gazing at me with looks of the greatest astonishment, as much as to ask what right I had to be there. But the most remarkable part of the matter to me was, that all the figures were those of men, and military men, to whom I was too well accustomed to be able to mistake. Some were officers and others soldiers, some were in uniform, others in undress, but they all belonged to the army, and they all seemed to labour under the same feeling of intense surprise at seeing *me* in the hotel. These apparitions were so life-like and appeared so frequently, that I grew quite uncomfortable about them, for however much one may be used to see "optical illusions," it is not pleasant to fancy there are about twenty strangers gazing at one every night as one lies asleep. Spiritualism is, or was, a tabooed subject in Dublin, and I had been expressly cautioned not to mention it before my new acquaintances. However, I could not keep entire silence on this subject, and dining *en famille* one day, with a hospitable family of the name of Robinson, I related to them my nightly experiences at the hotel. Father, mother, and son exclaimed simultaneously, "Good gracious," they said, "don't you know that that hotel was built on the site of the old barracks? The house immediately behind it, which formed part of the old building, was vacated by its last tenants on account of its being haunted. Every evening at the hour the soldiers used to be marched up to bed, they heard the tramp, tramp, tramp of the feet ascending the staircase."

"That may be," I replied, "but they *knew* their house stood on the site of the barracks, and *I didn't*."

My eldest daughter was spending a holiday with me once

after my second marriage, and during the month of August. She had been much overworked, and I made her lie in bed till noon. One morning I had been to her room at that hour to wake her, and on turning to leave it (in the broad daylight remember), I encountered a man on the landing outside her door. He was dressed in a white shirt with black studs down the front, and a pair of black cloth trousers. He had dark hair and eyes, and small features; altogether, he struck me as having rather a sinister and unpleasant appearance. I stood still, with the open door in my hand, and gazed at him. He looked at me also for a minute, and then turned and walked upstairs to an upper story where the nursery was situated, beckoning me, with a jerk of his hand, to follow him. My daughter (remarking a peculiar expression in my eyes, which I am told they assume on such occasions) said, "Mother! what do you see?"

"Only a spirit," I answered, "and he has gone upstairs."

"Now, what *is* the good of seeing them in that way," said Eva, rather impatiently (for this dear child always disliked and avoided Spiritualism), and I was fain to confess that I really did *not* know the especial good of encountering a sinister-looking gentleman in shirt and trousers, on a blazing noon in August. After which the circumstance passed from my mind, until recalled again.

A few months later I had occasion to change the children's nurse, and the woman who took her place was an Icelandic girl named Margaret Thommassen, who had only been in England for three weeks. I found that she had been educated far above the average run of domestic servants, and was well acquainted with the writings of Swedenborg and other authors. One day as I walked up the nursery stairs to visit the children in bed, I encountered the same man I had seen outside my daughter's room, standing on the upper landing, as though waiting my approach. He was dressed as before, but this time his arms were folded across his breast and his face downcast, as though he were unhappy about something. He disappeared as I reached the landing, and I mentioned the circumstance to no one. A few days later, Margaret Thommassen asked me timidly if I believed in the possibility of the spirits of the departed returning to this earth. When I replied that I did, she appeared overjoyed, and said she had never hoped to find anyone in England to whom she could speak about it. She then gave me a mass of evidence on the subject which forms a large part of the religion of the Icelanders. She told me that she felt uneasy about her eldest brother, to whom she was strongly attached. He had left Iceland a year before to become a waiter in Germany, and had promised faithfully that so long as he lived she should hear from him every month, and when he failed to write she must conclude he was dead. Margaret told me she had heard nothing from him now for three months, and each night when the nursery light was put out, someone came and sat at the foot of her bed and sighed. She then produced his photograph, and to my astonishment I recognized at once the man who had appeared to me some months before I knew that such a woman as Margaret Thommassen existed. He was taken in a shirt and trousers, just as I had seen him, and wore the same repulsive (to me) and sinister expression. I then told his sister that I had already seen him twice in that house, and she grew very excited and anxious to learn the truth. In consequence I sat with her in hopes of obtaining some news of her brother, who immediately came to the table, and told her that he was dead, with the circumstances under which he had died, and the address where she was to write to obtain particulars. And on Margaret Thommassen writing as she was directed, she obtained the practical proofs of her brother's death, without which this story would be worthless.

My sister Cecil lives with her family in Somerset, and many years ago I went down there to visit her for the first time since she had moved into a new house which I had never seen before. She put me to sleep in the guest chamber, a large, handsome room, just newly furnished by Oetzmann. But I could not sleep in it. The very first night some one walked up and down in the room, groaning and sighing close to my ears, and he, she, or it especially annoyed me by continually touching the new stiff counterpane with a "scrooping" sound that set my teeth on edge, and sent my heart up into my mouth. I kept on saying, "Go away! Don't come near me!" for its proximity inspired me with a horror and repugnance which I have seldom felt under similar circumstances. I did not say anything at first to my sister, who is rather nervous on the subject of "bogies," but on the third night I could stand it no longer, and told her plainly the room was haunted, and I wished she would put me in her dressing-room, or with her servants, sooner than let me remain there, as I could get no rest. Then the truth came out, and she confessed that the last owner of the house had committed suicide in that very room, and showed me the place on the boards, underneath the carpet, where the stain of his blood still remained. A lively sort of room to sleep all alone in.

Another sister of mine, Blanche, used to live in a haunted house in Bruges, of which a description will be found in the chapter headed "The Story of the Monk." Long, however, before the monk was heard of, I could not sleep in her house on account of the disturbances in my room, for which my sister used to laugh at me. But even when my husband, Colonel Lean, and I stayed there together, it was much the same. One night I waked him to see the figure of a woman, who had often visited me, standing at the foot of the bed. She was quaintly attired in a sort of leathern bodice or jerkin, laced up the front over a woollen petticoat of some dark colour. She wore a cap of Mechlin lace, with the large flaps at the side, adopted by Flemish women to this day; her hair was combed tightly off her forehead, and she wore a profusion of gold ornaments.

My husband could describe her as vividly as I did, which proves how plainly the apparition must have shown itself. I waked on several occasions to see this woman busy (apparently) with the contents of an old carved oak armoire which stood in a corner of the room, and which, I suppose, must have had something to do with herself. My eldest son joined me at Bruges on this occasion. He was a young fellow of twenty, who had never practised, nor even inquired into Spiritualism—fresh from sea, and about as free from fear or superstitious fancies as a mortal could be. He was put to sleep in a room on the other side of the house, and I saw from the first that he was grave about it, but I did not ask him the reason, though I felt sure, from personal experience, that he would hear or see something before long. In a few days he came to me and said—

"Mother! I'm going to take my mattress into the colonel's dressing-room to-night and sleep there." I asked him why. He replied, "It's impossible to stay in that room any longer. I wouldn't mind if they'd let me sleep, but they won't. There's something walks about half the night, whispering and muttering, and touching the bedclothes, and though I don't believe in any of your rubbishy spirits, I'll be 'jiggered' if I sleep there any longer." So he was not "jiggered" (whatever that may be), as he refused to enter the room again.

I cannot end this chapter more appropriately than by relating a very remarkable case of "optical illusion" which was seen by myself alone. It was in the month of July, 1880, and I had gone down alone to Brighton for a week's quiet. I had some important literary work to finish, and the exigencies of the London season made too many demands upon my time. So I packed up my writing materials, and took a lodging all to myself, and set hard to work. I used to write all day and walk in the evening. It was light then till eight or nine o'clock, and the Esplanade used to be crowded till a late hour. I was pushing my way, on the evening of the 9th of

July, through the crowd, thinking of my work more than anything else, when I saw, as I fully thought, my step-son, Francis Lean, leaning with his back against the palings at the edge of the cliff and smiling at me. He was a handsome lad of eighteen who was supposed to have sailed in his ship for the Brazils five months before. But he had been a wild young fellow, causing his father much trouble and anxiety, and my first impression was one of great annoyance, thinking naturally that, since I saw him there, he had never sailed at all but run away from his ship at the last moment. I hastened up to him, therefore, but as I reached his side, he turned round quite methodically, and walked quickly down a flight of steps that led to the beach. I followed him, and found myself amongst a group of ordinary seamen mending their nets, but I could see Francis nowhere. I did not know what to make of the occurrence, but it never struck me that it was not either the lad himself or some one remarkably like him. The same night, however, after I had retired to bed in a room that was unpleasantly brilliant with the moonlight streaming in at the window, I was roused from my sleep by someone turning the handle of my door, and there stood Francis in his naval uniform, with the peaked cap on his head, smiling at me as he had done upon the cliff. I started up in bed intending to speak to him, when he laid his finger on his lips and faded away. This second vision made me think something must have happened to the boy, but I determined not to say anything to my husband about it until it was verified. Shortly after my return to London, we were going, in company with my own son (also a sailor), to see his ship which was lying in the docks, when, as we were driving through Poplar, I again saw my step-son Francis standing on the pavement, and smiling at me. That time I spoke. I said to Colonel Lean, "I am sure I saw Francis standing there. Do you think it is possible he may not have sailed after all?" But Colonel Lean laughed at the idea. He believed it to be a chance likeness I had seen. Only the lad was too good-looking to have many duplicates in this world. We visited the seaside after that, and in September, whilst we were staying at Folkestone, Colonel Lean received a letter to say that his son Francis had been drowned by the upsetting of a boat in the surf of the Bay of Callao, in the Brazils, *on the 9th of July*—the day I had seen him twice in Brighton, two months before we heard that he was gone.

CHAPTER VI

ON SCEPTICISM

THERE are two classes of people who had done more harm to the cause of Spiritualism than the testimony of all the scientists has done good, and those are the enthusiasts and the sceptics. The first believe everything they see or hear. Without giving themselves the trouble to obtain proofs of the genuineness of the manifestations, they rush impetuously from one acquaintance to the other, detailing their experience with so much exaggeration and such unbounded faith, that they make the absurdity of it patent to all. They are generally people of low intellect, credulous dispositions, and weak nerves. They bow down before the influences as if they were so many little gods descended from heaven, instead of being, as in the majority of instances, spirits a shade less holy than our own, who, for their very shortcomings, are unable to rise above the atmosphere that surrounds this gross and material world. These are the sort of spiritualists whom *Punch* and other comic papers have very justly ridiculed. Who does not remember the picture of the afflicted widow, for whom the medium has just called up the departed Jones?

"Jones," she falters, "are you happy?"

"Much happier than I was down here," growls Jones.

"Oh! then you *must* be in heaven!"

"On the contrary, quite the reverse," is the reply.

Who also has not sat a *séance* where such people have not made themselves so ridiculous as to bring the cause they profess to adore into contempt and ignominy. Yet to allow the words and deeds of fools to affect one's inward and private conviction of a matter would be tantamount to giving up the pursuit of everything in which one's fellow creatures can take a part.

The second class to which I alluded—the sceptics—have not done so much injury to Spiritualism as the enthusiasts, because they are as a rule, so intensely bigoted and hardheaded, and narrow-minded, that they overdo their protestations, and render them harmless. The sceptic refuses to believe *anything*, because he has found out *one* thing to be a fraud. If one medium deceives, all the mediums must deceive. If one *séance* is a failure, none can be successful. If he gains no satisfactory test of the presence of the spirits of the departed, no one has ever gained such a test. Now, such reason is neither just nor logical. Again, a sceptic fully expects *his* testimony to be accepted and believed, yet he will never believe any truth on the testimony of another person. And if he is told that, given certain conditions, he can see this or hear the other, he says, "No! I will see it and hear it without any conditions, or else I will proclaim it all a fraud." In like manner, we might say to a savage, on showing him a watch, "If you will keep your eye on those hands, you will see them move round to tell the hours and minutes," and he should reply, "I must put the watch into boiling water—those are my conditions—and if it won't go then, I will not believe it can go at all."

Some years ago I was on friendly terms with a doctor, accounted clever in his profession, and I knew him to be an able arguist, and thought he had common sense enough not to eat his own words, but the sequel proved that I was mistaken. We had several conversations together on Spiritualism, and as Dr. H—— was a complete disbeliever in the existence of a God and a future life, I was naturally not surprised to find that he did not place any credence in the account I gave him of my spiritualistic experiences. Many medical men attribute such experiences entirely to a diseased condition of mind or body.

But when I asked Dr. H—— what he should think if he saw them with his own eyes, I confess I was startled to hear him answer that he should say his eyes deceived him. "But if you heard them speak?" I continued.

"I should disbelieve my ears."

"And if you touched and handled them?"

"I should mistrust my sense of feeling."

"Then by what means," I argued, "do you know that I am Florence Marryat? You can only see me and hear me and touch me! What is there to prevent your senses misleading you at the present moment?"

But to this argument Dr. H—— only returned a pitying smile, professing to think me, on this point at least, too feeble-minded to be worthy of reply, but in reality not knowing what on earth to say. He often, however, recurred to the subject of Spiritualism, and on several occasions told me that if I could procure him the opportunity of submitting a test which he might himself suggest, he should be very much obliged to me. It was about this time that a young medium, named William Haxby, now passed away, went to live with Mr. and Mrs. Olive in Ainger Terrace, and we were invited to attend a *séance* given by him. Mrs. Olive, when giving the invitation, informed me that Mr. Haxby had been very successful in procuring direct writing in sealed boxes, and she asked me, if I wished to try the experiment, to take a secured box, with writing materials in it, to the *séance*, and see what would happen to it.

Here was, I thought, an excellent opportunity for Dr. H——'s test, and I sent for him and told him what had been proposed. I urged him to prepare the test entirely by himself, and to accompany me to the *séance* and see what occurred—to all of which he readily consented. Indeed, he became quite excited on the subject, being certain it would prove a failure; and in my presence he made the following preparations:—

I. Half a sheet of ordinary cream-laid note-paper and half a cedar-wood black lead pencil were placed in a jeweller's cardwood box.

II. The lid of the box was carefully glued down all round to the bottom part.

III. The box was wrapt in white writing paper, which was gummed over it.

IV. It was tied eight times with a peculiar kind of silk made for tying up arteries, and the eight knots were knots known to (as Dr. H—— informed me) medical men only.

V. Each of the eight knots was sealed with sealing-wax, and impressed with Dr. H——'s crest seal, which he always wore on his watch-chain.

VI. The packet was again folded in brown paper, and sealed and tied to preserve the inside from injury.

When Dr. H—— had finished it, he said to me, "If the spirits (or anybody) can write on that paper without cutting the silk, *I will believe whatever you wish.*" I asked, "Are you *quite* sure that the packet could not be undone without your detecting it?" His answer was—"That silk is not to be procured except from a medical man; it is manufactured expressly for the tying of arteries; and the knots I have made are known only to medical men. They are the knots we use in tying arteries. The seal is my own crest, which never leaves my watch-chain, and I defy anyone to undo those knots without cutting them, or to tie them again, if cut. I repeat—if your friends can make, or cause to be made, the smallest mark on that paper, and return me the box in the condition it now is, *I will believe anything you choose.*" And I confess I was very dubious of the result myself, and almost sorry that I had subjected the doctor's incredulity to so severe a test.

On the evening appointed we attended the *séance*, Dr. H—— taking the prepared packet with him. He was directed to place it under his chair, but he tied a string to it and put it under his foot, retaining the other end of the string in his hand. The meeting was not one for favourably impressing an unbeliever in Spiritualism. There were too many people present, and too many strangers. The ordinary manifestations, to my mind, are worse than useless, unless they have been preceded by extraordinary ones; so that the doctor returned home more sceptical than before, and I repented that I had taken him there. One thing had occurred, however, that he could not account for. The packet which he had kept, as he thought, under his foot the whole time, was found, at the close of the meeting, to have disappeared. Another gentleman had brought a sealed box, with paper and pencil in it, to the *séance*; and at the close it was opened in the presence of all assembled, and found to contain a closely written letter from his deceased wife. But the doctor's box had evaporated, and was nowhere to be found. The door of the room had been locked all the time, and we searched the room thoroughly, but without success. Dr. H—— was naturally triumphant.

"They couldn't undo *my* knots and *my* seals," he said, exulting over me, "and so they wisely did not return the packet. Both packets were of course taken from the room during the sitting by some confederate of the medium. The other one was easily managed, and put back again—*mine* proved unmanageable, and so they have retained it. I *knew* it would be so!"

And he twinkled his eyes at me as much as to say, "I have shut *you* up. You will not venture to describe any of the marvels you have seen to me after this." Of course the failure did not discompose me, nor shake my belief. I never believed spiritual beings to be omnipotent, omnipresent, nor omniscient. They had failed before, and doubtless they would fail again. But if an acrobatic performer fails to turn a double somersault on to another man's head two or three times, it does not falsify the fact that he succeeds on the fourth occasion. I was sorry that the test had been a failure, for Dr. H——'s sake, but I did not despair of seeing the box again. And at the end of a fortnight it was left at my house by Mr. Olive, with a note to say that it had been found that morning on the mantel-piece in Mr. Haxby's bedroom, and he lost no time in returning it to me. It was wrapt in the brown paper, tied and sealed, apparently just as we had carried it to the *séance* in Ainger Terrace; and I wrote at once to Dr. H—— announcing its return, and asking him to come over and open it in my presence. He came, took the packet in his hand, and having stripped off the outer wrapper, examined it carefully. There were four tests, it may be remembered, applied to the packet.

I. The arterial silk, procurable only from a medical man.

II. The knots to be tied only by medical men.

III. Dr. H——'s own crest, always kept on his watch-chain, as a seal.

IV. The lid of the cardboard box, glued all round to the bottom part.

As the doctor scrutinized the silk, the knots, and the seals, I watched him narrowly.

"Are you *quite sure*," I asked, "that it is the same paper in which you wrapt it?"

"I am *quite sure*."

"And the same silk?"

"Quite sure."

"Your knots have not been untied?"

"I am positive that they have not."

"Nor your seal been tampered with?"

"Certainly not! It is just as I sealed it."

"Be careful, Dr. H——" I continued. "Remember I shall write down all you say."

"I am willing to swear to it in a court of justice," he replied.

"Then will you open the packet?"

Dr. H—— took the scissors and cut the silk at each seal and knot, then tore off the gummed white writing paper (which was as fresh as when he had put it on), and tried to pull open the cardboard box. But as he could not do this in consequence of the lid being glued down, he took out his penknife and cut it all round. As he did so, he looked at me and said, "Mark my words. There will be nothing written on the paper. It is impossible!"

He lifted the lid, and behold *the box was empty*! The half sheet of note-paper and the half cedar wood pencil had both *entirely disappeared*. Not a crumb of lead, nor a shred of paper remained behind. I looked at the doctor, and the doctor looked completely bewildered.

"*Well!*" I said, interrogatively.

He shifted about—grew red—and began to bluster.

"What do you make of it?" I asked. "How do you account for it?"

"In the easiest way in the world," he replied, trying to brave it out. "It's the most transparent deception I ever saw. They've kept the thing a fortnight and had time to do anything with it. A child could see through this. Surely your bright wits can want no help to an explanation."

"I am not so bright as you give me credit for," I answered. "Will you explain your meaning to me?"

"With pleasure. They have evidently made an invisible slit in the joining of the box cover, and with a pair of fine forceps drawn the paper through it, bit by bit. For the pencil, they drew that by the same means to the slit and then pared it, little by little, with a lancet, till they could shake out the fragments."

"That must have required very careful manipulation," I observed.

"Naturally. But they've taken a fortnight to do it in."

"But how about the arterial silk?" I said.

"They must have procured some from a surgeon."

"And your famous knots?"

"They got some surgeon to tie them!"

"But your crest and seal?"

"Oh! they must have taken a facsimile of that in order to reproduce it. It is very cleverly done, but quite explicable!"

"But you told me before you opened the packet that you would take your oath in a court of justice it had not been tampered with."

"I was evidently deceived."

"And you really believe, then, that an uneducated lad like Mr. Haxby would take the trouble to take impressions of seals and to procure arterial silk and the services of a surgeon, in order, not to mystify or convert *you*, but to gratify *me*, whose box he believes it to be."

"I am sure he has done so!"

"But just now you were equally sure he had *not* done so. Why should you trust your senses in one case more than in the other? And if Mr. Haxby has played a trick on me, as you suppose, why did you not discover the slit when you examined the box, before opening?"

"Because my eyes misled me!"

"Then after all," I concluded, "the best thing you can say of yourself is that you—a man of reputed science, skill, and sense, and with a strong belief in your own powers— are unable to devise a test in which you shall not be outwitted by a person so inferior to yourself in age, intellect and education as young Haxby. But I will give you another chance. Make up another packet in any way you like. Apply to it the severest tests which your ingenuity can devise, or other men of genius can suggest to you, and let me give it to Haxby and see if the contents can be extracted, or tampered with a second time."

"It would be useless," said Dr. H——. "If they were

extracted through the iron panels of a fireproof safe, I would not believe it was done by any but natural means."

"Because you do not *wish* to believe," I argued.

"You are right," he confessed, "I do *not* wish to believe. If you convinced me of the truth of Spiritualism, you would upset all the theories I have held for the best part of my life. I don't believe in a God, nor a soul, nor a future existence, and I would rather not believe in them. We have quite enough trouble, in my opinion, in this life, without looking forward to another, and I would rather cling to my belief that when we die we have done with it once and for ever."

So there ended my attempt to convince Dr. H——, and I have often thought since that he was but a type of the genus sceptic.

CHAPTER VII

THE STORY OF JOHN POWLES

On the 4th of April, 1860, there died in India a young officer in the 12th Regiment M.N.I., of the name of John Powles. He was an intimate friend of my first husband for several years before his death; indeed, on several occasions he shared our house and lived with us on the terms of a brother.

John Powles, however, though a careless and irreligious man, liked to discuss the Unseen. We talked continually on the subject, even when he was apparently in perfect health, and he often ended our conversation by assuring me that should he die first (and he always prophesied truly that he should not reach the age of thirty) he would (were such a thing possible) come back to me. I used to laugh at the absurdity of the idea, and remind him how many friends had made the same promise to each other and never fulfilled it. For though I firmly believed that such things *had* been, I could not realize that they would ever happen to me, or that I should survive the shock if they did. John Powles' death at the last was very sudden, although the diesase he died of was of long standing. He had been under the doctor's hands for a few days when he took an unexpected turn for the worse, and my husband and myself, with other friends, were summoned to his bedside to say good-bye to him. When I entered the room he said to me, "So you see it has come at last. Don't forget what I said to you about it." They were his last intelligible words to me, though for several hours he grasped my dress with his hand to prevent my leaving him, and became violent and umanageable if I attempted to quit his side. During this time, in the intervals of his delirium, he kept on entreating me to sing a certain old ballad, which had always been a great favourite with him, entitled "Thou art gone from my gaze." I am sure if I sung that song once during that miserable day, I must have sung it a dozen times. At last our poor friend fell into convulsions which recurred with little intermission until his death, which took place on the same evening.

His death and the manner of it caused me a great shock. He had been a true friend to my husband and myself for years, and we both mourned his loss very sincerely. That, and other troubles combined, had a serious effect upon my health, and the doctors advised my immediate return to England. When an officer dies in India, it is the custom to sell all his minor effects by auction. Before this took place, my husband asked me if there was anything belonging to John Powles that I should like to keep in remembrance of him. The choice I made was a curious one. He had possessed a dark green silk necktie, which was a favourite of his, and when it became soiled I offered to turn it for him, when it looked as good as new. Whereupon he had worn it so long that it was twice as dirty as before, so I turned it for him the second time, much to the amusement of the regiment. When I was asked to choose a keepsake of him, I said, "Give me the green tie," and I brought it to England with me.

3

The voyage home was a terrible affair. I was suffering mentally and physically, to such a degree that I cannot think of the time without a shudder. John Powles' death, of course, added to my distress, and during the many months that occupied a voyage "by long sea," I hoped and expected that his spirit would appear to me. With the very strong belief in the possibility of the return to earth of the departed— or rather, I should say, with my strong belief *in* my belief—I lay awake night after night, thinking to see my lost friend, who had so often promised to come back to me. I even cried aloud to him to appear and tell me where he was, or what he was doing, but I never heard or saw a single thing. There was silence on every side of me. Ten days only after I landed in England I was delivered of a daughter, and when I had somewhat recovered my health and spirits—when I had lost the physical weakness and nervous excitability, to which most medical men would have attributed any mysterious sights or sounds I might have experienced before—then I commenced to *know* and to *feel* that John Powles was with me again. I did not see him, but I felt his presence. I used to lie awake at night, trembling under the consciousness that he was sitting at my bedside, and I had no means of penetrating the silence between us. Often I entreated him to speak, but when a low, hissing sound came close to my ear, I would scream with terror and rush from my room. All my desire to see or communicate with my lost friend had deserted me. The very idea was a terror. I was horror-struck to think he had returned, and I would neither sleep alone nor remain alone. I was advised to try a livelier place than Winchester (where I then resided), and a house was taken for me at Sydenham. But there, the sense of the presence of John Powles was as keen as before, and so, at intervals, I continued to feel it for the space of several years—until, indeed, I became an inquirer into Spiritualism as a science.

I have related in the chapter that contains an account of

my first *séance*, that the only face I recognized as belonging to me was that of my friend John Powles, and how excited I became on seeing it. It was that recognition that brought back all my old longing and curiosity to communicate with the inhabitants of the Unseen World. As soon as I commenced investigations in my home circle, John Powles was the very first spirit who spoke to me through the table, and from that time until the present I have never ceased to hold communion with him. He is very shy, however (as he was whilst with us) of conversing before strangers, and seldom intimates his presence except I am alone. At such times, however, he will talk by the hour of all such topics as interested him during his earth life.

Soon after it became generally known that I was attending *séances*, I was introduced to Miss Showers, the daughter of General Showers of the Bombay Army. This young lady, besides being little more than a child—I think she was about sixteen when we met—was not a professional medium. The *séances* to which her friends were invited to witness the extraordinary manifestations that took place in her presence were strictly private. They offered therefore an enormous advantage to investigators, as the occurrences were all above suspicion, whilst Miss Showers was good enough to allow herself to be tested in every possible way. I shall have occasion to refer more particularly to Miss Showers' mediumship further on—at present, therefore, I will confine myself to those occasions which afforded proofs of John Powles' presence.

Mrs. and Miss Showers were living in apartments when I visited them, and there was no means nor opportunity of deceiving their friends, even had they had any object in doing so. I must add also, that they knew nothing of my Indian life nor experiences, which were things of the past long before I met them. At the first sitting Miss Showers gave me for "spirit faces," she merely sat on a chair behind the window curtains, which were pinned together half-way up, so as to leave a V-shaped opening at the top. The voice of "Peter" (Miss Showers' principal control) kept talking to us and the medium from behind the curtains all the time, and making remarks on the faces as they appeared at the opening. Presently he said to me, "Mrs. Ross-Church, here's a fellow says his name is Powles, and he wants to speak to you, only he doesn't like to show himself because he's not a bit like what he used to be." "Tell him not to mind that," I answered, "I shall know him under any circumstances." "Well! if he was anything like that, he was a beauty," exclaimed Peter; and presently a face appeared which I could not, by any stretch of imagination, decide to resemble in the slightest degree my old friend. It was hard, stiff and unlifelike. After it had disappeared, Peter said, "Powles says if you'll come and sit with Rosie (Miss Showers) often, he'll look quite like himself by-and-by," and of course I was only too anxious to accept the invitation.

As I was setting out another evening to sit with Miss Showers, the thought suddenly occurred to me to put the green necktie in my pocket. My two daughters accompanied me on that occasion, but I said nothing to them about the necktie. As soon as we had commenced, however, Peter called out, "Now, Mrs. Ross-Church, hand over that necktie. Powles is coming." "What necktie?" I asked, and he answered, "Why, Powles' necktie, of course, that you've got in your pocket. He wants you to put it round his neck." The assembled party looked at me inquisitively as I produced the tie. The face of John Powles appeared, very different from the time before, as he had his own features and complexion, but his hair and beard (which were auburn during life) appeared phosphoric, as though made of living fire. I mounted on a chair and tied the necktie round his throat, and asked him if he would kiss me. He shook his head. Peter called out, "Give him your hand." I did so, and as he kissed it, his moustaches *burned* me. I cannot account for it. I can only relate the fact. After which he disappeared with the necktie, which I have never seen since, though we searched the little room for it thoroughly.

When Mr. William Fletcher gave his first lecture in England, in the Steinway Hall, my husband, Colonel Lean, and I, went to hear him. We had never seen Mr. Fletcher before, nor any of his family, nor did he know we were amongst the audience. Our first view of him was when he stepped upon the platform, and we were seated quite in the body of the hall, which was full. It was Mr. Fletcher's custom, after his lecture was concluded, to describe such visions as were presented to him, and he only asked in return that if the people and places were recognized, those who recognized them would be brave enough to say so, for the sake of the audience and himself. I can understand that strangers who went there and heard nothing that concerned themselves would be very apt to imagine it was all humbug, and that those who claimed a knowledge of the visions were simply confederates of Mr. Fletcher. But there is nothing more true than that circumstances alter cases. I entered Steinway Hall as a perfect stranger, and as a press-writer, quite prepared to expose trickery if I detected it. And this is what I heard. After Mr. Fletcher had described several persons and scenes unknown to me, he took out a handkerchief and began to wipe his face, as though he were very warm.

"I am no longer in England now," he said. "The scene has quite changed, and I am taken over the sea thousands of miles away, and I am in a chamber with all the doors and windows open. Oh! how hot it is! I think I am somewhere in the tropics. O! I see why I have been brought here! It is to see a young man die! This is a death chamber. He is lying on a bed. He looks very pale, and he is very near death, but he has only been ill a short time. His hair is a kind of golden chestnut colour and he has no eyes. He is an Englishman, and I can see the letter 'P' above his head. He has not been happy on earth and he is quite content to die. He pushes all the influences that are round his bed away from him. Now I see a lady come and sit down beside him. He holds her hand, and appears to ask her to do something, and I hear a strain of sweet music. It is a song he has heard in happier times, and on the breath of it his spirit passes away. It is to this lady he seems to come now. She is sitting on my left about half-way down the hall. A little girl, with her hands full of blue flowers, points her out to me. The little girl holds up the flowers, and I see they are woven into a resemblance of the letter F. She tells me that is the initial letter of her mother's name and her own. And I see this message written.

" 'To my dearest friend, for such you ever were to me from the beginning. I have been with you through all your time of trial and sorrow, and I am rejoiced to see that a happier era is beginning for you. I am always near you. The darkness is fast rolling away, and happiness will succeed it. Pray for me, and I shall be near you in your prayers. I pray God to bless you and to bless me, and to bring us together again in the summer land.'

"And I see the spirit pointing with his hand far away, as though to intimate that the happiness he speaks of is only the beginning of some that will extend to a long distance of time. I see this scene more plainly than any I have ever seen before."

These words were written down at the time they were spoken. Colonel Lean and I were sitting in the very spot indicated by Mr. Fletcher, and the little girl with the blue flowers was my spirit child, "Florence," whose history I shall give in the next chapter. But my communications with John Powles, though very extraordinary, were not satisfactory to me. I am the "Thomas, surnamed Didymus," of the spiritualistic world, who wants to see and touch and handle before I can altogether believe. I wanted to meet John Powles and talk with him face to face, and it seemed such an impossibility for him to materialize in the light that, after his two failures with Miss Showers, he refused to try. I was always worrying him to tell me if we should meet in the body before I left this world, and his answer was always, "Yes! but not just yet!" I had no idea then that I should have to cross the Atlantic before I saw my dear old friend again.

CHAPTER VIII

MY SPIRIT CHILD

THE same year that John Powles died, 1860, I passed through the greatest trouble of my life. It is quite unnecessary to my narrative to relate what that trouble was, nor how it affected me, but I suffered terribly both in mind and body, and it was chiefly for this reason that the medical men advised my return to England, which I reached on the 14th of December, and on the 30th of the same month a daughter was born to me, who survived her birth for only ten days. The child was born with a most peculiar blemish, which it is necessary for the purpose of my argument to describe. On the left side of the upper lip was a mark as though a semi-circular piece of flesh had been cut out by a bullet-mould, which exposed part of the gum. The swallow also had been submerged into the gullet, so that she had for the short period of her earthly existence to be fed by artificial means, and the jaw itself had been so twisted that could she have lived to cut her teeth, the double ones would have been in front. This blemish was considered to be of so remarkable a type that Dr. Frederick Butler of Winchester, who attended me, invited several other medical men from Southampton and other places, to examine the infant with him, and they all agreed that *a similar case had never come under their notice before*. This is a very important factor in my narrative. I was closely catechized as to whether I had suffered any physical or mental shock, that should account for the injury to my child, and it was decided that the trouble I had experienced was sufficient to produce it. The case, under feigned names, was fully reported in the *Lancet* as something quite out of the common way. My little child, who was baptized by the name of "Florence," lingered until the 10th of January, 1861, and then passed quietly away, and when my first natural disappointment was over I ceased to think of her except as of something which "might have been," but never would be again. In this world of misery, the loss of an infant is soon swallowed up in more active trouble. Still I never quite forgot my poor baby, perhaps because at that time she was happily the "one dead lamb" of my little flock. In recounting the events of my first *séance* with Mrs. Holmes, I have mentioned how a young girl much muffled up about the mouth and chin appeared, and intimated that she came for me, although I could not recognize her. I was so ignorant of the life beyond the grave at that period, that it never struck me that the baby who had left me at ten days old had been growing since our separation, until she had reached the age of ten years.

The first *séance* made such an impression on my mind that two nights afterwards I again presented myself (this time alone) at Mrs. Holmes' rooms to attend another. It was a very different circle on the second occasion. There were about thirty people present, all strangers to each other, and the manifestations were proportionately ordinary. Another professional medium, a Mrs. Davenport, was present, as one of her controls, whom she called "Bell," had promised, if possible, to show her face to her. As soon, therefore, as the first spirit face appeared (which was that of the same little girl that I had seen before), Mrs. Davenport exclaimed, "There, 'Bell'." "Why!" I said, "that's the little nun we saw on Monday." "O! no! that's my 'Bell'," persisted Mrs. Davenport. But Mrs. Holmes took my side, and was positive the spirit came for me. She told me she had been trying to communicate with her since the previous *séance*. "I know she is nearly connected with you," she said. "Have you never lost a relation of her age?" "*Never!*" I replied; and at that declaration the little spirit moved away, sorrowfully as before.

A few weeks after I received an invitation from Mr. Henry Dunphy (the gentleman who had introduced me to Mrs. Holmes) to attend a private *séance*, given at his own house in Upper Gloucester Place, by the well-known medium Florence Cook. The double drawing-rooms were divided by velvet curtains, behind which Miss Cook was seated in an armchair, the curtains being pinned together half-way up, leaving a large aperture in the shape of a V. Being a complete stranger to Miss Cook, I was surprised to hear the voice of her control direct that *I* should stand by the curtains and hold the lower parts together whilst the forms appeared above, lest the pins should give way, and necessarily from my position I could hear every word that passed between Miss Cook and her guide. The first face that showed itself was that of a man unknown to me; then ensued a kind of frightened colloquy between the medium and her control. "Take it away. Go away! I don't like you. Don't touch me—you frighten me! Go away!" I heard Miss Cook exclaim, and then her guide's voice interposed itself, "Don't be silly, Florrie. Don't be unkind. It won't hurt you," etc., and immediately afterwards the same little girl I had seen at Mrs. Holmes' rose to view at the aperture of the curtains, muffled up as before, but smiling with her eyes at me. I directed the attention of the company to her, calling her again my "little nun." I was surprised, however, at the evident distaste Miss Cook had displayed towards the spirit, and when the *séance* was concluded and she had regained her normal condition, I asked her if she could recall the faces she saw under trance. "Sometimes," she replied. I told her of the "little nun," and demanded the reason of her apparent dread of her. "I can hardly tell you," said Miss Cook; "I don't know anything about her. She is quite a stranger to me, but her face is not fully developed, I think. There is *something wrong about her mouth*. She frightens me."

This remark, though made with the utmost carelessness, set me thinking, and after I had returned home, I wrote to Miss Cook, asking her to inquire of her guides *who* the little spirit was.

She replied as follows:

"Dear Mrs. Ross-Church, I have asked 'Katie King,' but she cannot tell me anything further about the spirit that came through me the other evening than that she is a young girl closely connected with yourself."

I was not, however, yet convinced of the spirit's identity, although "John Powles" constantly assured me that it *was* my child. I tried hard to communicate with her at home, but without success. I find in the memoranda I kept of our private *séances* at that period several messages from "Powles" referring to "Florence." In one he says, "Your child's want of power to communicate with you is not because she is too pure, but because she is too weak. She will speak to you some day. She is *not* in heaven." This last assertion, knowing so little as I did of a future state, both puzzled and grieved me. I could not believe that an innocent infant was not in the Beatific Presence—yet I could not understand what motive my friend could have in leading me astray. I had yet to learn that once received into Heaven no spirit could return to earth, and that a spirit may have a training to undergo, even though it has never committed a mortal sin. A further proof, however, that my dead child had never died was to reach me from a quarter where I least expected it. I was editor of the magazine *London Society* at that time, and amongst my contributors was Dr. Keningale Cook, who had married Mabel Collins, the now well-known writer of spiritualistic novels. One day Dr. Cook brought me an invitation from his wife (whom I had never met) to spend Saturday to Monday with them in their cottage at Redhill, and I accepted it, knowing nothing of the proclivities of either of them, and they knowing as little of my private history as I did of theirs. And I must take this opportunity to observe that, at this period, I had never made my lost child the subject of conversation even with my most intimate friends. The memory of her life and death, and the troubles that caused it, was not a happy one, and of no interest to any but myself. So little, therefore, had it been discussed amongst us that until "Florence" reappeared to revive the topic, my *elder children were ignorant* that their sister had been marked in any way differently from themselves. It may, therefore, be supposed how unlikely it was that utter strangers and public media should have gained any inkling of the matter. I went down to Redhill, and as I was sitting with the Keningale Cooks after dinner, the subject of Spiritualism came on the *tapis*, and I was informed that the wife was a powerful trance medium, which much interested me, as I had not, at that period, had any experience of her particular class of mediumship. In the evening we "sat" together, and Mrs. Cook having become entranced, her husband took shorthand notes of her utterances. Several old friends of their family spoke through her, and I was listening to them in the listless manner in which we hear the conversation of strangers, when my attention was aroused by the medium suddenly leaving her seat, and falling on her knees before me, kissing my hands and face, and sobbing violently the while. I waited in expectation of hearing who this might be, when the manifestations as suddenly ceased, the medium returned to her seat, and the voice of one of her guides said that the spirit was unable to speak through excess of emotion, but would try again later in the evening. I had almost forgotten the circumstances in listening to other communications, when I was startled by hearing the word "*Mother!*" sighed rather than spoken. I was about to make some excited reply, when the medium raised her hand to enjoin silence, and the following communication was taken down by Mr. Cook as she pronounced the words. The sentences in parentheses are my replies to her.

"Mother! I am 'Florence.' I must be very quiet. I want to feel I have a mother still. I am so lonely. Why should I be so? I cannot speak well. I want to be like one of you. I want to feel I have a mother and sisters. I am so far away from you all now."

("But I always think of you, my dear dead baby.")

"That's just it—your *baby*. But I'm not a baby now. I shall get nearer. They tell me I shall. I do not know if I can come when you are alone. It's all so dark. I know you are there, but *so dimly*. I've grown *all by myself*. I'm not really unhappy, but I want to get nearer you. I know you think of me, but you think of me as a baby. You don't know me as I *am*. You've seen me, because in my love I have forced myself upon you. I've not been amongst the flowers yet, but I shall be, very soon now; but I want *my mother* to take me there. All has been given me that can be given me, but I cannot receive it, except in so far——"

Here she seemed unable to express herself.

("Did the trouble I had before your birth affect your spirit, Florence?")

"Only as things cause each other. I was with you, Mother, all through that trouble. I should be nearer to you, *than any child you have*, if I could only get close to you."

("I can't bear to hear you speak so sadly, dear. I have always believed that *you*, at least, were happy in Heaven.")

"I am *not* in Heaven! But there will come a day, Mother— I can laugh when I say it—when we shall go to Heaven *together* and pick blue flowers—*blue flowers*. They are so good to me here, but if your eye cannot bear the daylight you cannot see the buttercups and daisies."

I did not learn till afterwards that in the spiritual language blue flowers are typical of happiness. The next question I asked her was if she thought she could write through me.

"I don't seem able to write through you, but why, I know not."

("Do you know your sisters, Eva and Ethel?")

"No! no!" in a weary voice. "The link of sisterhood is only through the mother. That kind of sisterhood does not last, because there is a higher."

("Do you ever see your father?")

"No! he is far, far away. I went once, not more. Mother dear, he'll love me when he comes here. They've told me so, and they always tell truth here! I am but a child, yet not so very little. I seem composed of two things—a child in ignorance and a woman in years. Why can't I speak at other places? I have wished and tried! I've come very near, but it seems so easy to speak now. This medium seems so different."

("I wish you could come to me when I am alone, Florence.")

"You *shall* know me! I *will* come, Mother dear. I shall always be able to come here. I *do* come to you, but not in the same way."

She spoke in such a plaintive, melancholy voice that Mrs. Cook, thinking she would depress my spirits, said, "Don't make your state out to be sadder than it really is." Her reply was very remarkable.

"*I am, as I am!* Friend! when you come here, if you find that sadness *is*, you will not be able to alter it by plunging into material pleasures. *Our sadness makes the world we live in.* It is not deeds that make us wrong. It is the state in which *we were born*. Mother! you say I died sinless. That is nothing. I was born *in a state*. Had I lived, I should have caused you more pain than you can know. I am better here. I was not fit to battle with the world, and they took me from it. Mother! you won't let this make you sad. You must not."

("What can I do to bring you nearer to me?")

"I don't know what will bring me nearer, but I'm helped

already by just talking to you. There's a ladder of brightness—every step. I believe I've gained just one step now. O! the Divine teachings are so mysterious. Mother! does it seem strange to you to hear your 'baby' say things as if she knew them? I'm going now. Good-bye!"

And so "Florence" went. The next voice that spoke was that of a guide of the medium, and I asked her for a personal description of my daughter as she then appeared. She replied, "Her face is downcast. We have tried to cheer her, but she is very sad. It is the *state in which she was born*. Every physical deformity is the mark of a condition. A weak body is not necessarily the mark of a weak spirit, but the *prison* of it, because the spirit might be too passionate otherwise. You cannot judge in what way the mind is deformed because the body is deformed. It does not follow that a canker in the body is a canker in the mind. But the mind may be too exuberant—may need a canker to restrain it."

I have copied this conversation, word for word, from the shorthand notes taken at the time of utterance; and when it is remembered that neither Mrs. Keningale Cook nor her husband knew that I had lost a child—that they had never been in my house nor associated with any of my friends—it will at least be acknowledged, even by the most sceptical, that it was a very remarkable coincidence that I should receive such a communication from the lips of a perfect stranger. Only once after this did "Florence" communicate with me through the same source. She found congenial media nearer home, and naturally availed herself of them. But the second occasion was almost more convincing than the first. I went one afternoon to consult my solicitor in the strictest confidence as to how I should act under some very painful circumstances, and he gave me his advice. The next morning as I sat at breakfast, Mrs. Cook, who was still living at Redhill, ran into my room with an apology for the unceremoniousness of her visit, on the score that she had received a message for me the night before which "Florence" had begged her to deliver without delay. The message was to this effect: "Tell my mother that I was with her this afternoon at the lawyer's, and she is *not* to follow the advice given her, as it will do harm instead of good." Mrs. Cook added, "I don't know to what 'Florence' alludes, of course, but I thought it best, as I was coming to town, to let you know at once."

The force of this anecdote does not lie in the context. The mystery is contained in the fact of a secret interview having been overheard and commented upon. But the truth is, that having greater confidence in the counsel of my visible guide than in that of my invisible one, I abided by the former, and regretted it ever afterwards.

The first conversation I held with "Florence" had a great effect upon me. I knew before that my uncontrolled grief had been the cause of the untimely death of her body, but it had never struck me that her spirit would carry the effects of it into the unseen world. It was a warning to me (as it should be to all mothers) not to take the solemn responsibility of maternity upon themselves without being prepared to sacrifice their own feelings for the sake of their children. "Florence" assured me, however, that communion with myself in my improved condition of happiness would soon lift her spirit from its state of depression and consequently I seized every opportunity of seeing and speaking with her. During the succeeding twelve months I attended numerous *séances* with various media, and my spirit child (as she called herself) never failed to manifest through the influence of any one of them, though, of course, in different ways. Through some she touched me only, and always with an infant's hand, that I might recognize it as hers, or laid her mouth against mine that I might feel the scar upon her lips; through others she spoke, or wrote, or showed her face, but I never attended a *séance* at which she omitted to notify her presence. Once at a dark circle, held with Mr. Charles Williams, after having had my dress and that of my next neighbour, Lady Archibald Campbell, pulled several times, as if to attract our attention, the darkness opened before us, and there stood my child, smiling at us like a happy dream, her fair hair waving about her temples, and her blue eyes fixed on me. She was clothed in white, but we saw no more than her head and bust, about which her hands held her drapery. Lady Archibald Campbell saw her as plainly as I did. On another occasion Mr. William Eglinton proposed to me to try and procure the spirit-writing on his arm. He directed me to go into another room and write the name of the friend I loved best in the spirit world upon a scrap of paper, which I was to twist up tightly and take back to him. I did so, writing the name of "John Powles." When I returned to Mr. Eglinton, he bared his arm, and holding the paper to the candle till it was reduced to tinder, rubbed his flesh with the ashes. I know what was expected to ensue. The name written on the paper was to reappear in red or white letters on the medium's arm. The sceptic would say it was a trick of thought-reading, and that, the medium knowing what I had written, had prepared the writing during my absence. But to his surprise and mine, when, at last he shook the ashes from his arm, we read, written in a bold, clear hand, the words—"Florence is the dearest," as though my spirit child had given me a gentle rebuke for writing any name but her own. It seems curious to me now to look back and remember how melancholy she used to be when she first came back to me, for as soon as she had established an unbroken communication between us, she developed into the merriest little spirit I have ever known, and though her childhood has now passed away, and she is more dignified and thoughtful and womanly, she always appears joyous and happy. She has manifested largely to me through the mediumship of Mr. Arthur Colman. I had known her during a dark *séance* with a very small private circle (the medium being securely held and fastened the while) run about the room, like the child she was, and speak to and kiss each sitter in turn, pulling off the sofa and chair covers and piling them up in the middle of the table, and changing the ornaments of everyone present—placing the gentlemen's neckties round the throats of the ladies, and hanging the ladies' earrings in the buttonholes of the gentlemen's coats—just as she might have done had she been still with us, a happy, petted child, on earth. I have known her come in the dark and sit on my lap and kiss my face and hands, and let me feel the defect in her mouth with my own. One bright evening on the 9th of July—my birth-day—Arthur Colman walked in quite unexpectedly to pay me a visit, and as I had some friends with me, we agreed to have a *séance*. It was impossible to make the room dark, as the windows were only shaded by venetian blinds, but we lowered them, and sat in the twilight. The first thing we heard was the voice of "Florence" whispering—"A present for dear Mother's birthday," when something was put into my hand. Then she crossed to the side of a lady present and dropped something into her hand, saying, "And a present for dear Mother's friend!" I knew at once by the feel of it that what "Florence" had given me was a chaplet of beads, and knowing how often, under similar circumstances, articles are merely carried about a room, I concluded it was one which lay upon my drawing-room mantelpiece, and said as much. I was answered by the voice of "Aimée," the medium's nearest control.

"You are mistaken," she said, " 'Florence' has given you a chaplet you have never seen before. She was exceedingly anxious to give you a present on your birthday, so I gave her the beads which were buried with me. They came from my coffin. I held them in my hand. All I ask is that you will not show them to Arthur until I give you leave. He is not well at present, and the sight of them will upset him."

I was greatly astonished, but, of course, I followed her instructions, and when I had an opportunity to examine the beads, I found that they really were strangers to me, and had not been in the house before. The present my lady friend had received was a large, unset topaz. The chaplet was made of carved wood and steel. It was not till months had elapsed that I was given permission to show it to Arthur Colman. He immediately recognized it as the one he had himself placed in the hands of "Aimée" as she lay in her coffin, and when I saw how the sight affected him, I regretted I had told him anything about it. I offered to give the beads up to him, but he refused to receive them, and they remain in my possession to this day.

But the great climax that was to prove beyond all question the personal identity of the spirit who communicated with me, with the body I had brought into the world, was yet to come. Mr. William Harrison, the editor of the *Spiritualist* (who, after seventeen years' patient research into the science of Spiritualism, had never received a personal proof of the return of his own friends, or relations) wrote me word that he had received a message from his lately deceased friend, Mrs. Stewart, to the effect that if he would sit with the medium Florence Cook, and one or two harmonious companions, she would do her best to appear to him in her earthly likeness and afford him the test he had so long sought after. Mr. Harrison asked me, therefore, if I would join him and Miss Kidlingbury—the secretary to the British National Association of Spiritualists—in holding a *séance* with Miss Cook, to which I agreed, and we met in one of the rooms of the Association for that purpose. It was a very small room, about 8 feet by 16 feet, was uncarpeted and contained no furniture, so we carried in three cane-bottomed chairs for our accommodation. Across one corner of the room, about four feet from the floor, we nailed an old black shawl, and placed a cushion behind it for Miss Cook to lean her head against. Miss Florence Cook, who is a brunette, of a small, slight figure, with dark eyes and hair which she wore in a profusion of curls, was dressed in light grey merino, ornamented with crimson ribbons. She informed me previous to sitting, that she had become restless during her trances lately, and in the habit of walking out amongst the circle, and she asked me as a friend (for such we had by that time become) to scold her well should such a thing occur, and order her to go back into the cabinet as if she were "a child or a dog"; and I promised her I would do so. After Florence Cook had sat down on the floor, behind the black shawl (which left her grey merino skirt exposed), and laid her head against the cushion, we lowered the gas a little, and took our seats on the three cane chairs. The medium appeared very uneasy at first, and we heard her remonstrating with the influences for using her so roughly. In a few minutes, however, there was a tremulous movement of the black shawl, and a large white hand was several times thrust into view and withdrawn again. I had never seen Mrs. Stewart (for whom we were expressly sitting) in this life, and could not, therefore, recognize the hand; but we all remarked how large and white it was. In another minute the shawl was lifted up, and a female figure crawled on its hands and knees from behind it, and then stood up and regarded us. It was impossible, in the dim light and at the distance she stood from us, to identify the features, so Mr. Harrison asked if she were Mrs. Stewart. The figure shook its head. I had lost a sister a few months previously, and the thought flashed across me that it might be her. "Is it you, Emily?" I asked; but the head was still shaken to express a negative, and a similar question on the part of Miss Kidling-bury, with respect to a friend of her own, met with the same response. "Who *can* it be?" I remarked curiously to Mr. Harrison.

"Mother! don't you know me?" sounded in "Florence's" whispering voice. I started up to approach her exclaiming, "O! my darling child! I never thought I should meet you here!" But she said, "Go back to your chair, and I will come to you?" I reseated myself, and "Florence" crossed the

room and sat down *on my lap*. She was more unclothed on
that occasion than any materialized spirit I have ever seen.
She wore nothing on her head, only her hair, of which she
appears to have an immense quantity, fell down her back
and covered her shoulders. Her arms were bare and her feet
and part of her legs, and the dress she wore had no shape or
style, but seemed like so many yards of soft thick muslin,
wound round her body from the bosom to below the knees.
She was a heavy weight—perhaps ten stone—and had well-
covered limbs. In fact, she was then, and has appeared for several years past, to be, in point of size and shape, so like her
eldest sister Eva, that I always observe the resemblance
between them. This *séance* took place at a period when
"Florence" must have been about seventeen years old.

"Florence, my darling," I said, "is this *really* you?" "Turn
up the gas," she answered, "and look at my mouth." Mr.
Harrison did as she desired, and we all saw distinctly *that
peculiar defect on the lip* with which she was born—a defect, be
it remembered, which some of the most experienced members
of the profession had affirmed to be "*so rare as never to have
fallen under their notice before.*" She also opened her mouth that
we might see she had no gullet. I promised at the commencement of my book to confine myself to facts, and leave the
deductions to be drawn from them to my readers, so I will
not interrupt my narrative to make any remarks upon this
incontrovertible proof of identity. I know it struck me
dumb, and melted me into tears. At this juncture Miss Cook,
who had been moaning and moving about a good deal behind
the black shawl, suddenly exclaimed, "I can't stand this any
longer," and walked out into the room. There she stood in her
grey dress and crimson ribbons whilst "Florence" sat on my
lap in white drapery. But only for a moment, for directly the
medium was fully in view, the spirit sprung up and darted
behind the curtain. Recalling Miss Cook's injunctions to me, I
scolded her heartily for leaving her seat, until she crept back,

whimpering, to her former position. The shawl had scarcely closed behind her before "Florence" reappeared and clung to me saying, "Don't let her do that again. She frightens me so." She was actually trembling all over. "Why, Florence," I replied, "do you mean to tell me you are frightened of your medium? In this world it is we poor mortals who are frightened of the spirits." "I am afraid she will send me away, Mother," she whispered. However, Miss Cook did not disturb us again, and "Florence" stayed with us for some time longer. She clasped her arms round my neck, and laid her head upon my bosom, and kissed me dozens of times. She took my hand and spread it out, and said she felt sure I should recognize her hand when she thrust it outside the curtain, because it was so much like my own. I was suffering much trouble at that time, and "Florence" told me the reason God had permitted her to show herself to me in her earthly deformity was so that I might be sure that she was herself, and that Spiritualism was a truth to comfort me. "Sometimes you doubt, Mother," she said, "and think your eyes and ears have misled you; but after this you must never doubt again. Don't fancy I am like this in the spirit land. The blemish left me long ago. But I put it on to-night to make you certain. Don't fret, dear Mother. Remember I am always near you. No one can take me away. Your earthly children may grow up and go out into the world and leave you, but you will always have your spirit child close to you." I did not, and cannot, calculate for how long "Florence" remained visible on that occasion. Mr. Harrison told me afterwards that she had remained for nearly twenty minutes. But her undoubted presence was such a stupendous fact to me, that I could only think that *she was there*—that I actually held in my arms the tiny infant I had laid with my own hands in her coffin—that she was no more dead than I was myself, but had grown to be a woman. So I sat, with my arms tight round her, and my heart beating against hers, until the power decreased, and "Florence" was compelled to give me a last kiss and leave me stupefied and bewildered by what had so unexpectedly occurred. Two other spirits materialized and appeared after she had left us, but as neither of them was Mrs. Stewart, the *séance*, as far as Mr. Harrison was concerned, was a failure. I have seen and heard "Florence" on numerous occasions since the one I have narrated, but not with the mark upon her mouth, which she assures me will never trouble either of us again. I could fill pages with accounts of her pretty, caressing ways and her affectionate and sometimes solemn messages; but I have told as much of her story as will interest the general reader. It has been wonderful to me to mark how her ways and mode of communication have changed with the passing years. It was a simple child who did not know how to express itself that appeared to me in 1873. It is a woman full of counsel and tender warning that comes to me in 1890. But yet she is only nineteen. When she reached that age, "Florence" told me she should never grow any older in years or appearance, and that she had reached the climax of womanly perfection in the spirit world. Only to-night—the night before Christmas Day—as I write her story, she comes to me and says, "Mother! you must not give way to sad thoughts. The Past is past. Let it be buried in the blessings that remain to you."

And amongst the greatest of those blessings I reckon my belief in the existence of my spirit-child.

CHAPTER IX

THE STORY OF EMILY

My sister Emily was the third daughter of my late father, and several years older than myself. She was a handsome woman —strictly speaking, perhaps, the handsomest of the family, and quite unlike the others. She had black hair and eyes, a pale complexion, a well-shaped nose, and small, narrow hands and feet. But her beauty had slight detractions—so slight, indeed, as to be imperceptible to strangers, but well known to her intimate friends. Her mouth was a little on one side, one shoulder was half an inch higher than the other, her fingers were not quite straight, nor her toes, and her hips corresponded with her shoulders. She was clever, with a versatile, all-round talent, and of a very happy and contented disposition. She married Dr. Henry Norris of Charmouth, in Dorset, and lived there many years before her death. She was an excellent wife and mother, a good friend, and a sincere Christian; indeed, I do not believe that a more earnest, self-denying, better woman ever lived in this world. But she had strong feelings, and in some things she was very bigoted. One was Spiritualism. She vehemently opposed even the mention of it, declared it to be diabolical, and never failed to blame me for pursuing such a wicked and unholy occupation. She was therefore about the last person whom I should have expected to take advantage of it to communicate with her friends.

My sister Emily died on the 20th of April, 1875. Her death resulted from a sudden attack of pleurisy, and was most unexpected. I was sitting at an early dinner with my children on the same day when I received a telegram from my brother-in-law to say, "Emily very ill; will telegraph when change occurs," and I had just despatched an answer to ask if I should go down to Charmouth, or could be of any use, when a second message arrived, "All is over. She died quietly at two o'clock." Those who have received similar shocks will understand what I felt. I was quite stunned, and could not realize that my sister had passed away from us, so completely unanticipated had been the news. I made the necessary arrangements for going down to her funeral, but my head was filled with nothing but thoughts of Emily the while, and conjectures of *how* she had died and of *what* she had died (for that was, as yet, unknown to me), and what she had thought and said; above all, what she was thinking and feeling at that moment. I retired to rest with my brain in a whirl, and lay half the night wide awake, staring into the darkness, and wondering where my sister was. *Now* was the time (if any) for my cerebral organs to play me a trick, and conjure up a vision of the person I was thinking of. But I saw nothing; no sound broke the stillness; my eyes rested only on the darkness. I was quite disappointed, and in the morning I told my children so. I loved my sister Emily dearly, and I hoped she would have come to wish me good-bye. On the following night I was exhausted by want of sleep and the emotion I had passed through, and when I went to bed I was very sleepy. I had not been long asleep, however, before I was waked up—I can hardly say by what—and there at my bedside stood Emily, smiling at me. When I lost my little "Florence," Emily had been unmarried, and she had taken a great interest in my poor baby, and nursed her during her short lifetime, and, I believe, really mourned her loss, for (although she had children of her own) she always wore a little likeness of "Florence" in a locket on her watch-chain. When Emily died I had of course been for some time in communication with my spirit-child, and when my sister appeared to me that night, "Florence" was in her arms, with her head resting on her shoulder. I recognized them both at once, and the only thing which looked strange to me was that Emily's long black hair was combed right back in the Chinese fashion, giving her forehead an unnaturally high appearance. This circumstance made the greater impression on me, because we all have such high foreheads with the hair growing off the temples that we have never been able to wear it in the style I speak of. With this exception my sister looked beautiful and most happy, and my little girl clung to her lovingly. Emily did not speak aloud, but she kept on looking down at "Florence," and up at me, whilst her lips formed the words, "Little Baby," which was the name by which she had always mentioned my spirit-child. In the morning I mentioned what I had seen to my elder girls, adding, "I hardly knew dear Aunt Emily, with her hair scratched back in that fashion."

This apparition happened on the Wednesday night, and on the Friday following I travelled down to Charmouth to be present at the funeral, which was fixed for Saturday. I found my sister Cecil there before me. As soon as we were alone, she said to me, "I am so glad you came to-day. I want you to arrange dear Emily nicely in her coffin. The servants had laid her out before my arrival, and she doesn't look a bit like herself. But I haven't the nerve to touch her." It was late at night, but I took a candle at once and accompanied Cecil to the death-chamber. Our sister was lying, pale and calm, with a smile upon her lips, much as she had appeared to me, and with *all her black hair combed back from her forehead*. The servants had arranged it so, thinking it looked neater. It was impossible to make any alteration till the morning, but when our dear sister was carried to her grave, her hair framed her dead face in the wavy curls in which it always fell when loose; a wreath of flowering syringa was round her head, a cross of violets on her breast, and in her waxen, beautifully-moulded hands, she held three tall, white lilies. I mention this because she has come to me since with the semblance of these very flowers to ensure her recognition. After the funeral, my brother-in-law gave me the details of her last illness. He told me that on the Monday afternoon, when her illness first took a serious turn and she became (as he said) delirious, she talked continually to her father, Captain Marryat (to whom she had been most reverentially attached), and who, she affirmed, was sitting by the side of the bed. Her conversation was perfectly rational, and only disjointed when she waited for a reply to her own remarks. She spoke to him of Langham and all that had happened there, and particularly expressed her surprise at his having *a beard*, saying, "Does hair grow up there, Father?" I was the more impressed by this account, because Dr. Norris, like most medical men, attributed the circumstance entirely to the distorted imagination of a wandering brain. And yet my father (whom I have never seen since his death) has been described to me by various clairvoyants, and always as *wearing a beard*, a thing he never did during his lifetime, and it was the fashion then for naval officers to wear only side whiskers. In all his pictures he is represented as clean shorn, and as he was so well known a man, one would think that (were they dissembling) the clairvoyants, in describing his personal characteristics, would follow the clue given by his portraits.

For some time after my sister Emily's death I heard nothing more of her, and for the reasons I have given, I never expected to see her again until we met in the spirit-world. About two years after her death, however, my husband, Colonel Lean, bought two tickets for a series of *séances* to be held in the rooms of the British National Association of Spiritualists under the mediumship of Mr. William Eglinton. This was the first time we had ever seen or sat with Mr. Eglinton, but we had heard a great deal of his powers, and were curious to test them. On the first night, which was a Saturday, we assembled with a party of twelve, all complete strangers, in the rooms I have mentioned, which were comfortably lighted with gas. Mr. Eglinton, who is a young man inclined to stoutness, went into the cabinet, which was placed in the centre of us, with spectators all round it. The cabinet was like a large cupboard, made of wood and divided into two parts, the partition being of wire-work, so that the medium might be padlocked into it, and a curtain drawn in front of both sides. After a while, a voice called out to us not to be frightened, as the medium was coming out to get more power, and Mr. Eglinton, in a state of trance and dressed in a suit of evening clothes, walked out of the cabinet and commenced a tour of the circle. He touched every one in turn, but did not stop until he reached Colonel Lean, before whom he remained for some time, making magnetic passes down his face and figure. He then turned to re-enter the cabinet, but as he did so, some one moved the curtain from inside and Mr. Eglinton *actually held the curtain to one side to permit the materialized form to pass out* before he went into the cabinet himself. The figure that appeared was that of a woman clothed in loose white garments that fell to her feet. Her eyes were black and her long black hair fell over her shoulders. I suspected at the time who she was, but each one in the circle was so certain she came for him or for her, that I said nothing, and only mentally asked if it were my sister that I might receive a proof of her identity. On the following evening (Sunday) Colonel Lean and I were "sitting" together, when Emily came to the table to assure us that it was she whom we had seen, and that she would appear again on Monday and show herself more clearly. I asked her to think of some means by which she could prove her identity with the spirit that then spoke to us, and she said, "I will hold up my right hand." Colonel Lean cautioned me not to mention this promise to any one, that we might be certain of the correctness of the test. Accordingly, on the Monday evening we assembled for our second *séance* with Mr. Eglinton, and the same form appeared, and walking out much closer to us, *held up the right hand*. Colonel Lean, anxious not to be deceived by his own senses, asked the company what the spirit was doing. "Cannot you see?" was the answer. "She is holding up her hand." On this occasion Emily came with all her old characteristics about her, and there would have been no possibility of mistaking her (at least on my part) without the proof she had promised to give us.

The next startling assurance we received of her proximity happened in a much more unexpected manner. We were staying, in the autumn of the following year, at a boarding-house in the Rue de Vienne at Brussels, with a large party of

English visitors, none of whom we had ever seen till we entered the house. Amongst them were several girls, who had never heard of Spiritualism before, and were much interested in listening to the relation of our experiences on the subject. One evening when I was not well, and keeping my own room, some of these young ladies got hold of Colonel Lean and said, "Oh! do come and sit in the dark with us and tell us ghost stories." Now sitting in the dark and telling ghost stories to five or six nice looking girls is an occupation few men would object to and they were all soon ensconced in the dark and deserted *salle-à-manger*. Amongst them was a young girl of sixteen, Miss Helen Hill, who had never shown more interest than the rest in such matters. After they had been seated in the dark for some minutes, she said to Colonel Lean, "Do you know, I can see a lady on the opposite side of the table quite distinctly, and she is nodding and smiling at you." The colonel asked what the lady was like. "She is very nice looking," replied the girl, "with dark eyes and hair, but she seems to want me to notice her ring. She wears a ring with a large blue stone in it, of such a funny shape, and she keeps on twisting it round and round her finger, and pointing to it. Oh! now she has got up and is walking round the room. Only fancy! she is holding up her feet for me to see. They are bare and very white, but her toes are crooked!" Then Miss Hill became frightened and asked them to get a light. She declared that the figure had come up, close to her, and torn the lace off her wrists. And when the light was procured and her dress examined, a frill of lace that had been tacked into her sleeve that morning had totally disappeared. The young ladies grew nervous and left the room, and Colonel Lean, thinking the description Helen Hill had given of the spirit tallied with that of my sister Emily, came straight up to me and surprised me by an abrupt question as to whether she had been in the habit of wearing any particular ring (for he had not seen her for several years before her death).

I told him that her favourite ring was an uncut turquoise—so large and uneven that she used to call it her "potato." "Had she any peculiarity about her feet?" he went on, eagerly. "Why do you wish to know?" I said. "She had crooked toes, that is all." "Good heavens!" he exclaimed, "then she has been with us in the *salle-à-manger*." I have never met Miss Hill since, and I am not in a position to say if she has evinced any further possession of clairvoyant power; but she certainly displayed it on that occasion to a remarkable degree; for she had never even heard of the existence of my sister Emily, and was very much disturbed and annoyed when told that the apparition she had described was reality and not imagination.

CHAPTER X

THE STORY OF THE GREEN LADY

THE story I have to tell now happened a very short time ago, and every detail is as fresh in my mind as if I had heard and seen it yesterday. Mrs. Guppy-Volckman has been long known to the spiritualistic world as a very powerful medium, also as taking a great private interest in Spiritualism, which all media do not. Her means justify her, too, in gratifying her whims; and hearing that a certain house in Broadstairs was haunted, she became eager to ascertain the truth. The house being empty, she procured the keys from the landlord, and proceeded on a voyage of discovery alone. She had barely recovered, at the time, from a most dangerous illness, which had left a partial paralysis of the lower limbs behind it; it was therefore with considerable difficulty that she gained the drawing-room of the house, which was on the first floor, and when there she abandoned her crutches, and sat down on the floor to recover herself. Mrs. Volckman was now perfectly alone. She had closed the front door after her, and she was moreover almost helpless, as it was with great difficulty that she could rise without assistance. It was on a summer's evening towards the dusky hour, and she sat on the bare floor of the empty house waiting to see what might happen. After some time (I tell this part of the story as I received it from her lips) she heard a rustling or sweeping sound, as of a long silk train coming down the uncarpeted stairs from the upper story. The room in which she sat communicated with another, which led out upon the passage, and it was not long before the door between these two apartments opened and the figure of a woman appeared. She entered the room in which Mrs. Volckman sat, very cautiously, and commenced to walk round it, feeling her way along the walls as though she were blind or tipsy. She was dressed in a green satin robe that swept behind her—round the upper part of her body was a kind of scarf of glistening white material, like silk gauze—and on her head was a black velvet cap, or coif, from underneath which her long black hair fell down her back. Mrs. Volckman, although used all her life to manifestations and apparitions of all sorts, told me she had never felt so frightened at the sight of one before. She attempted to rise, but feeling her incapability of doing so quickly, she screamed with fear. As soon as she did so, the woman turned round and ran out of the room, apparently as frightened as herself. Mrs. Volckman got hold of her crutches, scrambled to her feet, found her way downstairs, and reached the outside of the house in safety. Most people would never have entered it again. She, on the contrary, had an interview with the landlord, and actually, then and there, purchased a lease of the house and entered upon possession, and as soon as it was furnished and ready for occupation, she invited a party of friends to go down and stay with her at Broadstairs, and make the acquaintance of the "Green Lady," as we had christened her. Colonel Lean and I were amongst the visitors, the others consisting of Lady Archibald Campbell, Miss Shaw, Mrs.

Olive, Mrs. Bellew, Colonel Greck, Mr. Charles Williams, and Mr. and Mrs. Henry Volckman, which, with our host and hostess, made up a circle of twelve. We assembled there on a bright day in July, and the house, with its large rooms and windows facing the sea, looked cheerful enough. The room in which Mrs. Volckman had seen the apparition was furnished as a drawing-room, and the room adjoining it, which was divided by a *portière* only from the larger apartment, she had converted for convenience sake into her bedroom. The first evening we sat it was about seven o'clock, and so light that we let down all the venetians, which, however, did little to remedy the evil. We had no cabinet, nor curtains, nor darkness, for it was full moon at the time, and the dancing, sparkling waves were quite visible through the interstices of the venetians. We simply sat round the table, holding hands in an unbroken circle and laughing and chatting with each other. In a few minutes Mrs. Volckman said something was rising beside her from the carpet, and in a few more the "Green Lady" was visible to us all standing between the medium and Mr. Williams. She was just as she had been described to us, both in dress and appearance, but her face was as white and as cold as that of a corpse, and her eyes were closed. She leaned over the table and brought her face close to each of us in turn, but she seemed to have no power of speech. After staying with us about ten minutes, she sunk as she had risen, through the carpet, and disappeared. The next evening, under precisely similar circumstances, she came again. This time she had evidently gained more vitality in a materialized condition, for when I urged her to tell me her name she whispered, though with much difficulty, "Julia!" and when Lady Archibald observed that she thought she had no hands, the spirit suddenly thrust out a little hand, and grasped the curls on her forehead with a violence that gave her pain. Unfortunately, Mr. Williams' professional engagements compelled him to leave us on the following day, and Mrs.

Volckman had been too recently ill to permit her to sit alone, so that we were not able to hold another *séance* for the "Green Lady" during our visit. But we had not seen the last of her. One evening Mrs. Bellew and I were sitting in the bay window of the drawing-room, just "between the lights," and discussing a very private matter indeed, when I saw (as I thought) my hostess' maid raise the *portière* that hung between the apartments and stand there in a listening attitude. I immediately gave Mrs. Volckman the hint. "Let us talk of something else," I said in a low voice. "Jane is in your bedroom." "O! no! she's not," was the reply. "But I saw her lift the *portière*," I persisted; "she has only just dropped it." "You are mistaken," replied my hostess, "for Jane has gone on the beach with the child." I felt sure I had *not* been mistaken, but I held my tongue and said no more. The conversation was resumed, and as we were deep in the delicate matter, the woman appeared for the second time.

"Mrs. Volckman," I whispered, "Jane is really there. She has just looked in again."

My friend rose from her seat. "Come with me," she said, "and I will convince you that you are wrong."

I followed her into the bedroom, where she showed me that the door communicating with the passage was locked *inside*.

"Now, do you see," she continued, "that no one but the 'Green Lady' could enter this room but through the one we are sitting in."

"Then it must have been the 'Green Lady'," I replied, 'for I assuredly saw a woman standing in the doorway."

"That is likely enough," said Mrs. Volckman; "but if she comes again she shall have the trouble of drawing back the curtains."

And thereupon she unhooped the *portière*, which consisted of two curtains, and drew them right across the door. We had hardly regained our seats in the bay window before the two curtains were sharply drawn aside, making the brass rings rattle on the rod, and the "Green Lady" stood in the opening we had just passed through. Mrs. Volckman told her not to be afraid, but to come out and speak to us; but she was apparently not equal to doing so, and only stood there for a few minutes gazing at us. I imprudently left my seat and approached her, with a view to making overtures of friendship, when she dropped the curtains over her figure. I passed through them immediately to the other side, and found the bedroom empty and the door locked inside, as before.

CHAPTER XI

THE STORY OF THE MONK

A LADY named Uniacke, a resident in Bruges, whilst on a visit to my house in London, met and had a *séance* with William Eglinton, with which she was so delighted that she immediately invited him to go and stay with her abroad, and as my husband and I were about to cross over to Bruges to see my sister, who also resided there, we travelled in company—Mr. Eglinton living at Mrs. Uniacke's home, whilst we stayed with our own relations. Mrs. Uniacke was a medium herself, and had already experienced some very noisy and violent demonstrations in her own house. She was, therefore, quite prepared for her visitor, and had fitted up a spare room with a cabinet and blinds to the windows, and everything that was necessary. But, somewhat to her chagrin, we were informed at the first sitting by Mr. Eglinton's control, "Joey," that all future *séances* were to take place at my sister's house instead. We were given no reason for the change; we were simply told to obey it. My sister's house was rather a peculiar one, and I have already alluded to it, and some of the sights and sounds by which it was haunted, in the chapter

4

headed "Optical Illusions." The building is so ancient that the original date has been completely lost. A stone set into one of the walls bore an inscription to the effect that it was restored in the year 1616. And an obsolete plan of the city shows it to have stood in its present condition in 1562. Prior to that period, however, probably about the thirteenth century, it is supposed, with three houses on either side of it, to have formed a convent, but no printed record remains of the fact. Beneath it are subterraneous passages, choked with rubbish, which lead, no one knows whither. I had stayed in this house several times before, and always felt unpleasant influences from it, as I have related, especially in a large room on the lower floor, then used as a drawing-room, but which is said to have formed, originally, the chapel to the convent. Others had felt the influence beside myself, though we never had had reason to suppose that there was any particular cause for it. When we expressed curiosity, however, to learn why "Joey" desired us to hold our *séance* in my sister's house, he told us that the medium had not been brought over to Bruges for *our* pleasure or edification, but that there was a great work to be done there, and Mrs. Uniacke had been expressly influenced to invite him over, that the purposes of a higher power than his own should be accomplished. Consequently, on the following evening Mrs. Uniacke brought Mr. Eglinton over to my sister's house, and "Joey" having been asked to choose a room for the sitting, selected an *entresol* on the upper floor, which led by two short passages to the bedrooms. The bedroom doors being locked a dark curtain was hung at the entrance of one of these passages, and "Joey" declared it was a first-rate cabinet. We then assembled in the drawing-room, for the purposes of music and conversation, for we intended to hold the *séance* later in the evening. The party consisted only of the medium, Mrs. Uniacke, my sister, my husband, and myself. After I had sung a song or two, Mr. Eglinton became restless and moved away from the piano, saying the influence was too strong for him. He began walking up and down the room, and staring fixedly at the door, before which hung a *portière*. Several times he exclaimed with knitted brows, "What is the matter with that door? There is something very peculiar about it." Once he approached it quickly, but "Joey's" voice was heard from behind the *portière*, saying, "Don't come too near." Mr. Eglinton then retreated to a sofa, and appeared to be fighting violently with some unpleasant influence. He made the sign of the cross, then extended his fingers towards the door, as though to exorcise it: finally he burst into a mocking, scornful peal of laughter that lasted for some minutes. As it concluded, a diabolical expression came over his face. He clenched his hands, gnashed his teeth, and commenced to grope in a crouching position towards the door. We concluded he wished to get up to the room where the cabinet was, and let him have his way. He crawled, rather than walked, up the steep turret stairs, but on reaching the top, came to himself suddenly and fell back several steps. My husband, fortunately, was just behind him and saved him from a fall. He complained greatly of the influence and of a pain in his head, and we sat at the table to receive directions. In a few seconds the same spirit had taken possession of him. He left the table and groped his way towards the bedrooms, listening apparently to every sound, and with his hand holding an imaginary knife which was raised every now and then as if to strike. The expression on Mr. Eglinton's face during this possession is too horrible to describe. The worst passions were written as legibly there as though they had been labelled. There was a short flight of stairs leading from the *entresol* to the corridor, closed at the head by a padded door which we had locked for fear of accident. When, apparently in pursuit of his object, the spirit led the medium up to this door and he found it fastened, his moans were terrible. Half a dozen times he made his weary round of the room, striving to get downstairs to accomplish some end, and to return to us moaning and baffled. At this juncture, he was so exhausted that one of his controls, "Daisy," took possession of him and talked with us for some time. We asked "Daisy" what the spirit was like that had controlled Mr. Eglinton last, and she said she did not like him—he had a bad face, no hair on the top of his head, and a long black frock. From this we concluded he had been a monk or a priest. When "Daisy" had finished speaking to us "Joey" desired Mr. Eglinton to go into the cabinet; but as soon as he rose, the same spirit got possession again and led him grovelling as before towards the bedrooms. His "guides" therefore carried him into the cabinet before our eyes. He was elevated far above our heads, his feet touching each of us in turn; he was then carried past the unshaded window, which enabled us to judge the height he was from the ground, and finally over a large table, into the cabinet.

Nothing, however, of consequence occurred, and "Joey" advised us to take the medium downstairs to the supper room.

Accordingly we adjourned there, and during supper Mr. Eglinton appeared to be quite himself, and laughed with us over what had taken place. As soon as the meal was over, however, the old restlessness returned on him, and he began pacing up and down the room, walking out every now and then into the corridor. In a few minutes we perceived that the uneasy spirit again controlled him, and we all followed. He went steadily towards the drawing-room, but, on finding himself pursued, turned back, and three times pronounced emphatically the word "Go." He then entered the drawing-room, which was in darkness and closed the door behind him, whilst we waited outside. In a little while he reopened it, speaking in quite a different voice, said, "Bring a light! I have something to say to you." When we reassembled with a lamp we found the medium controlled by a new spirit, whom "Joey" afterwards told us was one of his highest guides.

Motioning us to be seated, he stood before us and said, "I have been selected from amongst the controls of this medium to tell you the history of the unhappy being who has so disturbed you this evening. He is present now, and the confession of his crime through my lips will help him to throw off the earthbound condition to which it has condemned him. Many years ago, the house in which we now stand was a convent, and underneath it were four subterraneous passages running north, south, east, and west, which communicated with all parts of the town. (I must here state that Mr. Eglinton had not previously been informed of any particulars relating to the former history of my sister's home, neither were Mrs. Uniacke or myself acquainted with it.)

"In this convent there lived a most beautiful woman—a nun, and in one of the neighbouring monasteries a priest who, against the strict law of his Church, had conceived and nourished a passion for her. He was an Italian who had been obliged to leave his own country, for reasons best known to himself, and nightly he would steal his way to this house, by means of one of the subterraneous passages, and attempt to overcome the nun's scruples, and make her listen to his tale of love; but she, strong in the faith, resisted him. At last, maddened one day by her repeated refusals, and his own guilty passion, he hid himself in one of the northern rooms in the upper story of this house, and watched there in the dark for her to pass him on her way from her devotions in the chapel; but she did not come. Then he crept downstairs stealthily, with a dagger hid beneath his robes, and met her in the hall. He conjured her again to yield to him, but again she resisted, and he stabbed her within the door on the very spot where the medium first perceived him. Her pure soul sought immediate consolation in the spirit spheres, but his has been chained down ever since to the scene of his awful crime. He dragged her body down the secret stairs (which are still existent) to the vaults beneath, and hid it in the subterraneous passage.

"After a few days he sought it again, and buried it. He lived many years after, and committed many other crimes, though none so foul as this. It is his unhappy spirit that asks your prayers to help it to progress. It is for this purpose that we were brought to this city, that we might aid in releasing the miserable soul that cannot rest."

I asked, "By what name shall we pray for him?"

"Pray for 'the distressed Being.' Call him by no other name."

"What is your own name?"

"I prefer to be unknown. May God bless you all and keep you in the way of prayer and truth and from all evil courses, and bring you to everlasting life. Amen."

The medium then walked up to the spot he had indicated as the scene of the murder, and knelt there for some minutes in prayer.

Thus concluded the first *séance* at which the monk was introduced to us. But the next day as I sat at the table with my sister only, the name of "Hortense Dupont" was given us, and the following conversation was rapped out.

"Who are you?"

"I am the nun. I did love him. I couldn't help it. It is such a relief to think that he will be prayed for."

"When did he murder you?"

"In 1498."

"What was his name?"

"I cannot tell you."

"His age."

"Thirty-five!"

"And yours?"

"Twenty-three."

"Are you coming to see us to-morrow?"

"I am not sure."

On that evening, by "Joey's" orders, we assembled at

seven. Mr. Eglinton did not feel the influence in the drawing-room that day, but directly he entered the *séance* room, he was possessed by the same spirit. His actions were still more graphic than on the first occasion. He watched from the window for the coming of his victim through the courtyard, and then recommenced his crawling stealthy pursuit, coming back each time from the locked door that barred his egress with such heart-rending moans that no one could have listened to him unmoved. At last, his agony was so great, as he strove again and again, like some dumb animal, to pass through the walls that divided him from the spot he wished to visit, whilst the perspiration streamed down the medium's face with the struggle, that we attempted to make him speak to us. We implored him in French to tell us his trouble, and believe us to be his friends; but he only pushed us away. At last we were impressed to pray for him, and kneeling down, we repeated all the well-known Catholic prayers. As we commenced the "De Profundis" the medium fell prostrate on the earth, and seemed to wrestle with his agony. At the "Salve Regina" and "Ave Maria" he lifted his eyes to Heaven and clasped his hands, and in the "Pater Noster" he appeared to join. But directly we ceased praying the evil passions returned, and his face became distorted in the thirst for blood. It was an experience that no one who had seen could ever forget. At last my sister fetched a crucifix, which we placed upon his breast. It had not been there many seconds before a different expression came over his face. He seized it in both hands, straining it to his eyes, lips, and heart, holding it from him at arm's length, then passionately kissing it, as we repeated the "Anima Christi." Finally, he held the crucifix out for each of us to kiss; a beautiful smile broke out on the medium's face, and the spirit passed out of him.

Mr. Eglinton awoke on that occasion terribly exhausted. His face was as white as a sheet, and he trembled violently. His first words were: "They are doing something to my forehead. Burn a piece of paper, and give me the ashes." He rubbed them between his eyes, when the sign of the cross became distinctly visible, drawn in deep red lines upon his forehead. The controls then said, exhausted as Mr. Eglinton was, we were to place him in the cabinet, as their work was not yet done. He was accordingly led in trance to the arm-chair behind the curtain, whilst we formed a circle in front of him. In a few seconds the cabinet was illuminated, and a cross of fire appeared outside of it. This manifestation having been seen twice, the head and shoulders of a nun appeared floating outside the curtain. Her white coif and "chin-piece" were pinned just as the "*religieuses*" are in the habit of pinning them, and she seemed very anxious to show herself, coming close to each of us in turn, and reappearing several times. Her face was that of a young and pretty woman. "Joey" said, "That's the nun, but you'll understand that this is only a preliminary trial, preparatory to a more perfect materializa-tion." I asked the apparition if she were the "Hortense Dupont" that had communicated through me, and she nodded her head several times in acquiescence. Thus ended our second *séance* with the Monk of Bruges.

On the third day we were all sitting at supper in my sister's house at about ten o'clock at night, when loud raps were heard about the room, and on giving the alphabet, "Joey" desired us to go upstairs and sit, and to have the door at the head of the staircase (which we had hitherto locked for fear of accidents) left open; which we accordingly did. As soon as we were seated at the table, the medium became entranced, and the same pantomime which I have related was gone through. He watched from the window that looked into the courtyard, and silently groped his way round the room, until he had crawled on his stomach up the stairs that led to the padded door. When he found, however, that the obstacle that had hitherto stood in his way was removed (by its being open) he drew a long breath and started away for the winding turret staircase, listening at the doors as he passed to find out if he were overheard. When he came to the stairs, in descending which we had been so afraid he might hurt himself, he was carried down them in the most wonderful manner, only placing his hand on the balustrades, and swooping to the bottom in one flight. We had placed a lamp in the hall, so that as we followed him we could observe all his actions. When he reached the bottom of the staircase he crawled on his stomach to the door of the drawing-room (originally the chapel) and there waited and listened, darting back into the shadow every time he fancied he heard a sound. Imagine our little party of four in that sombre old house, the only ones waking at that time of night, watching by the ghastly light of a turned-down lamp the acting of that terrible tragedy. We held our breath as the murderer crouched by the chapel door, opening it noiselessly to peep within, and then, retreating with his imaginary dagger in his hand, ready to strike as soon as his victim appeared. At last she seemed to come. In an instant he had sprung to meet her, stabbing her first in a half-stooping attitude, and then, apparently, finding her not dead, he rose to his full height and stabbed her twice, straight downwards. For a moment he seemed paralysed at what he had done, starting back with both hands clasped to his forehead. Then he flung himself prostrate on the supposed body, kissing the ground frantically in all directions. Presently he woke to the fear of detection, and raised the corpse suddenly in his arms. He fell once beneath the supposed weight, but staggering to his feet again, seized and dragged it, slipping on the stone floor as he went, to the head of the staircase that led to the cellars below, where the mouth of one of the subterraneous passages was still to be seen. The door at the head of this flight was modern, and he could not undo the lock, so, prevented from dragging the body down the steps, he cast himself again upon it, kissing the stone floor of the hall and moaning. At last he dragged himself on his knees to the spot of the murder, and began to pray. We knelt with him, and as he heard our voices he turned on his knees towards us with outstretched hands. I suggested that he wanted the crucifix again, and went upstairs to fetch it, when the medium followed me. When I had found what I sought, he seized it from me eagerly, and carrying it to the window, whence he had so often watched, fell down again upon his knees. After praying for some time he tried to speak to us. His lips moved and his tongue protruded, but he was unable to articulate. Suddenly he seized each of our hands in turn in both of his own, and wrung them violently. He tried to bless us, but the words would not come. The same beautiful smile we had seen the night before broke out over his countenance, the crucifix dropped from his hands, and he fell prostrate on the floor. The next moment Mr. Eglinton was asking us where he was and what on earth had happened to him, as he felt so queer. He declared himself fearfully exhausted, but said he felt that a great calm and peace had come over him notwithstanding the weakness, and he believed some great good had been accomplished. He was not again entranced, but "Joey" ordered the light to be put out, and spoke to us in the direct voice as follows:—

"I've just come to tell you what I know you will be very glad to hear, that through the medium's power, and our power, and the great power of God, the unhappy spirit who has been confessing his crime to you is freed to-night from the heaviest part of his burden—the being earth-chained to the spot. I don't mean to say that he will go away at once to the spheres, because he's got a lot to do still to alter the conditions under which he labours, but the worst is over. This was the special work Mr. Eglinton was brought to Bruges to do, and Ernest and I can truly say that, during the whole course of our control of him, we have never had to put forth our own powers, nor to ask so earnestly for the help of God, as in the last three days. You have all helped in a good work—

to free a poor soul from earth, and to set him on the right road, and *we* are grateful to you and to the medium, as well as he. He will be able to progress rapidly now until he reaches his proper sphere, and hereafter the spirits of himself and the woman he murdered will work together to undo for others the harm they brought upon themselves. She is rejoicing in her high sphere at the work we have done for him, and will be the first to help and welcome him upward. There are many more earthbound spirits in this house and the surrounding houses who are suffering as he was, though not to the same extent, nor for the same reason. But they all ask for and need your help and your prayers, and this is the greatest and noblest end of Spiritualism—to aid poor, unhappy spirits to free themselves from earth and progress upwards. After a while when this spirit can control the medium with calmness, he will come himself and tell you, through him, all his history and how he came to fall. Meanwhile, we thank you very much for allowing us to draw so much strength from you and helping us with your sympathy, and I hope you will believe me always to remain, your loving friend, Joey."

.   .   .   .

This account, with very little alteration, was published in the *Spiritualist* newspaper, August 29th, 1879, when the *séances* had just occurred. There is a sequel to the story, however, which is almost as remarkable as itself, and which has not appeared in print till now. From Bruges on this occasion my husband and I went to Brussels, where we diverted ourselves by means very dissimilar to anything so grave as Spiritualism. There were many sales going on in Brussels at that moment, and one of our amusements was to make a tour of the salerooms and inspect the articles put up for competition. During one of these visits I was much taken by a large oil painting, in a massive frame, measuring some six or seven feet square. It represented a man in the dress of a Franciscan monk—*i.e.*, a brown serge robe, knotted with cords about the waist—kneeling in prayer with outstretched hands upon a mass of burning embers. It was labelled in the catalogue as the picture of a Spanish monk of the order of Saint Francis Xavier, and was evidently a painting of some value. I was drawn to go and look at it several days in succession before the sale, and I told my husband that I coveted its possession. He laughed at me and said it would fetch a great deal more money than we could afford to give for it, in which opinion I acquiesced. The day of the sale, however, found us in our places to watch the proceedings, and when the picture of the monk was put up I bid a small sum for it. Colonel Lea looked at me in astonishment, but I whispered to him that I was only in fun, and I should stop at a hundred francs. The bidding was very languid, however, and to my utter amazement, the picture was knocked down to me for *seventy-two francs*. I could hardly believe that it was true. Directly the sale was concluded, the brokers crowded round me to ask what I would take for the painting, and they told me they had not thought of bidding until it should have reached a few hundred francs. But I told them I had got my bargain and I meant to stick by it. When we returned the next day to make arrangements for its being sent to us, the auctioneer informed us that the frame alone in which it had been sent for sale had cost three hundred francs, so that I was well satisfied with my purchase. This occurrence took place a short time before we returned to England, where we arrived long before the painting, which, with many others, was left to follow us by a cheaper and slower route.

The Sunday after we reached home (having seen no friends in the meanwhile), we walked into Steinway Hall to hear Mr. Fletcher's lecture. At its conclusion he passed as usual into a state of trance, and described what he saw before him. In the midst of mentioning people, places, and incidents unknown to us, he suddenly exclaimed: "Now I see a very strange thing, totally unlike anything I have ever seen before, and I hardly know how to describe it. A man comes before me—a foreigner—and in a dress belonging to some monastic order, a brown robe of coarse cloth or flannel, with a rope round his waist and beads hanging, and bare feet and a shaved head. He is dragging a picture on to the platform, a very large painting in a frame, and it looks to me like a portrait of himself, kneeling on a carpet of burning wood. No! I am wrong. The man tells me the picture is *not* a portrait of himself, but of the founder of his Order, and it is in the possession of some people in this hall to-night. The man tells me to tell these people that it was *his* spirit that influenced them to buy this painting at some place over the water, and he did so in order that they might keep it in remembrance of what they have done for him. And he desires that they shall hang that picture in some room where they may see it every day, that they may never forget the help which spirits on this earth may render by their prayers to spirits that have passed away. And he offers them through me his heartfelt thanks for the assistance given him, and he says the day is not far off when he shall pray for himself and for them, that their kindness may return into their own bosoms."

.   .   .   .

The, oil painting reached England in safety some weeks afterwards, and was hung over the mantelpiece in our dining-room, where it remained, a familiar object to all our personal acquaintances.

CHAPTER XII

THE MEDIUMSHIP OF MISS SHOWERS

SOME time before I had the pleasure of meeting Miss Showers, I heard, through friends living in the west of England, of the mysterious and marvellous powers possessed by a young lady of their acquaintance, who was followed by voices in the air, which held conversations with her, and the owners of which were said to have made themselves visible. I listened with curiosity, the more so, as my informants utterly disbelieved in Spiritualism, and thought the phenomena were due to trickery. At the same time I conceived a great desire to see the girl of sixteen, who, for no gain or apparent object of her own, was so clever as to mystify everyone around her; and when she and her mother came to London, I was amongst the first to beg for an introduction, and I shall never forget the experiences I had with her. She was the first *private* medium through whom my personal friends returned to converse with me; and no one but a Spiritualist can appreciate the blessing of spiritual communications through a source that is above the breath of suspicion. I have already written at length about Miss Showers in "The Story of John Powles." She was a child, compared to myself, whose life had hardly commenced when mine was virtually over, and neither she, nor any member of her family, had ever had an opportunity of becoming acquainted with even the names of my former friends. Yet (as I have related) John Powles made Miss Showers his especial mouthpiece, and my daughter, "Florence" (then a little child) also appeared through her, though at long intervals, and rather timidly. Her own controls, however, or cabinet spirits (as they call them in America)—*i.e.*, such spirits as are always about the medium, and help the strangers to appear—"Peter," "Florence," "Lenore," and "Sally," were very familiar with me, and afforded me such facilities of testing their medium as do not often fall to the lot of inquirers. Indeed, at one time, they always requested that I should be present at their *séances*, so that I considered myself to be highly favoured. And I may mention here that Miss Showers and I were so much *en rapport* that her manifestations were always much stronger in my presence. We could not sit next each other at an ordinary tea or supper table, when we had no thought of, or desire to hold a *séance*, without manifestations occurring in the full light. A hand, that did not belong to either of us, would make itself apparent under the table-cloth between us—a hand with power to grasp ours—or feet would be squeezed or kicked beneath the table, or fingers would suddenly appear, and whisk the food off our plates. Some of their jests were inconvenient. I have had the whole contents of a tumbler, which I was raising to my lips, emptied over my dress. It was generally known that our powers were sympathetic, and at last "Peter" gave me leave, or, rather, ordered me to sit in the cabinet with "Rosie," whilst the manifestations went on outside. He used to say he didn't care for me any more than if I had been "a spirit myself." One evening "Peter" called me into the cabinet (which was simply a large box cupboard at one end of the dining-room) before the *séance* began, and told me to sit down at the medium's feet and "be a good girl and keep quiet." Miss Showers was in a low chair, and I sat with my arms resting on her lap. She did not become entranced, and we talked the whole time together. Presently, without any warning, two figures stood beside us. I could not have said where they came from. I neither saw them rise from the floor nor descend from the ceiling. There was no beginning to their appearance. In a moment they were simply *there*—"Peter" and "Florence" (not my child, but Miss Showers' control of the same name).

"Peter" sent "Florence" out to the audience, where we heard her speaking to them and their remarks upon her (there being only a thin curtain hung before the entrance of the cabinet), but he stayed with us himself. We could not see him distinctly in the dim light, but we could distinctly hear and feel him. He changed our ornaments and ribbons, and pulled the hair-pins out of our hair, and made comments on what was going on outside. After a while "Florence" returned to get more power, and both spirits spoke to and touched us at the same time. During the whole of this *séance* my arms rested on Miss Showers' lap, and she was awake and talking to me about the spirits.

One evening, at a sitting at Mr. Luxmore's house in Hyde Park, the spirit "Florence" had been walking amongst the audience in the lighted front drawing-room for a considerable time—even sitting at the piano and accompanying herself whilst she sung as a song in what she called "the planetary language." She greatly resembled her medium on that occasion, and several persons present remarked that she did so. I suppose the inferred doubt annoyed her, for before she finally left us she asked for a light, and a small oil lamp was brought to her which she placed in my hand, telling me to follow her and look at her medium, which I accordingly did. "Florence" led the way back into the back drawing-room, where I found Miss Showers reposing in an arm-chair. The first sight of her terrified me. For the purpose of making any change in her dress as difficult as possible, she wore a high, tight-fitting black velvet frock, fastened at the back, and high Hessian boots, with innumerable buttons. But she now appeared to be shrunk to half her usual size, and the dress hung loosely on her figure. Her arms had disappeared, but putting my hands up the dress sleeves, I found them diminished to the size of those of a little child—the fingers reaching only to where the elbows had been. The same miracle had happened to her feet, which only occupied half her boots. She looked in fact like the mummy of a girl of four or six years old. The spirit told me to feel her face. The forehead was dry, rough, and burning hot, but from the chin water was dropping freely on to the bosom of her dress. "Florence" said to me, "I wanted *you* to see her, because I know you are brave enough to tell people what you have seen."

There was a marked difference in the personality of the two influences "Florence" and "Lenore," although both at times resembled Miss Showers, and sometimes more than others. "Florence" was taller than her medium, and a very beautiful woman. "Lenore" was much shorter and smaller, and not so pretty, but more vivacious and pert. By the invitation of Mrs. Macdougal Gregory, I attended several *séances* with Miss Showers at her residence in Green Street, when these spirits appeared. "Lenore" was fond of saying that she wouldn't or couldn't come out unless *I* held her hand, or put my arm round her waist. To tell the truth, I didn't care for the distinction, for this influence was very peculiar in some things, and to me she always appeared "uncanny," and to leave an unpleasant feeling behind her. She was seldom completely formed, and would hold up a foot which felt like wet clay, and had no toes to it, or not the proper quantity. On occasions, too, there was a charnel-house smell about her, as if she had been buried a few weeks and dug up again, an odour which I have never smelt from any materialized spirit before or after. One evening at Mrs. Gregory's, when "Lenore" had insisted upon walking round the circle supported by my arm, I nearly fainted from the smell. It resembled nothing but that of a putrid corpse, and when she returned to the cabinet, I was compelled to leave the room and retch from the nausea it had caused me. It was on this occasion that the sitters called "Lenore" so many times back into the circle, that all the power was gone, and she was in danger of melting away before their eyes. Still they entreated her to remain with them a little longer. At last she grew impatient, and complained to me of their unreasonableness. She was then raised from the floor—actually floating just outside the curtain—and she asked me to put my hands up her skirts and convince myself that she was half-dematerialized. I did as she told me, and felt that she had *no legs*, although she had been walking round the room a few minutes before. I could feel nothing but the trunk of a body, which was completely lifted off the ground. Her voice, too, had grown faint, and her face indistinct, and in another moment she had totally disappeared.

One evening at Mrs. Gregory's, after the *séance* was concluded, "Florence" looked round the curtain and called to me to come inside it. I did so and found myself in total darkness. I said, "What's the good of my coming here? I can't see anything." "Florence" took me by one hand, and answered, "I will lead you! Don't be afraid." Then someone else grasped my other hand, and "Peter's" voice said, "We've got you safe. We want you to feel the medium." The two figures led me between them to the sofa on which Miss Showers was lying. They passed my hand all over her head and body. I felt, as before, her hands and feet shrunk to half their usual size, but her heart appeared to have become proportionately increased. When my hand was placed upon it, it was leaping up and down violently, and felt like a rabbit or some other live animal bounding in her bosom. Her brain was burning as before, but her extremities were icy cold. There was no doubt at all of the abnormal condition into which the medium had been thrown, in order to produce these strong physical manifestations which were borrowed, for the time being, from her life, and could never (so they informed me) put the *whole* of what they borrowed back again. This seems to account for the invariable deterioration of health and strength that follows physical manifestations in both sexes. These were the grounds alone on which they explained to me the fact that, on several occasions, when the materialized spirit has been violently seized and held apart from the medium, it has been found to have become, or been changed into the medium, and always with injury to the latter—as in the case of Florence Cook being seized by Mr. Volckman and Sir George Sitwell. Mr. Volckman concluded because when he seized the spirit "Katie King," he found he was holding Florence Cook, that the latter must have impersonated the former; yet I shall tell you in its proper place how I have sat in the same room with "Katie King," whilst Miss Cook lay in a trance between us. The medium nearly lost her life on the occasion alluded to, from the sudden disturbance of the mysterious link that bound her to the spirit. I have had it from the lips of the Countess of Caithness, who was one of the sitters, and stayed with Miss Cook till she was better, that she was in convulsions the whole night after, and that it was some time before they believed she would recover. If a medium could simulate a materialized spirit, it is hardly likely that she would (or could) simulate convulsions with a medical man standing by her bedside. "You see," said Miss Showers' "Florence," whilst pointing out to me the decreased size of her medium under trance, "that 'Rosie' is half her usual size and weight. I have borrowed the other half from her, which, combined with contributions from the sitters, goes to make up the body in which I show myself to you. If you seize and hold me tight, you are holding her, i.e., half of her, and you increase the action of the vital half to such a degree that, if the two halves did not reunite, you would kill her. You see that I can detach certain particles from her organism for my own use, and when I dematerialize, I restore these particles to her, and she becomes once more her normal size. You only hurry the reunion by violently detaining me, so as to injure her. But you might drive her mad, or kill her in the attempt, because the particles of brain, or body, might become injured by such a violent collision. If you believe I can take them from her (as you see I do) in order to render my invisible body visible to you, why can't you believe I can make them fly together again on the approach of danger. And granted the one power, I see no difficulty in acknowledging the other."

One day Mrs. Showers invited me to assist at a *séance* to be given expressly for friends living at a distance. When I reached the house, however, I found the friends were unable to be present, and the meeting was adjourned. Mrs. Showers apologized for the alteration of plan, but I was glad of it. I had often sat with "Rosie" in company with others, and I wanted to sit with her quite alone, or rather to sit with her in a room quite alone, and see what would spontaneously occur without any solicitation on our parts. We accordingly annexed the drawing-room for our sole use—locked the door, extinguished the lights, and sat down on a sofa side by side, with our arms round each other. The manifestations that followed were not all nice ones. They formed an experience to be passed through once, but not willingly repeated, and I should not relate them here, excepting that they afford so strong a proof that they were produced by a power outside and entirely distinct from our own—a power, which having once called into action, we had no means of repressing. We had sat in the dark for some minutes, without hearing or seeing anything, when I thoughtlessly called out, "Now, Peter, do your worst," and extending my arms, singing, "Come! for my arms are empty." In a moment a large, heavy figure fell with such force into my outstretched arms as to bruise my shoulder—it seemed like a form made of wood or iron, rather than flesh and blood—and the rough treatment that ensued for both of us is almost beyond description. It seemed as if the room were filled with materialized creatures, who were determined to let us know they were not to be trifled with. Our faces and hands were slapped, our hair pulled down, and our clothes nearly torn off our backs. My silk skirt being separate from the bodice was torn off at the waistband, and the trimming ripped from it, and Miss Showers' muslin dress was also much damaged. We were both thoroughly frightened, but no expostulations or entreaties had any effect with our tormentors. At the same time we heard the sound as of a multitude of large birds or bats swooping about the room." The fluttering of wings was incessant, and we could hear them "scrooping" up and down the walls. In the midst of the confusion, "Rosie" was whisked out of my arms (for fright had made us cling tighter than ever together) and planted on the top of a table at some distance from me, at which she was so frightened, she began to cry, and I called out, "Powles, where are you? Can't you stop them?" My appeal was heard. Peter's voice exclaimed, "Hullo! here's Powles coming!" and all the noise ceased. We heard the advent of my friend, and in another moment he was smoothing down the ruffled hair and arranging the disordered dresses and telling me to light the gas and not be frightened. As soon as I could I obeyed his directions and found Rosie sitting doubled up in the centre of the table, but the rest of the room and furniture in its usual condition. "Peter" and his noisy crowd had vanished—so had "Powles," and there was nothing but our torn skirts and untidy appearance to prove that we had not been having an unholy dream. "Peter" is not a wicked spirit—far from it—but he is a very earthly and frivolous one. But when we consider that nine-tenths of the spirits freed from the flesh are both earthly and frivolous (if not worse), I know not what right we have to expect to receive back angels in their stead.

At one time when my sister Blanche (who was very sceptical as to the possibility of the occurrences I related having taken place before me) was staying in my house at Bayswater, I asked Miss Showers if she would give us a *séance* in my own home, to which she kindly assented. This was an unusual concession on her part, because, in consequence of several accidents and scandals that had occurred from media being forcibly detained (as I have just alluded to), her mother was naturally averse to her sitting anywhere but in their own circle. However, on my promising to invite no strangers, Mrs. Showers herself brought her daughter to my house. We had made no preparation for the *séance* except by opening part of the folding doors between the dining-room and study, and hanging a curtain over the aperture. But I had carefully locked the door of the study, so that there should be no egress from it excepting through the dining-room, and had placed against the locked door a heavy writing-table laden with books and ornaments to make "assurance doubly sure." We sat first in the drawing-room above, where there was a piano. The lights were extinguished, and Miss Showers sat down to the instrument and played the accompaniment to a very simple melody, "Under the willow she's sleeping." Four voices, sometimes alone and sometimes *all together*, accompanied her own. One was a baritone, supposed to proceed from "Peter," the second, a soprano, from "Lenore." The third was a rumbling bass, from an influence who called himself "The Vicar of Croydon," and sung in a fat, unctuous and conceited voice; and the fourth was a cracked and quavering treble, from another spirit called "The Abbess." These were the voices, Mrs. Showers told me, that first followed her daughter about the house in Devonshire, and gained her such an unenviable notoriety there. The four voices were perfectly distinct from one another, and sometimes blended most ludicrously and tripped each other up in a way which made the song a medley—upon which each one would declare it was the fault of the other. "The Vicar of Croydon" always required a great deal of solicitation before he could be induced to exhibit his powers, but having once commenced, it was difficult to make him leave off again, whereas "The Abbess" was always complaining that they would not allow her to sing the solos. An infant's voice also sung some baby songs in a sweet childish treble, but she was also very shy and seldom was heard, in comparison with the rest. "All ventriloquism!" I hear some reader cry. If so, Miss Showers ought to have made a fortune in exhibiting her talent in public. I have heard the best ventriloquists in the world, but I never heard one who could produce *four* voices at the same time.

After the musical portion of the *séance* was over, we descended to the dining-room, where the gas was burning, and the medium passed through it to the secured study, where a mattress was laid upon the floor for her accommodation. "Florence" was the first to appear, tall and beautiful in appearance, and with upraised eyes like a nun. She measured her height against the wall with me, and we found she was the taller of the two by a couple of inches—my height being five feet six, and the medium's five feet, and the spirit's five feet eight, an abnormal height for a woman. "Lenore" came next, very short indeed, looking like a child of four or six, but she grew before our eyes, until her head was on a level with mine. She begged us all to observe that she had *not* got on "Rosie's" petticoat body. She said she had borrowed it on one occasion, and Mrs. Showers had recognized it, and slipped upstairs in the middle of the *séance* and found it missing from her daughter's chest of drawers, and that she had been so angry in consequence (fearing Rosie's honour might be impeached) that she said if "Lenore" did not promise never to to do so again, she should not be allowed to assist at the *séances* at all. So Miss "Lenore," in rather a pert and defiant mood, begged Mrs. Showers to see that what she wore was her own property, and not that of the medium. She was succeeded on that occasion by a strange being, totally different from the other two, who called herself "Sally," and said she had been a cook. She was one of those extraordinary influences for whose return to earth one can hardly account; quick, and clever, and amusing as she could be, but with an unrefined wit and manner, and to all appearance, more earthly-minded than ourselves. But do we not often ask the same question with respect to those still existent here below? What were they born for? What good do they do? Why were they ever permitted to come? God, without whose permission nothing happens, alone can answer it.

We had often to tease "Peter" to materialize and show himself, but he invariably refused, or postponed the work to another occasion. His excuse was that the medium being so small, he could not obtain sufficient power from her to make himself appear as a big man, and he didn't like to come "looking like a girl in a billycock hat." "I came once to Mrs. Showers," he said, "and she declared I was 'Rosie' dressed up, and so I have resolved never to show myself again." At the close of that *séance*, however, "Peter" asked me to go into the study and see him wake the medium. When I entered it and made my way up to the mattress, I found Miss Showers extended on it in a deep sleep, whilst "Peter," materialized, sat at her feet. He made me sit down next to him and take his hand and feel his features with my own hand. Then he proceeded to rouse "Rosie" by shaking her and calling her by name, holding me by one hand as he did so. As Miss Showers yawned and woke up from her trance, the hand slipped from mine, and "Peter" evaporated. When she sat up I said to her gently, "I am here! Peter brought me in and was sitting on the mattress by my side till just this moment." "Ha, ha!" laughed his voice close to my ear, "and I'm here still, my dears, though you can't see me."

Who can account for such things? I have witnessed them over and over again, yet I am unable, even to this day, to do more than believe and wonder.

CHAPTER XIII

THE MEDIUMSHIP OF WILLIAM EGLINTON

In the stories I have related of "Emily" and "The Monk" I have alluded freely to the wonderful powers exhibited by William Eglinton, but the marvels there spoken of were by no means the only ones I have witnessed through his mediumship. At the *séance* which produced the apparition of my sister Emily, Mr. Eglinton's control "Joey" made himself very familiar. "Joey" is a remarkably small man—perhaps two-thirds lighter in weight than the medium—and looks more like a little jockey than anything else, though he says he was a clown whilst in this world, and claims to be the spirit of the immortal Joe Grimaldi. He has always appeared to us clothed in a tight-fitting white dress like a woven jersey suit, which makes him look still smaller than he is. He usually keeps up a continuous chatter, whether visible or invisible, and is one of the cleverest and kindest controls I know. He is also very devotional, for which the public will perhaps give him as little credit now as they did whilst he was on earth. On the first occasion of our meeting in the Russell Street Rooms he did not show himself until quite the last, but he talked incessantly of and for the other spirits that appeared. My sister was, as I have said, the first to show herself—then came an extraordinary apparition. On the floor, about three feet from the cabinet, appeared a head—only the head and throat of a dark man, with black beard and moustaches, surmounted by a white turban usually worn by natives. It did not speak, but the eyes rolled and the lips moved, as if it tried to articulate, but without success. "Joey" said the spirit came for Colonel Lean, and was that of a foreigner who had been decapitated. Colonel Lean could not recognize the features; but, strange to say, he had been present at the beheading of two natives in Japan who had been found guilty of murdering some English officers, and we concluded from "Joey's" description that this must be the head of one of them. I knelt down on the floor and put my face on a level with that of the spirit, that I might assure myself there was no body attached to it and concealed by the curtain of the cabinet, and I can affirm that it was *a head only*, resting on the neck—that its eyes moved and its features worked, but that there was nothing further on the floor. I questioned it, and it evidently tried hard to speak in return. The mouth opened and the tongue was thrust out, and made a sort of dumb sound, but was unable to form any words, and after a while the head sunk through the floor and disappeared. If this was not one of the pleasantest apparitions

I have seen, it was one of the most remarkable. There was no possibility of trickery or deception. The decapitated head rested in full sight of the audience, and had all the peculiarities of the native appearance and expression. After this the figures of two or three Englishmen came, friends of others of the audience—then "Joey" said he would teach us how to "make muslin." He walked right outside the cabinet, a quaint little figure, not much bigger than a boy of twelve or thirteen, with a young, old face, and dressed in the white suit I have described. He sat down by me and commenced to toss his hands in the air, as though he were juggling with balls, saying the while, "This is the way we make ladies' dresses." As he did so, a small quantity of muslin appeared in his hands, which he kept on moving in the same manner, whilst the flimsy fabric increased and increased before our eyes, until it rose in billows of muslin above "Joey's" head and fell over his body to his feet, and enveloped him until he was completely hidden from view. He kept on chattering till the last moment from under the heap of snowy muslin, telling us to be sure and "remember how he made ladies' dresses"—when, all of a sudden, in the twinkling of an eye, the heap of muslin rose into the air, and before us stood the tall figure of "Abdullah," Mr. Eglinton's Eastern guide. There had been no darkness, no pause to effect this change. The muslin had remained on the spot where it was fabricated until "Joey" evaporated, and "Abdullah" rose up from beneath it. Now "Abdullah" is not a spirit to be concealed easily. He is six foot two—a great height for a native—and his high turban adds to his stature. He is a very handsome man, with an aquiline nose and bright black eyes—a Persian, I believe, by birth, and naturally dark in complexion. He does not speak English, but "salaams" continually, and will approach the sitters when requested, and let them examine the jewels, of which he wears a large quantity in his turban and ears and round his throat, or to show them and let them feel that he has lost one arm, the stump being plainly discernible through his thin clothing. "Abdullah" possesses all the characteristics of the Eastern nation, which are unmistakable to one who, like myself, has been familiar with them in the flesh. His features are without doubt those of a Persian; so is his complexion. His figure is long and lithe and supple, as that of a cat, and he can bend to the ground and rise again with the utmost ease and grace. Anybody who could pretend for a moment to suppose that Mr. Eglinton by "making up" could personate "Abdullah" must be a fool. It would be an impossibility, even were he given unlimited time and assistance, to dress for the character. There is a peculiar boneless elasticity in the movements of a native which those who have lived in the East know that no Englishmen can imitate successfully. "Abdullah's" hands and feet also possess all the characteristics of his nationality, being narrow, long and nerveless, although I have heard that he can give rather too good a grip with his one hand when he chooses to exert his power or to show his dislike to any particular sitter. He has always, however, shown the utmost urbanity towards us, but he is not a particularly friendly or familiar spirit. When "Abdullah" had retired on this occasion, "Joey" drew back the curtain that shaded the cabinet, and showed us his medium and himself. There sat Mr. Eglinton attired in evening dress, with the front of his shirt as smooth and spotless as when it left the laundress' hands, lying back in his chair in a deep sleep, whilst little Joey sat astride his knee, his white suit contrasting strangely with his medium's black trousers. Whilst in this position he kissed Mr. Eglinton several times, telling him to wake up, and not look so sulky; then, having asked if we all saw him distinctly, and were satisfied he was not the medium, he bade God bless us, and the curtains closed once more upon this incomprehensible scene. Mr. Eglinton subsequently became an intimate friend of ours, and we often had the pleasure of sitting with him, but we never saw anything more wonderful (to my mind) than we did on our first acquaintance. When he accompanied us to Bruges (as told in the history of the "Monk"), "Joey" took great trouble to prove to us incontrovertibly that he is not an "emanation," or double, of his medium, but a creature completely separate and wholly distinct. My sister's house being built on a very old-fashioned principle, had all the bedrooms communicating with each other. The *entresol* in which we usually assembled formed the connecting link to a series of six chambers, all of which opened into each other, and the entrance to the first and last of which was from the *entresol*.

We put Mr. Eglinton into No. 1, locking the connecting door with No. 2, so that he had no exit except into our circle as we sat round the curtain, behind which we placed his chair. "Joey" having shown himself outside the curtain, informed us he was going through the locked door at the back into our bedrooms, Nos. 2, 3 and 4, and would bring us something from each room.

Accordingly, in another minute we heard his voice in No. 2, commenting on all he saw there; then he passed into No. 3, and so on, making a tour of the rooms, until he appeared at the communicating door of No. 5, and threw an article taken from each room into the *entresol*. He then told us to lift the curtain and inspect the medium, which we did, finding him fast asleep in his chair, with the door behind him locked. "Joey" then returned by the way he had gone, and presented himself once more outside the cabinet, the key of the locked door being all the time in our possession.

"Ernest" is another well-known control of Mr. Eglinton's, though he seldom appears, except to give some marvellous test or advice. He is a very earnest, deep-feeling spirit, like his name, and his symbol is a cross of light; sometimes large and sometimes small, but always bright and luminous. "Ernest" seldom shows his whole body. It is generally only his face that is apparent in the midst of the circle, a more convincing manifestation for the sceptic or inquirer than any number of bodies which are generally attributed to the chicanery of the medium. "Ernest" always speaks in the direct voice in a gentle, bass tone, entirely distinct from "Joey's" treble, and his appearance is usually indicative of a harmonious and successful meeting. "Daisy," a North American Indian girl, is another control of William Eglinton's, but I have only heard her speak in trance. I do not know which of these spirits it is who conducts the manifestations of writing on the arm, with which Mr. Eglinton is very successful; sometimes it seems to be one, and sometimes the other. As he was sitting with our family at supper one evening, I mentally asked "Joey" to write something on some part of his body where his hand could not reach. This was in order to prove that the writing had not been prepared by chemical means beforehand, as some people are apt to assert. In a short time Mr. Eglinton was observed to stop eating, and grow very fidgety and look uncomfortable, and on being questioned as to the cause, he blushed and stammered, and could give no answer. After a while he rose from table, and asked leave to retire to his room. The next morning he told us that he had been so uneasy at supper, it had become impossible for him to sit it out; that on reaching his room he had found that his back, which irritated him as though covered with a rash, *had a sentence written across it*, of which he could only make out a few words by looking at it backwards in a glass; and as there were only ladies in the house beside himself, he could not call in an interpreter to his assistance. One day, without consulting him, I placed a small card and a tiny piece of black lead between the leaves of a volume of the *Leisure Hour*, and asked him to hold the book with me on the dining-table. I never let the book out of my hand, and it was so thick that I had difficulty afterwards in finding my card (from the corner of which I had torn a piece) again. Mr. Eglinton sat with me in the daylight with the family about, and all he did was to place his hand on mine, which rested on the book. The perspiration ran down his face whilst he did so, but there was no other sign of power, and, honestly, I did not expect to find any writing on my card. When I had shaken it out of the leaves of the book, however, I found a letter closely written on it from my daughter "Florence" to this effect:—

"DEAR MAMA,—I am so glad to be able to communicate with you again, and to demonstrate by actual fact that I am really present. Of course, you quite understand that I do not write this myself. 'Charlie' is present with me, and so are many more, and we all unite in sending you our love.

"Your daughter, FLORENCE."

Mr. Eglinton's mediumship embraces various phases of phenomena, as may be gathered from his own relations of them, and the testimony of his friends. A narrative of his spiritual work, under the title of " 'Twixt two Worlds," has been written and published by Mr. John T. Farmer, and contains some exhaustive descriptions of, and testimonies to, his undoubtedly wonderful gifts. In it appear several accounts written by myself, and which, for the benefit of such of my readers as have not seen the book in question, I will repeat here. The first is that of the "Monk," given *in extenso*, as I have given it in the eleventh chapter of this book. The second is of a *séance* held on the 5th September, 1884. The circle consisted of Mr. and Mrs. Stewart, Colonel and Mrs. Wych, Mr. and Mrs. Russell-Davies, Mr. Morgan, and Colonel Lean and myself, and was held in Mr. Eglinton's private chambers in Quebec Street. We sat in the front drawing-room, with one gas-burner alight, and the door having been properly secured, Mr. Eglinton went into the back room, which was divided by curtains from the front. He had not left us a couple of minutes before a man stepped out through the *portière*, and walked right into the midst of us. He was a large, stout man, and very dark, and most of the sitters remarked that he had a very peculiar smell. No one recognized him, and after appearing two or three times he left, and was *immediately* succeeded by a woman, very much like him, who also had to leave us without any recognition. These two spirits, before taking a final leave, came out *together*, and seemed to examine the circle curiously. After a short interval a much smaller and slighter man came forward, and darted in a peculiar slouching attitude round the circle. Colonel Lean asked him to shake hands. He replied by seizing his hand, and nearly dragging him off his seat. He then darted across the room, and gave a similar proof of his muscular power to Mr. Stewart. But when I asked him to notice *me*, he took my hand and squeezed it firmly between his own. He had scarcely disappeared before "Abdullah," with his one arm and his six feet two of height, stood before us, and salaamed all round. Then came my daughter Florence, a girl of nineteen by that time, very slight and feminine in appearance. She advanced two or three times, near enough to touch me with her hand, but seemed fearful to approach nearer. But the next moment she returned, dragging Mr. Eglinton after her. He was in deep trance, breathing with difficulty, but "Florence" held him by the hand and brought him up to my side, when he detached my hands from those of the sitters either side of me, and making me stand up, he placed my daughter in my arms. As she stood folded in my embrace, she whispered a few words to me relative to a subject *known to no one but myself*, and she placed my hand upon her heart, that I might feel she was a living woman. Colonel Lean asked her to go to him. She tried and failed, but having retreated behind the curtain to gather strength, she appeared the second time *with Mr. Eglinton*, and calling Colonel Lean to her, embraced him. This is one of the most perfect instances on record of a spirit form being seen distinctly by ten witnesses with the medium under gas. The next materialization that appeared was for Mr. Stewart. This gentleman was newly arrived from Australia, and a stranger to Mr. Eglinton. As soon as he saw the female form, who beckoned him to the *portière* to speak to her, he exclaimed, "My God! Pauline," with such genuine surprise and conviction as were unmistakable. The spirit then whispered to him, and putting her arms round his neck affectionately kissed him. He turned after a while, and addressing his wife, told her that the spirit bore the very form and features of their niece Pauline, whom they had lost the year before. Mr. Stewart expressed himself entirely satisfied with the identity of his niece, and said she looked just as she had done before she was taken ill. I must not omit to say that the medium also appeared with this figure, making the third time of showing himself in one evening with the spirit form.

The next apparition, being the seventh that appeared, was that of a little child apparently about two years old, who supported itself in walking by holding on to a chair. I stooped down, and tried to talk to this baby, but it only cried in a fretful manner, as though frightened at finding itself with strangers, and turned away. The attention of the circle was diverted from this sight by seeing "Abdullah" dart between the curtains, and stand with the child in our view, whilst Mr. Eglinton appeared at the same moment between the two forms, making a *tria juncta in uno*.

Thus ended the *séance*. The second one of which I wrote took place on the 27th of the same month, and under very similar circumstances. The circle this time consisted of Mrs. Wheeler, Mr. Woods, Mr. Gordon, The Honourable Gordon Sandeman, my daughter Eva, my son Frank, Colonel Lean, and myself. Mr. Eglinton appeared on this occasion to find some difficulty in passing under control, and he came out so frequently into the circle to gather power, that I guessed we were going to have uncommonly good manifestations. The voice of "Joey," too, begged us under *no circumstances whatever*, to lose hands, as they were going to try something very difficult, and we might defeat their efforts at the very moment of victory. When the medium was at last under control in the back drawing-room, a tall man, with an uncovered head of dark hair, and a large beard, appeared and walked up to a lady in the company. She was very much affected by the recognition of the spirit, which she affirmed to be that of her brother. She called him by name and kissed him, and informed us that he was just as he had been in earth life. Her emotion was so great, we thought she would have fainted, but after a while she became calm again. We next heard the notes of a clarionet. I had been told that Mr. Woods (a stranger just arrived from the Antipodes) had lost a brother under peculiarly distressing circumstances, and that he hoped (though hardly expected) to see his brother that evening. It was the first time I had ever seen Mr. Woods; yet so remarkable was the likeness between the brothers, that when a spirit appeared with a clarionet in his hand, I could not help knowing who it was, and exclaimed, "Oh, Mr. Woods, there is your brother!" The figure walked up to Mr. Woods and grasped his hand. As they appeared thus with their faces turned to one another, they were *strikingly* alike both in feature and expression. This spirit's head was also bare, an unusual occurrence, and covered with thick, crisp hair. He appeared twice, and said distinctly, "God bless you!" each time to his brother. Mrs. Wheeler, who had known the spirit in earth life, was startled by the tone of the voice, which she recognized at once; and Mr. Morgan, who had been an intimate friend of his in Australia, confirmed the recognition. We asked Mr. Woods the meaning of the clarionet, which was a black one, handsomely inlaid with silver. He told us his brother had been an excellent musician, and had won a similar instrument as a prize at some musical competition. "But," he added wonderingly, "his clarionet is locked up in my house in Australia." My daughter "Florence" came out next, but only a little way, at which I was disappointed, but "Joey" said they were reserving the strength for a manifestation further on. He then said, "Here comes a friend

5

for Mr. Sandeman," and a man, wearing a masonic badge and scarf, appeared, and made the tour of the circle, giving the masonic grip to those of the craft present. He was a good looking young man, and said he had met some of those present in Australia, but no one seemed to recognize him. He was succeeded by a male figure, who had materialized on the previous occasion. As he passed through the curtain, a female figure appeared beside him, bearing a very bright light, as though to show him the way. She did not come beyond the *portière*, but every one in the room saw her distinctly. On account of the dress and complexion of the male figure, we had wrongly christened him "The Bedouin"; but my son, Frank Marryat, who is a sailor, now found out he was an East Indian by addressing him in Hindustani, to which he responded in a low voice. Some one asked him to take a seat amongst us, upon which he seized a heavy chair in one hand and flourished it above his head. He then squatted, native fashion, on his haunches on the floor and left us, as before, by vanishing suddenly.

"Joey" now announced that they were going to try the experiment of "*showing us how the spirits were made from the medium.*" This was the crowning triumph of the evening. Mr. Eglinton appeared in the very midst of us in trance. He entered the room backwards, and as if fighting with the power that pushed him in, his eyes were shut, and his breath was drawn with difficulty. As he stood thus, holding on to a chair for support, an airy mass like a cloud of tobacco smoke was seen on his left hip, his legs became illuminated by lights travelling up and down them, and a white film settled about his head and shoulders. The mass increased, and he breathed harder and harder whilst invisible hands *pulled the filmy drapery out of his hip* in long strips, that amalgamated as soon as formed, and fell to the ground to be succeeded by others. The cloud continued to grow thicker, and we were eagerly watching the process, when, in the twinkling of an eye, the mass had evaporated, and a spirit, full formed, stood beside him. No one could say *how* it had been raised in the very midst of us, nor whence it came, but *it was there*. Mr. Eglinton then retired with the new-born spirit behind the curtains, but in another moment he came (or was thrown out) amongst us again, and fell upon the floor. The curtains opened again, and the full figure of "Ernest" appeared and raised the medium by the hand. As he saw him, Mr. Eglinton fell on his knees, and "Ernest" drew him out of sight. Thus ended the second of these two wonderful *séances*. The published reports of them were signed with the full names and addresses of those who witnessed them.

William Eglinton's powers embrace various phases of phenomena, amongst which levitation is a common occurrence; indeed, I do not think I have ever sat with him at a *séance* during which he had *not* been levitated. I have seen him on several occasions rise, or be carried, into the air, so that his head touched the ceiling, and his feet were above the sitters' heads. On one occasion whilst sitting with him a perfectly new manifestation was developed. As each spirit came the name was announced, written on the air in letters of fire, which moved round the circle in front of the sitters. As the names were those of friends of the audience and not of friends of Mr. Eglinton, and the phenomenon ended with a letter written to me in the same manner on private affairs, it could not be attributed to a previously arranged trick. I have accompanied Mr. Eglinton, in the capacity of interpreter, to a professional *séance* in Paris consisting of some forty persons, not one of whom could speak a word of English whilst he was equally ignorant of foreign languages. And I have heard French and German spirits return through him to converse with their friends, who were radiant with joy at communicating with them again, whilst their medium could not (had he been conscious) have understood or pronounced a single word of all the news he was so glibly repeating. I

will conclude this testimony to his powers by the account of
a sitting with him for slate writing—that much abused and
much maligned manifestation. Because a few ignorant pig-
headed people who have never properly investigated the
science of Spiritualism decide that a thing cannot be, "because
it can't," men of honour and truth are voted charlatans and
tricksters, and those who believe in them fools and blind.
The day will dawn yet when it will be seen which of the two
classes best deserve the name.

Some years ago, when I first became connected in business
with Mr. Edgar Lee of the *St. Stephen's Review*, I found him
much interested in the subject of Spiritualism, though he
had never had an opportunity of investigating it, and through
my introduction I procured him a test *séance* with William
Eglinton. We met one afternoon at the medium's house in
Nottingham Place for that purpose, and sat at an ordinary
table in the back dining-room for slate-writing. The slate
used on the occasion (as Mr. Lee had neglected to bring his
own slate as requested) was one which was presented to
Mr. Eglinton by Mr. Gladstone. It consisted of two slates
of medium size, set in mahogany frames, with box hinges,
and which, when shut, were fastened with a Bramah lock
and key. On the table cloth was a collection of tiny pieces
of different coloured chalk. In the front room, which was
divided from us by folding doors, were some bookcases. Mr.
Eglinton commenced by asking Mr. Lee to go into the front
room by himself, and select, in his mind's eye, any book he
chose as the one from which extracts should be given. Mr.
Lee having done as he was told, returned to his former place
beside us, without giving a hint as to which book he had
selected. Mr. Gladstone's slate was then delivered over to
him to clean with sponge and water; that done, he was
directed to choose four pieces of chalk and place them
between the slates, to lock them and retain the key. The
slates were left on the table in the sight of all; Mr. Lee's hand

remained on them all the time. All that Mr. Eglinton did was to place *his* hand above Mr. Lee's.

"You chose, I think," he commenced, "four morsels of chalk—white, blue, yellow and red. Please say which word, on which line, on which page of the book you selected just now, the white chalk shall transcribe."

Mr. Lee answered (I forget the exact numbers) some-what in this wise, "The 3rd word on the 15th line of the 102nd page," he having, it must be remembered, no know-ledge of the contents of the volume, which he had not even touched with his hand. Immediately he had spoken, a scratching noise was heard between the two slates. When it ceased, Mr. Eglinton put the same question with regard to the blue, yellow and red chalks, which was similarly responded to. He then asked Mr. Lee to unlock the slates, read the words, and then fetch the book he had selected, and compare notes, and in each instance the word had been given correctly. Several other experiments were then made, equally curious, the number of Mr. Lee's watch, which he had not taken from his pocket, and which he said he did not know himself, being amongst them. Then Mr. Eglinton said to Mr. Lee, "Have you any friend in the spirit-world from whom you would like to hear? If so, and you will mentally recall the name, we will try and procure some writing from him or her." (I must say here that these two were utter strangers to each other, and had met for the first time that afternoon, and indeed as will be seen by the context *I* had a very slight knowledge of Mr. Edgar Lee myself at that time.) Mr. Lee thought for a moment, and then replied that there was a dead friend of his from he should like to hear. The cleaning and locking process was gone through again, and the scratching re-commenced, and when it concluded, Mr. Lee unlocked the slates and read a letter to this effect:—

"My Dear Will,—I am quite satisfied with your decision respect-ing Bob. By all means, send him to the school you are thinking of.

He will get on better there. His education requires more pushing than it gets at present. Thanks for all you have done for him. God bless you.—Your affectionate cousin,   R. TASKER."

I do not pretend to give the exact words of this letter; for though they were afterwards published, I have not a copy by me. But the gist of the experiment does not lie in the exactitude of the words. When I saw the slate, I looked at Mr. Lee in astonishment.

"Who is it for?" I asked.

"It is all right," he replied; "it is for me. It is from my cousin, who left his boy in my charge. *My real name is William Tasker.*"

Now, I had never heard it hinted before that Edgar Lee was only a *nom de plume*, and the announcement came on me as a genuine surprise. So satisfied was Mr. William Tasker Edgar Lee with his experimental *séance*, that he had the slate photographed and reproduced in the *St. Stephen's Review*, with an account of the whole proceedings which were sufficient to make any one stop for a moment in the midst of the world's harassing duties and think.

CHAPTER XIV

THE MEDIUMSHIP OF ARTHUR COLMAN

ARTHUR COLMAN was so intimate a friend of Mr. Eglinton's, and so much associated with him in my thoughts in the days when I first knew them both, that it seems only natural that I should write of him next. His powers were more confined to materialization than Eglinton's, but in that he excelled. He is the most wonderful materializing medium I ever met in England; but of late years, owing to the injury it did him in his profession, he has been compelled, in justice to himself, to give up sitting for physical manifestations, and, indeed, sitting at all, except to oblige his friends. I cannot but consider this decision on his part as a great public loss; but until the public takes more interest in the next world than they do in this, it will not make it worth the while of such as Mr. Colman to devote their lives, health and strength to their enlightenment.

Arthur Colman is a young man of delicate constitution and appearance, who was at one time almost brought down to death's door by the demands made by physical phenomena upon his strength; but since he has given up sitting, he has regained his health, and looks quite a different person. This fact proves of itself what a tax is laid upon the unfortunate medium for such manifestations. Since he has resolved, however, never to sit again, I am all the more anxious to record what I have seen through him, probably for the last time. When I first knew my husband Colonel Lean, he had seen nothing of Spiritualism, and was proportionately curious, and naturally a little sceptical on the subject, or, rather let me say, incredulous. He was hardly prepared to receive all the marvels I told him of without proof; and Mr. Colman's guide, "Aimée," was very anxious to convince him of their truth. She arranged, therefore, a *séance* at which he was to be present, and which was to be held at the house of Mr. and Mrs. George Neville. The party dined there together previously, and consisted only of Mr. and Mrs. Neville, Arthur Colman, Colonel Lean, and myself. As we were in the drawing-room, however, after dinner, and before we had commenced the *séance*, an American lady, who was but slightly known to any of us, was announced. We had particularly wished to have no strangers present, and her advent proportionately annoyed us, but we did not know on what excuse to get rid of her. She was a pushing sort of person; and when Mrs. Neville told her we were going to hold a *séance*, as a sort of hint that she might take her leave, it only made her resolve to stay; indeed, she declared she had had a premonition of the fact. She said that whilst in her own room that morning, a figure had appeared standing by her bed, dressed in blue and white, like the pictures of the Virgin Mary, and that all day she had had an impression that she must spend the evening with the Nevilles, and she should hear something more about it. We could not get rid of the lady, so we were obliged to ask her to remain and assist at the *séance*, which she had already made up her mind to do, so we commenced our preparations. The two drawing-rooms communicated by folding doors, which were opened and a *portière* drawn across the opening. In the back room we placed Mr. Colman's chair. He was dressed in a light grey suit, which we secured in the following manner: His hands were first sewn inside the sleeves of the coat, then his arms were placed behind his back, and the coat sleeves sewn together to the elbow. We then sewed his trouser legs together in the same way. We then tied him round the throat, waist and legs with *white cotton*, which the least movement on his part would break, and the ends of each ligament were sealed to the wall of the room with wax, and stamped with my seal with "*Florence Marryat*" on it. Considering him thus secure, without any *possibility* of escape unless we discovered it, we left him in the back room, and arranged ourselves on a row of five chairs before the *portière* in the front one, which was lighted by a single gas-burner. I sat at the head of the row, then the American lady, Mrs. Neville, Colonel Lean and Mr. Neville. I am not sure how long we waited for the manifestations; but I do not think it was many minutes before a female figure glided from the side of the curtain and took a vacant chair by my side. I said, "*Who is this?*" and she whispered, "*Florence,*" and laid her head down on my shoulder, and kissed my neck. I was turning towards her to distinguish her features more fully, when I became aware that a second figure was standing in front of me, and "Florence" said, "Mother, there is Powles"; and at the same time, as he bent down to speak to me, his beard touched my face. I had not had time to draw the attention of my friends to the spirits that stood by me, when I was startled by hearing one exclamation after another from the various sitters. The American lady called out, "There's the woman that came to me this morning." Mr. Neville said, "That is my father," and Colonel Lean was asking some one if he would not give his name. I looked down the line of sitters. Before Colonel Lean there stood an old man with a long, white beard; a somewhat similar figure was in front of Mr. Neville. Before the dark curtain appeared a woman dressed in blue and white, like a nun; and meanwhile, "Florence" and "Powles" still maintained their station by my side. As if this were not enough of itself to turn a mortal's brain, the *portière* was at the same moment drawn aside, and there stood Arthur Colman in his grey suit, freed from all his bonds, but under the control of "Aimée," who called out joyously to my husband, *"Now, Frank, will you believe?"* She dropped the curtain, the apparitions glided or faded away, and we passed into the back drawing-room, to find Mr. Colman still in trance, just as we had left him, and *with all the seals and stitches* intact. Not a thread of them all was broken. This is the largest number of spirits I have ever seen at one time with one medium. I have seen two materialized spirits at a time, and even three, from Mr. Williams and Miss Showers and Katie Cook; but on this occasion there were five apparent with the medium, all standing together before us. And this is the sort of thing that the majority of people do not consider it worth their while to take a little trouble to see. I have already related how successfully "Florence" used to materialize through this medium, and numerous friends, utterly unknown to him, have revisited us through his means. His trance mediumship is as wonderful as his physical phenomena; some people might think more so. Amongst others, two spirits have come back to us through Mr. Colman, neither of whom he knew in this life, and both of whom are, in their way, too characteristic to be mistaken. One is Phillis Glover the actress; the other my stepson, Francis Lean, who was drowned by an accident at sea. Phillis Glover was a woman who led a very eventful life, chiefly in America, and was a versatile genius in conversation, as in everything else. She was peculiar also, and had a half-Yankee way of talking, and a store of familiar sayings and anecdotes, which she constantly introduced into her conversation. She was by no means an ordinary person whilst in this life, and in order to imitate her manner and speech successfully one would need to be as clever a person as herself. And, without wishing to derogate from the powers of Mr. Colman's mind, he knows, and I know, that Phillis Glover was cleverer than either of us. When her influence or spirit therefore returns through him, it is quite unmistakable. It is not only that she retains all her little tricks of voice and feature and manner (which Mr. Colman has never seen), but she alludes to circumstances that took place in this life and people she was associated with here that he has never heard of. More, she will relate her old stories and anecdotes, and sing her old songs, and give the most incontrovertible tests of her identity, even to recalling facts and incidents that have entirely passed from our minds. When she appears through him, it is Phillis Glover we are sitting with again and talking with, as familiarly as we did in the days gone by. "Francis," in his way too, is quite as remarkable. The circumstances of his death and the events leading to it were unknown to us, till he related them through Mr. Colman; and he speaks to us of the contents of private letters, and repeats conversations and alludes to circumstances and names that are known only to him and ourselves. He had a peculiar manner also—quick and nervous—and a way of cutting his words short, which his spirit preserves to the smallest particular, and which furnish the strongest proofs possible of his identity to those who knew him here below.

CHAPTER XV

THE MEDIUMSHIP OF MRS. GUPPY VOLCKMAN

THE mediumship of this lady is so well known, and has been so universally attested, that nothing I can write of could possibly add to her fame; and as I made her acquaintance but a short time before she relinquished sitting for manifestations, I have had but little experience of her powers, but such as I enjoyed were very remarkable. I have alluded to them in the story of "The Green Lady," whose apparition was due solely to Mrs. Guppy Volckman's presence, and on that occasion she gave us another wonderful proof of her mediumship. A sheet was procured and held up at either end by Mr. Charles Williams and herself. It was held in the light, in the centre of the room, forming a white wall of about five feet high, *i.e.*, as high as their arms could conveniently reach. *Both* the hands of Mrs. Volckman and Mr. Williams were placed *outside* the sheet, so that no trickery might be suspected through their being concealed. In a short time the head of a woman appeared above the sheet, followed by that of a man, and various pairs of hands, both large and small which bobbed up and down, and seized the hands of the spectators, whilst the faces went close to the media, as if with the intention of kissing them. This frightened Mrs. Volckman, so that she frequently screamed and dropped her end of the sheet, which, had there been any deception, must inevitably have exposed it. It seemed to make no difference to the spirits, however, who reappeared directly they had the opportunity, and made her at last so nervous that she threw the sheet down and refused to hold it any more. The faces were life-size, and could move their eyes and lips; the hands were some as large as a man's, and covered with hair, and others like those of a woman or child. They had all the capability of working the fingers and grasping objects presented to them; whilst the four hands belonging to the media were kept in sight of the audience and could not have worked machinery even if they could have concealed it.

The first time I was introduced to Mrs. Volckman (then Mrs. Guppy) was at a *séance* at her own house in Victoria Road, where she had assembled a large party of guests, including several names well known in art and literature. We sat in a well-lighted drawing-room, and the party was so large that the circle round the table was three deep. Mrs. Mary Hardy, the American medium (since dead), was present. and the honours of the manifestations may be therefore, I conclude, divided between the two ladies. The table, a common deal one, made for such occasions, with a round hole of about twenty inches in diameter in the middle of it, was covered with a cloth that hung down, and was nailed to the ground, leaving only the aperture free. (I must premise that this cloth had been nailed down by a committee of the gentlemen visitors, in order that there might be no suspicion of a confederate hidden underneath it.) We then sat round the table, but without placing our hands on it. In a short time hands began to appear through the open space in the table, all sorts of hands, from the woman's taper fingers and the baby's dimpled fist, to the hands of old and young men, wrinkled or muscular. Some of the hands had rings on the fingers, by which the sitters recognized them, some stretched themselves out to be grasped; and some appeared in pairs, clasped together or separate. One hand took a glove from a sitter and put it on the other, showing the muscular force it possessed by the way in which it pressed down each finger and then buttoned the glove. Another pair of hands talked through the dumb alphabet to us, and a third played on a musical instrument. I was leaning forward, before I had witnessed the above, peering inquisitively down the hole, and saying, "I wonder if they would have strength to take anything down with them, when a large hand suddenly appeared and very nearly took *me* down, by seizing my nose as if it never meant to let go again. At all events, it took me a peg or two down, for I remember it brought tears into my eyes with the force it exhibited. After the hands had ceased to appear, the table was moved away, and we sat in a circle in the light. Mrs. Guppy did not wish to take a part in the *séance*, except as a spectator, so she retired to the back drawing-room with the Baroness Adelma Vay and other visitors, and left Mrs. Hardy with the circle in the front. Suddenly, however, she was levitated and carried in the sight of us all into the midst of our circle. As she felt herself rising in the air, she called out, "Don't let go hands for Heaven's sake." We were standing in a ring, and I had hold of the hand of Prince Albert of Solms. As Mrs. Guppy came sailing over our heads, her feet caught his neck and mine, and in our anxiety to do as she had told us, we gripped tight hold of each other, and were thrown forward on our knees by the force with which she was carried past us into the centre. This was a pretty strong proof to us, whatever it may be to others, that our senses did not deceive us when we thought we saw Mrs. Guppy over our heads in the air. The influence that levitated her, moreover, placed her on a chair with such a bump that it broke the two front legs off. As soon as Mrs. Guppy had rejoined us, the order was given to put out the light and to wish for something. We unanimously asked for flowers, it being the middle of December, and a hard frost. Simultaneously we smelt the smell of fresh earth, and were told to light the gas again, when the following extraordinary sight met our view. In the middle of the sitters, still holding hands, was piled up *on the carpet* an immense quantity of mould, which had been torn up apparently with the roots that accompanied it. There were laurestinus, and laurels, and holly, and several others, just as they had been pulled out of the earth and thrown down in the midst of us. Mrs. Guppy looked anything but pleased at the state of her carpet, and begged the spirits would bring something cleaner next time. They then told us to extinguish the lights again, and each sitter was to wish *mentally* for something for himself. I wished for a yellow butterfly, knowing it was December; and as I thought of it, a little cardboard box was put into my hand. Prince Albert whispered to me, "Have you got anything?" "Yes," I said; "but not what I asked for. I expect they have given me a piece of jewellery." When the gas was re-lit, I opened the box, and there lay *two yellow butterflies;* dead, of course, but none the less extraordinary for that. I wore at that *séance* a tight-fitting, high white muslin dress, over a tight petticoat body. The dress had no pocket, and I carried my handkerchief, a fine cambric one, in my hand. When the *séance* was over, I found this handkerchief had disappeared, at which I was vexed, as it had been embroidered for me by my sister Emily, then dead. I inquired of every sitter if they had seen it, even making them turn out their pockets in case they had taken it in mistake for their own, but it was not to be found, and I returned home, as I thought, without it. What was my surprise on removing my dress and petticoat bodice to find the handkerchief, neatly folded into a square of about four inches, *between* my stays and the garment beneath them; placed, moreover, over the smallest part of my waist, where no fingers could have penetrated even had my dress been loose. My woman readers may be able better than the men to appreciate the difficulty of such a manœuvre by mortal means; indeed it would have been quite impossible for myself or anybody else to place the handkerchief in such a position without removing the stays. And it was folded so neatly also, and placed so smoothly, that there was not a crumple in the cambric.

CHAPTER XVI

THE MEDIUMSHIP OF FLORENCE COOK

IN writing of my own mediumship, or the mediumship of any other person, I wish it particularly to be understood that I do not intend my narrative to be, by any means, an account of *all séances* held under that control (for were I to include everything that I have seen and heard during my researches into Spiritualism, this volume would swell to unconscionable dimensions), but only of certain events which I believe to be remarkable, and not enjoyed by every one in like measure. Most people have read of the ordinary phenomena that take place at such meetings. My readers, therefore, will find no description here of marvels which—whether true or false—can be accounted for upon natural grounds. Miss Florence Cook, now Mrs. Elgie Corner, is one of the media who have been most talked of and written about. Mr. Alfred Crookes took an immense interest in her, and published a long account of his investigation of Spiritualism under her mediumship. Mr. Henry Dunphy, of the *Morning Post*, wrote a series of papers for *London Society* (of which magazine I was then the editor), describing her powers, and the proof she gave of them. The first time I ever met Florence Cook was in his private house, when my little daughter appeared through her (*vide* "The Story of my Spirit Child"). On that occasion, as we were sitting at supper after the *séance*—a party of perhaps thirty people—the whole dinner-table, with everything upon it, rose bodily in the air to a level with our knees, and the dishes and glasses swayed about in a perilous manner, without, however, coming to any permanent harm. I was so much astonished at, and interested by, what I saw that evening, that I became most anxious to make the personal acquaintance of Miss Cook. She was the medium for the celebrated spirit, "Katie King," of whom so much has been believed and disbelieved, and the *séances* she gave at her parents' house in Hackney for the purpose of seeing this figure alone used to be crowded by the cleverest and most scientific men of the day, Sergeants Cox and Ballantyne, Mr. S. C. Hall, Mr. Alfred Crookes, and many others, being on terms of the greatest intimacy with her. Mr. William Harrison, of the *Spiritualist* paper, was the one to procure me an introduction to the family and an entrance to the *séances*, for which I shall always feel grateful to him.

For the benefit of the unitiated, let me begin by telling *who* "Katie King" was supposed to be. Her account of herself was that her name was "Annie Owens Morgan"; that she was the daughter of Sir Henry Morgan, a famous buccaneer who lived about the time of the Commonwealth, and suffered death upon the high seas, being, in fact, a pirate; that she herself was about twelve years old when Charles the First was beheaded; that she married and had two little children; that she committed more crimes than we should like to hear of, having murdered men with her own hands, but yet died quite young, at about two or three and twenty. To all questions concerning the reason of her reappearance on earth, she returned but one answer, that it was part of the work given her to do to convince the world of the truth of Spiritualism. This was the information I received from her own lips. She had appeared to the Cooks some years before I saw her, and had become so much one of the family as to walk about the house at all times without alarming the inmates. She often materialized and got into bed with her medium at night, much to Florrie's annoyance; and after Miss Cook's marriage to Captain Corner, he told me himself that he used to feel at first as if he had married two women, and was not quite sure which was his wife of the two.

The order of these *séances* was always the same. Miss Cook retired to a back room, divided from the audience by a thin damask curtain, and presently the form of "Katie King" would appear dressed in white, and walk out amongst the sitters in gaslight, and talk like one of themselves. Florence Cook (as I mentioned before) is a very small, slight brunette, with dark eyes and dark curly hair and a delicate aquiline nose. Sometimes "Katie" resembled her exactly; at others, she was totally different. Sometimes, too, she measured the same height as her medium; at others, she was much taller. I have a large photograph of "Katie" taken under limelight. In it she appears as the double of Florrie Cook, yet Florrie was looking on whilst the picture was taken. I have sat for her several times with Mr. Crookes, and seen the tests applied which are mentioned in his book on the subject. I have seen Florrie's dark curls *nailed down to the floor*, outside the curtain, in view of the audience, whilst "Katie" walked about and talked with us. I have seen Florrie placed on the scale of a weighing machine constructed by Mr. Crookes for the purpose, behind the curtain, whilst the balance remained in sight. I have seen under these circumstances that the medium weighed eight stone in a normal condition, and that as soon as the materialized form was fully developed, the balance ran up to four stone. Moreover, I have seen both Florrie and "Katie" together on several occasions, so I can have no doubt on the subject that they were two separate creatures. Still, I can quite understand how difficult it must have been for strangers to compare the strong likeness that existed between the medium and the spirit, without suspecting they were one and the same person. One evening "Katie" walked out and perched herself upon my knee. I could feel she was a much plumper and heavier woman than Miss Cook, but she wonderfully resembled her in features, and I told her so. "Katie" did not seem to consider it a compliment. She shrugged her shoulders, made a grimace, and said, "I know I am; I can't help it, but I was much prettier than that in earth life. You shall see, some day—you shall see." After she had finally retired that evening, she put her head out at the curtain again and said, with the strong lisp she always had, "I want Mrs. Ross-Church." I rose and went to her, when she pulled me inside the curtain, when I found it was so thin that the gas shining through it from the outer room made everything in the inner quite visible. "Katie" pulled my dress impatiently and said, "Sit down on the ground," which I did. She then seated herself in my lap, saying, "And now, dear, we'll have a good 'confab,' like women do on earth." Florence Cook, meanwhile, was lying on a mattress on the ground close to us, wrapped in a deep trance. "Katie" seemed very anxious I should ascertain beyond doubt that it was Florrie. "Touch her," she said, "take her hand, pull her curls. Do you see that it is Florrie lying there?" When I assured her I was quite satisfied there was no doubt of it, the spirit said, "Then look round this way, and see what I was like in earth life." I turned to the form in my arms, and what was my amazement to see a woman fair as the day, with large grey or blue eyes, a white skin, and a profusion of golden red hair. "Katie" enjoyed my surprise, and asked me, "Ain't I prettier than Florrie now?" She then rose and procured a pair of scissors from the table, and cut off a lock of her own hair and a lock of the medium's, and gave them to me. I have them safe to this day. One is almost black, soft and silky; the other a coarse golden red. After she had made me this present, "Katie" said, "Go back now, but don't tell the others to-night, or they'll all want to see me." On another very warm evening she sat on my lap amongst the audience, and I felt perspiration on her arm. This surprised me; and I asked her if, for the time being, she had the veins, nerves, and secretions of a human being; if blood ran through her body, and she had a heart and lungs. Her answer was, "I have everything that Florrie has." On that occasion also she called me after her into the back room, and dropping her white garment, stood perfectly naked before me. "Now," she said, "you can see that I am a woman." Which indeed she was, and a most beautifully-made woman too; and I examined her well, whilst Miss Cook lay beside us on the floor. Instead of dismissing me this time, "Katie" told me to sit down by the medium, and, having brought me a candle and matches, said I was to strike a light as soon as she gave three knocks, as Florrie would be hysterical on awaking, and need my assistance. She then knelt down and kissed me, and I saw she was still naked. "Where is your dress, Katie?" I asked. "Oh, that's gone," she said; "I've sent it on before me." As she spoke thus, kneeling beside me, she rapped three times on the floor. I struck the match almost simultaneously with the signal; but as it flared up, "Katie King" was gone like a flash of lightning, and Miss Cook, as she had predicted, awoke with a burst of frightened tears, and had to be soothed into tranquillity again. On another occasion "Katie King" was asked at the beginning of the *séance*, by one of the company, to say *why* she could not appear in the light of more than one gas-burner. The question seemed to irritate her, and she replied, "I have told you all, several times before, that I can't stay under a searching light. I don't know *why*; but I can't, and if you want to prove the truth of what I say, turn up all the gas and see what will happen to me. Only remember, if you do there will be no *séance* to-night, because I shan't be able to come back again, and you must take your choice."

Upon this assertion it was put to the vote if the trial should be made or not, and all present (Mr. S. C. Hall was one of the party) decided we would prefer to witness the effect of a full glare of gas upon the materialized form than to have the usual sitting, as it would settle the vexed question of the necessity of gloom (if not darkness) for a materializing *séance* for ever. We accordingly told "Katie" of our choice, and she consented to stand the test, though she said afterwards we had put her to much pain. She took up her station against the drawing-room wall, with her arms extended as if she were crucified. Then the gas-burners were turned on to their full extent in a room about sixteen feet square. The effect upon "Katie King" was marvellous. She looked like herself for the space of a second only, then she began gradually to melt away. I can compare the dematerialization of her form to nothing but a wax doll melting before a hot fire. First, the features became blurred and indistinct; they seemed to run into each other. The eyes sunk in the sockets, the nose disappeared, the frontal bone fell in. Next the limbs appeared to give way under her, and she sank lower and lower on the carpet like a crumbling edifice. At last there was *nothing but her head* left above the ground—then a heap of white drapery only, which disappeared with a whisk, as if a hand had pulled it after her—and we were left staring by the light of three gas-burners at the spot on which "Katie King" had stood.

She was always attired in white drapery, but it varied in quality. Sometimes it looked like long cloth; at others like mull muslin or jaconet; oftenest it was a species of thick cotton net. The sitters were much given to asking "Katie" for a piece of her dress to keep as a souvenir of their visit, and when they received it, would seal it up carefully in an envelope and convey it home; and were much surprised on examining their treasure to find it had totally disappeared.

"Katie" used to say that nothing material about her could be made to last without taking away some of the medium's vitality, and weakening her in consequence. One evening, when she was cutting off pieces of her dress rather lavishly, I remarked that it would require a great deal of mending. She answered, "I'll show you how we mend dresses in the Spirit World." She then doubled up the front breadth of her garment a dozen times, and cut two or three round holes in it. I am sure when she let it fall again there must have been thirty of forty holes, and "Katie" said, "Isn't that a nice cullender?"

She then commenced, whilst we stood close to her, to shake her skirt gently about, and in a minute it was as perfect as before, without a hole to be seen. When we expressed our astonishment, she told me to take the scissors and cut off her hair. She had a profusion of ringlets falling to her waist that night. I obeyed religiously, hacking the hair wherever I could, whilst she kept on saying, "Cut more! cut more! not for yourself, you know, because you can't take it away."

So I cut off curl after curl, and as fast as they fell to the ground, *the hair grew again upon her head.* When I had finished, "Katie" asked me to examine her hair, to see if I could detect any place where I had used the scissors, and I did so without any effect. Neither was the severed hair to be found. It had vanished out of sight. "Katie" was photographed many times, by limelight, by Mr. Alfred Crookes, but her portraits are all too much like her medium to be of any value in establishing her claim to a separate identity. She had always stated she should not appear on this earth after the month of May, 1874; and accordingly, on the 21st, she assembled her friends to say "Good-bye" to them, and I was one of the number. "Katie" had asked Miss Cook to provide her with a large basket of flowers and ribbons, and she sat on the floor and made up a bouquet for each of her friends to keep in remembrance of her.

Mine, which consists of lilies of the valley and pink geranium, looks almost as fresh to-day, nearly seventeen years after, as it did when she gave it to me. It was accompanied by the following words, which "Katie" wrote on a sheet of paper in my presence:—

"From Annie Owen de Morgan (*alias* 'Katie') to her friend Florence Marryat Ross-Church. With love. *Pensez a moi.*

"*May* 21*st*, 1874."

The farewell scene was as pathetic as if we had been parting with a dear companion by death. "Katie" herself did not seem to know how to go. She returned again and again to have a last look, especially at Mr. Alfred Crookes, who was as attached to her as she was to him. Her prediction has been fulfilled, and from that day, Florence Cook never saw her again nor heard anything about her. Her place was shortly filled by another influence, who called herself "Marie" and who danced and sung in a truly professional style, and certainly as Miss Cook never either danced or sung. I should not have mentioned the appearance of this spirit, whom I only saw once or twice, excepting for the following reason. On one occasion Miss Cook (then Mrs. Corner) was giving a public *séance* at the rooms of the National British Association of Spiritualists, at which a certain Sir George Sitwell, a very young man, was present, and at which he declared that the medium cheated, and that the spirit "Marie" was herself, dressed up to deceive the audience. Letters appeared in the newspapers about it, and the whole press came down upon Spiritualists, and declared them all to be either knaves or fools. These notices were published on the morning of a day on which Miss Cook was engaged to give another public *séance*, at which I was present. She was naturally very much cut up about them. Her reputation was at stake; her honour had been called into question, and being a proud girl, she resented it bitterly. Her present audience was chiefly composed of friends; but, before commencing, she put it to us whether, whilst under such a stigma, she had better not sit at all. We, who had all tested her and believed in her, were unanimous in repudiating the vile charges brought against her, and in begging the *séance* should proceed. Florrie refused, however, to sit unless some one remained in the cabinet with her, and she chose me for the purpose. I was therefore tied to her securely with a stout rope, and we remained thus fastened together for the whole of the evening. Under which conditions "Marie" appeared and sung and danced outside the cabinet, just as she had done to Sir George Sitwell whilst her medium remained tied to me. So much for men who decide a matter before they have sifted it to the bottom. Mrs. Elgie Corner has long since given up mediumship either private or public, and lives deep down in the heart of Wales, where the babble and scandal of the city affect her no longer. But she told me, only last year, that she would not pass through the suffering she had endured on account of Spiritualism again for all the good this world could give her.

CHAPTER XVII

THE MEDIUMSHIP OF KATIE COOK

IN the matter of producing physical phenomena the Cooks are a most remarkable family, all three daughters being powerful media, and that without any solicitation on their part. The second one, Katie, is by no means the least powerful of the three, although she has sat more privately than her sister Florence, and not had the same scientific tests (I believe) applied to her. The first time I had an opportunity of testing Katie's mediumship was at the private rooms of Signor Rondi, in a circle of nine or ten friends. The apartment was small and sparsely furnished, being an artist's studio. The gas was kept burning and before the sitting commenced the door was locked and strips of paper pasted over the opening inside. The cabinet was formed of a window curtain nailed across one corner of the room, behind which a chair was placed for the medium, who is a remarkably small and slight girl—much slighter than her sister Florence—with a thin face and delicate features. She was dressed, on this occasion, in a tight-fitting black gown and Hessian boots that buttoned half-way to her knee, and which, she informed me, she always wore when sitting (just as Miss Showers· did), because they had each eighteen buttons, which took a long time to fasten and unfasten. The party sat in a semicircle, close outside the curtain, and the light was lowered, but not extinguished. There was no darkness, and no holding of hands. I mention these facts to show how very simple the preparations were. In a few minutes the curtain was lifted, and a form, clothed in white, who called herself "Lily," was presented to our view. She answered several questions relative to herself and the medium; and perceiving some doubt on the part of some of the sitters, she seated herself on my knee, I being nearest the curtain, and asked me to feel her body, and tell the others how differently she was made from the medium. I had already realized that she was much heavier than Katie Cook, as she felt like a heavy girl of nine or ten stone. I then passed my hand up and down her figure. She had full breasts and plump arms and legs, and could not have been mistaken by the most casual observers for Miss Cook. Whilst she sat on my knee, however, she desired my husband and Signor Rondi to go inside the curtain and feel that the medium was seated in her chair. When they did so, they found Katie was only half entranced. She thrust her feet out to view, and said, "I am not 'Lily'; feel my boots." My husband had, at the same moment, one hand on Miss Cook's knee, and the other stretched out to feel the figure seated on my lap. There remained no doubt in *his* mind of there being two bodies there at the same time. Presently "Lily" passed her hand over my dress, and remarked how nice and warm it was, and how she wished she had one on too. I asked her, "Are you cold?" and she said, "Wouldn't you be cold if you had nothing but this white thing on?" Half-jestingly, I took my fur cloak, which was on a sofa close by, and put it round her shoulders, and told her to wear it. "Lily" seemed delighted. She exclaimed, "Oh, how warm it is! May I take it away with me?" I said, "Yes, if you will bring it back before I go home. I have nothing else to wear, remember." She promised she would, and left my side. In another moment she called out, "Turn up the gas!" We did so. "Lily" was gone, and so was my large fur cloak! We searched the little room round for it. It had entirely disappeared. There was a locked cupboard in which Signor Rondi kept drawing materials. I insisted on its being opened, although he declared it had not been unlocked for weeks, and we found it full of dust and drawing blocks, but nothing else, so the light was again lowered, and the *séance* resumed. In a short time the heavy cloak was flung, apparently from the ceiling, evidently from somewhere higher than my head, and fell right over it.

I laid it again on the sofa, and thought no more about it until I returned home. I then found, to my astonishment, and considerably to my annoyance, that the fur of my cloak (which was a new one) was all coming out. My dress was covered with it, and from that day I was never able to wear the cloak again. "Lily" said she had *de*-materialized it, to take it away. Of the truth of that assertion I had no proof, but I am quite sure that she did not put it together again when she brought it back. An army of moths encamped in it could not have damaged it more, and I can vouch that until that evening the fur had been as perfect as when I purchased it.

I think my next sitting with Katie Cook was at a *séance* held in Museum Street, and on the invitation of Mr. Chas. Blackburn, who is one of the most earnest friends of Spiritualism, and has expended a large amount of money in its research. The only other guests were my husband, and General and Mrs. Maclean. We sat round a small uncovered table with the gas burning and *without a cabinet*. Miss Katie Cook had a seat between General Maclean and myself, and we made sure of her proximity to us during the whole *séance*. In fact, I never let go of her hand, and even when she wished to use her pocket handkerchief, she had to do it with my hand clinging to her own. Neither did she go into a trance. We spoke to her occasionally during the sitting, and she answered us, though in a very subdued voice, as she complained of being sick and faint. In about twenty minutes, during which the usual manifestations occurred, the materialized form of "Lily"

appeared *in the middle of the table*, and spoke to us and kissed
us all in turn. Her face was very small, and she was *only formed
to the waist*, but her flesh was quite firm and warm. Whilst
"Lily" occupied the table in the full sight of all the sitters, and
I had my hand upon Miss Cook's figure (for I kept passing my
hand up and down from her face to her knees, to make sure
it was not only a hand I held), some one grasped my chair
from behind and shook it, and when I turned my head and
spoke, in a moment one arm was round my neck and one
round the neck of my husband, who sat next to me, whilst the
voice of my daughter "Florence" spoke to us both and her
long hair and her soft white dress swept over our faces and
hands. Her hair was so abundant and long, that she shook it
out over my lap, that I might feel its length and texture. I
asked "Florence" for a piece of her hair and dress, and
scissors not being forthcoming, "Lily" materialized more
fully, and walked round from the other side of the table and
cut off a piece of "Florence's" dress herself with my husband's
penknife, but said they could not give me the hair that time.
The two spirits remained with us for, perhaps, half an hour or
more, whilst General Maclean and I continued to hold Miss
Cook a prisoner. The power then failing, they disappeared,
but every one present was ready to take his oath that two
presences had been with us that never entered at the door. The
room was small and unfurnished, the gas was burning, the
medium sat for a whole time in our sight. Mrs. Maclean and I
were the only other women present, yet two girls bent over
and kissed us, spoke to us, and placed their bare arms on our
necks at one and the same time. There was again also a marked
difference between the medium and the materializations. I
have already described her appearance. Both of these spirits
had plump faces and figures, my daughter "Florence's"
hands especially being large and firm, and her loose hair
nearly down to her knees.

I had the pleasure of holding another *séance* with Katie

Cook in the same rooms, when a new manifestation occurred. She is (as I have said) a very small woman, with very short arms. I am, on the contrary, a very large woman, with very long arms, yet the arm of the hand I held was elongated to such an extent that it reached the sitters on the other side of the table, where it would have been impossible for mine to follow it. I should think the limb must have been stretched to thrice its natural length, and that in the sight of everybody. I sat again with Katie Cook in her own house, where, if trickery is employed, she had every opportunity of tricking us, but the manifestations were much the same, and certainly not more marvellous than those she had exhibited in the houses of strangers. "Lily" and "Florence" both appeared at the same time, under circumstances that admitted of no possibility of fraud. My husband and I were accompanied on that occasion by our friends, Captain and Mrs. Kendal, and the order of sitting round the table was as follows: Myself, Katie, Captain K., Florence Cook, my husband, Mrs. Cook, Mrs. Kendal. Each member of the family, it will be observed, was held between two detectives, and their hands were not once set free. I must say also that the *séance* was a free one, courteously accorded us on the invitation of Mrs. Cook; and if deception had been intended, we and our friends might just as well have been left to sit with Katie alone, whilst the other members of the family superintended the manifestation of the "ghosts" outside. Miss Florence Cook, indeed (Mrs. Corner) objected at first to sitting with us, on the score that her mediumship usually neutralized that of her sister, but her mother insisted on her joining the circle, lest any suspicion should be excited by her absence. The Cooks, indeed, are, all of them, rather averse to sitting than not, and cordially agree in disliking the powers that have been thrust upon them against their own will.

These influences take possession of them, unfitting them for more practical work, and they must live. This is, I believe, the sole reason that they have never tried to make money by the exercise of their mediumship. But I, for one, fully believe them when they tell me that they consider the fact of their being media as the greatest misfortune that has ever happened to them. On the occasion of this last *séance*, cherries and rosebuds were showered in profusion on the table during the evening. These may easily be believed to have been secreted in the room before the commencement of the sitting, and produced at the proper opportunity, although the hands of everybody interested in their production were fast held by strangers. But it is less easy to believe that a lady of limited income, like Mrs. Cook, should go to such an expense for an unpaid *séance*, for the purpose of making converts of people who were strangers to her. Mediumship pays very badly as it is. I am afraid it would pay still worse if the poor media had to purchase the means for producing the phenomena, especially when, in a town like London, they run (as in this instance) to hothouse fruit and flowers.

One more example of Katie Cook's powers and I have done. We were assembled one evening by the invitation of Mr. Charles Blackburn at his house, Elgin Crescent. We sat in a small breakfast room on the basement floor, so small indeed, for the size of the party, that as we encircled a large round table, the sitters' backs touched the wall on either side, thus entirely preventing any one crossing the room whilst we were established there. The only piece of furniture of any consequence in the room, beside the chairs and table, was a trichord cabinet piano, belonging to Mrs. Cook (who was keeping house at the time for Mr. Blackburn), and which she much valued.

Katie Cook sat amongst us as usual. In the middle of the *séance* her control "Lily," who was materialized, called out, "Keep hands fast. Don't let go, whatever you do!" And at the same time, without seeing anything (for we were sitting in complete darkness), we became conscious that something large and heavy was passing or being carried over our heads. One of the ladies of the party became nervous, and dropped her neighbour's hand with a cry of alarm, and, at the same moment, a weighty body fell with a fearful crash on the other side of the room. "Lily" exclaimed, "Some one has let go hands," and Mrs. Cook called out, "Oh! it's my piano." Lights were struck, when we found the cabinet piano had actually been carried from its original position right over our heads to the opposite side of the room, where it had fallen on the floor and been seriously damaged. The two carved legs were broken off, and the sounding board smashed in. Any one who had heard poor Mrs. Cook's lamentations over the ruin of her favourite instrument, and the expense it would entail to get it restored, would have felt little doubt as to whether *she* had been a willing victim to this unwelcome proof of her daughter's physical mediumship.

CHAPTER XVIII

THE MEDIUMSHIP OF BESSIE FITZGERALD

One evening I went to have a cup of tea with my friend Miss Schonberg at Shepherd's Bush, when she proposed that we should go and have a *séance* with Mrs. Henry Jencken (Kate Fox), who lived close by. I hailed the idea, as I had heard such great things of the medium in question, and never had an opportunity of testing them. Consequently, I was proportionately disappointed when, on sending round to her house to ask if she could receive us that evening, we received a message to say that Mr. Jencken, her husband, had died that morning, and she could see no one. Miss Schonberg and I immediately cast about in our minds to see what we should do with our time, and she suggested we should call on Mrs. Fitzgerald. "Who is Mrs. Fitzgerald?" I queried. "A wonderful medium," replied my friend, "whom I met at Mrs. Wilson's last week, and who gave me leave to call on her. Let us go together. And accordingly we set forth for Mrs. Fitzgerald's residence in the Goldhawk Road. I only mention these circumstances to show how utterly unpremeditated was my first visit to her. We arrived at her house, and were ushered into a sitting-room, Miss Schonberg only sending up her name. In a few minutes the door opened, and a small, fair woman, dressed in black velvet, entered the room. Miss Schonberg saluted her, and was about to tender some explanation regarding *my* presence there, when Mrs. Fitzgerald walked straight up to me and took my hand. Her eyes seemed to dilate and contract, like the opening and shutting off of a light, in a manner which I have often seen since, and she uttered rapidly, "You have been married once; you have been married twice; and you will be married a third time." I answered, "If you know anything, Mrs. Fitzgerald, you must know that I am very much attached to my husband, and that your information can give me no pleasure to hear." "No!" she said, "no! I suppose not, but you cannot alter Fate." She then proceeded to speak of things in my past life which had had the greatest influence over the whole of it, occurrences of so private and important a nature that it becomes impossible to write them down here, and for that very reason doubly convincing to the person whom they concern. Presently Mrs. Fitzgerald wandered to her piano, and commenced to play the air of the ballad so firmly connected in my mind with John Powles, "Thou art gone from my gaze," whilst she turned and nodded at me saying, "*He's* here!" In fact, after a couple of hours' conversation with her, I felt that this stranger in the black velvet dress had turned out every secret of my life, and laid it naked and bare before me. I was wonderfully attracted to her. Her personality pleased me; her lonely life, living with her two babies in the Goldhawk Road, made me anxious to give her society and pleasure, and her wonderful gifts of clairvoyance and trance mediumship, all combined to make me desire her friendship, and I gave her a cordial invitation to my house in the Regent's Park, where for some years she was a constant visitor, and always sure of a hearty welcome. It was due to her kindness that I first had the opportunity to study trance mediumship at my leisure, and in a short time we became so familiar with her most constant control, "Dewdrop," a Red Indian girl, and so accustomed to speak through Mrs. Fitzgerald with our own friends gone before, that we welcomed her advent to our house as the signal for holding a spiritual party. For the sake of the uninitiated and curious, I think I had better here describe what is meant by trance mediumship. A person thus gifted has the power of giving him or herself up to the control of the influences in command, who send him or her off to sleep, a sleep so deep and so like death that the spirit is actually parted *pro tem* from the body, which other spirits, sometimes living, but far oftener dead, enter and use as if it were their own. I have mentioned in my chapter on "Embodied Spirits" how my living friend in India conversed with me through Bessie Fitzgerald in this way, also how "Florence" spoke to me through the unconscious lips of Mabel Keningale Cook.

Of course, I am aware that it would be so easy for a medium simply to close her eyes, and, professing to be entranced, talk a lot of commonplaces, which open-mouthed fools might accept as a new gospel, that it becomes imperative to test this class of media strictly by *what they utter*, and to place no faith in them, until you are convinced that the matters they speak of cannot possibly have been known to any one except the friend whose mouthpiece they profess to be. All this I fully proved for myself from repeated trials and researches; but the unfortunate part of it is, that the more forcible and convincing the private proof, the more difficult it is to place it before the public. I must content myself, therefore, with saying that some of my dead friends (so called) came back to me so frequently through Bessie Fitzgerald, and familiarized themselves so completely with my present life, that I forgot sometimes that they had left this world, and flew to them (or rather to Bessie) to seek their advice or ask their sympathy as naturally as if she were their earthly form. Of these my daughter "Florence" was necessarily the most often with me, and she and "Dewdrop" generally divided the time which Mrs. Fitzgerald spent with us between them. I never saw a control so completely identified with its medium as "Dewdrop" was with Bessie. It was difficult at times to know which was which, and one could never be certain until she spoke whether the spirit or the medium had entered the house. When she *did* speak, however, there was no mistaking them. Their characters were so different. Bessie Fitzgerald, a quiet, soft-spoken little woman, devoted to her children, and generally unobtrusive; "Dewdrop," a Sioux Indian girl, wary and deep as her tribe and cute and saucy as a Yankee, with an amount of devilry in her that must at times have proved very inconvenient. She used to play Mrs. Fitzgerald tricks in those days that might have brought her into serious trouble, such as controlling her whilst travelling in an omnibus and talking her Yankee Indian to the passengers until she had made their hair stand on end, with the suspicion that they had a lunatic for a companion. One evening we had a large and rather "swell" evening party, chiefly composed of ladies and gentlemen of the theatrical profession, and entirely of non-spiritualists, excepting ourselves. Mrs. Fitzgerald had been invited to this party, and declined, because it was out of her line. We were therefore rather astonished, when all the guests were assembled to hear her name announced and see her enter the room in a morning dress. Directly I cast eyes upon her however, I saw that it was not herself, but "Dewdrop." The stride with which she walked, the waggish way she rolled from side to side, the devilry in her eye, all betokened the Indian control. To make matters worse, she went straight up to Colonel Lean, and, throwing herself on the ground at his feet, affectionately laid her head upon his knee, and said, "I'se come to the party." Imagine the astonishment of our guests! I was obliged at once, in defence of my friend, to explain to them how matters stood; and though they looked rather incredulous, they were immensely interested, and "Dewdrop's" visit proved to be *the* event of the evening. She talked to each one separately, telling them home truths, and prophesying their future in a way that made their cheeks go pale with fright, or red with conscious shame, and there was quite a contest between the men as to who should take "Dewdrop" down to the supper table. When there, she made herself particularly lively, making personal remarks aloud that were, in some instances, rather trying to listen to, and which Bessie Fitzgerald would have cut out her tongue sooner than utter. She ate, too, of dishes which would have made Bessie ill for a week. This was another strange peculiarity of "Dewdrop's" control. She had not only ousted the spirit; she regulated the internal machinery of her medium's body. Bessie in her normal condition was a very delicate woman with a weak heart and lungs, and obliged to be most careful in her diet. She ate like a sparrow, and of the simplest things. "Dewdrop," on the other hand, liked indigestible food, and devoured it freely; yet Bessie has told me that she never felt any inconvenience from the food amalgamated with her system whilst under "Dewdrop's" control. One day when Mrs. Fitzgerald was dining with us, we had some apples as dessert, which she would have liked to partake of, but was too much afraid of the after consequences. "I *dare* not," she said; "if I were to eat a raw apple, I should have indigestion for a week." She took some preserved ginger instead; and we were proceeding with our dessert, when I saw her hand steal out and grasp an apple. I looked in her face. "Dewdrop" had taken her place. "Dewdrop," I said, authoritatively, "you must not eat that. You will hurt Bessie. Put it down directly."

6

"I shan't," replied "Dewdrop," drawing the dish towards her; "I like apples. I'm always wanting 'Medy' to eat them, and she won't, so she must go away till I've had as many as I want." And in effect she ate three or four of them, and Bessie would never have been cognizant of the fact unless I had informed her. On the occasion of the party to which she came uninvited, "Dewdrop" remained with us to the very last, and went home in a cab, and landed Mrs. Fitzgerald at her house without her being aware that she had ever left it. At that time we were constantly at each other's houses, and many an evening have I spent alone with Bessie in the Goldhawk Road, her servant out marketing and her little children asleep in the room overhead. Her baby was then a great fat fellow of about fifteen months old, who was given to waking and crying for his mother. If "Dewdrop" were present, she was always very impatient with these interruptions. "Both dat George," she would say; "I must go up and quiet him." Then she would disappear for a few minutes, while Bessie woke and talked to me, and then, in the twinkling of an eye, "Dewdrop" would be back again. One day, apparently, "George" would not be comforted, for on "Dewdrop's" return she said to me, "It's no good; I've had to bring him down. He's on the mat outside the door"; and there, sure enough, we found the poor baby wailing in his nightshirt. Not being able to walk, how he had been spirited from the top storey to the bottom I leave my readers to determine. Bessie's little girl Mabel promised to be as wonderful a medium as her mother. She would come in from the garden flushed from her play with the "spirit-children," of whom she talked as familiarly as of her little neighbours next door. I have watched her playing at ball with an invisible child, and have seen the ball thrown, arrested half-way in the air, and then tossed back again just as if a living child had been Mab's opponent. I had lost several infants from premature birth during my second marriage, and the eldest of these, a girl, appeared to be a constant companion of Mabel's. She was always talking of what "Mrs. Lean's girl" (as she called her) had done and said; and one day she had a violent fit of weeping because her mother would not promise to buy her a frock like the one "Mrs. Lean's girl" wore.

Apropos of these still-born children, I had a curious experience with Mrs. Fitzgerald. I had had no idea until then that children so born possessed any souls, or lived again, but "Florence" undeceived me when she told me she had charge of her little brothers and sisters. She even professed to know the names by which they were known in the spirit world. When a still-born baby is launched upon the other side, she said it is delivered to the nearest relative of its parent, to be called by what name he may choose. Thus my first girl was christened by Colonel Lean's mother "Gertrude," after a bosom friend of her's, and my second my father named "Joan," as he said it was his favourite female name. Upon subsequent inquiry, we found that Mrs. Lean *had* a friend called "Gertrude," and that "Joan" was distinctly Captain Marryat's *beau ideal* of a woman's name. However, that signified but little. I became very curious to see or speak with these unknown babies of mine, and used to worry "Florence" to bring them to me. She would expostulate with me after this fashion: "Dear mother, be reasonable. Remember what babies they are, and that this world is quite strange to them. When your earthly children were small you never allowed them to be brought down before strangers, for fear they should cry. 'Gertie' and 'Yonnie' would behave just the same if I brought them back to you now." However, I went on teasing her till she made the attempt, and "Gertie" returned through Mrs. Fitzgerald. It was a long time before we could coax her to remain with us, and when she overcame her first shyness, it was like talking to a little savage. "Gertie" didn't know the meaning of anything, or the names of anything. Her incessant questions of "What's a father?" "What's a mother?" "What's a dog?"

were very difficult to answer; but she would chatter about the spirit-world, and what she did there, as glibly as possible. She told us that she knew her brother Francis (the lad who was drowned at sea) very well, and she "ran races, and Francis 'chivied' her; and when he caught her he held her under the fountain, and the spray wetted her frock, and made it look like silver." The word "*chivied*" sounding to me very much of a mundane character, I asked "Gertie" where she learned it; and she said, "Francis says 'chivy,' so *I* may," and it was indeed a common expression with him. "Gertie" took, after a while, such a keen interest in my ornaments and china, rather to their endangerment, that I bought a doll to see if she would play with it. At first she was vastly delighted with the "little spirit," as she called it, and nursed it just as a mortal child would have done. But when she began to question me as to the reason the doll did not look at her, or answer her, or move about, and I said it was because it was not alive, she was dreadfully disappointed. "*Not alive!*" she echoed; "didn't God make it?" and when I replied in the negative, she threw it to the other end of the room, and would never look at it again.

"Gertie" was about five years old at this period, and seemed to have a great idea of her own importance. She always announced herself as "The Princess Gertie," and was very dignified in her behaviour. One day, when a lady friend was present when "Gertie" came and asked her to kiss her, she extended her hand instead of her face, saying, "You may kiss my hand."

"Yonnie" (as "Joan" called herself) was but eighteen months old, and used to manifest herself, *roaring* like a child forcibly dragged before strangers, and the only word we could ever extract from her was "Sugar-plums." Accordingly, I invested in some for her benefit, with which she filled her mouth so full as nearly to choke the medium, and "Florence" rebuked me seriously for my carelessness, and threatened never to bring "Yonnie" down to this earth again. There had been three other children—boys—whom I was equally anxious to see again, but, for some inexplicable reason, "Florence" said it was impossible that they could manifest. The little girls, however, came until we were quite familiar with them. I am aware that all this must sound very childish, but had it not borne a remarkable context, I should not have related it. All the wonder of it will be found later on.

Mrs. Fitzgerald suffered very much at this time from insomnia, which she always declared was benefited after a visit to me. I proposed one night, therefore, when she had stayed with us later than usual, that she should remain and share my bed, and return home in the morning. She consented, and at the usual hour we retired to rest together, I taking care to lock the bedroom door and keep the gas burning; indeed, Bessie was so nervous of what she might see that she would not have remained in the dark for any consideration. The bed we occupied was what is called a half tester, with a canopy and curtains on either side. As soon as ever Bessie got into it, she burrowed under the clothes like a dormouse, and went fast asleep. I was too curious to see what might happen to follow her example, so my head remained on the pillow, and my eyes wide open, and turning in every direction. Presently I saw the curtains on the opposite side of the bed gently shaken, next a white hand and arm appeared round them, and was passed up and down the ridge that represented Bessie Fitzgerald's body; finally, after several times stepping forward and retreating again, a female figure emerged and walked to the foot of the bedstead and stood there regarding me. She was, to all appearance, as solidly formed as any human creature could be, and she was as perfectly distinct as though seen by daylight. Her head and bust reminded me at once of the celebrated "Clytie," they were so classically and beautifully formed. Her hair and skin were fair, her eyes luminously liquid and gentle, her whole attitude one of modest dignity. She was clothed in some creamy white material, thick and soft, and intermixed with dull gold. She wore no ornaments, but in her right hand she carried a long branch of palm, or olive, or myrtle, something tall and tapering, and of dark green. She scarcely could be said to smile at me, but there was an indescribable appearance of peace and tranquillity about her. When I described this apparition to Bessie in the morning, she recognized it at once as that of her control, "Goodness," whom she had seen clairvoyantly, but she affirmed that I was the only person who had ever given her a correct description of this influence, which was the best and purest about her. After "Goodness" had remained in the same position for a few minutes, she walked back again behind the curtain, which served as a cabinet, and "Florence" came out and had a whispered conversation with me. Next a dark face, but only a face, said to be that of "Dewdrop," peeped out four or five times, and disappeared again; then a voice said, "No more! good night," and I turned round to where Bessie lay sleeping beside me, and went to sleep myself. After that, she often came, when suffering worse than usual from insomnia, to pass the night with me, as she said my magnetism caused her to sleep, and similar manifestations always occurred when we were alone and together.

Mrs. Fitzgerald's mediumship was by no means used, however, for the sole purpose of gratifying curiosity, or foretelling the future. She was a wonderful medical diagnoser, and sat for a long time in the service of a well-known medical man. She would be ensconced in a corner of his waiting-room and tell him the exact disease of each patient that entered. She told me she could see the inside of everybody as perfectly as though they were made of glass. This gift, however, induced her to take on a reflection (as it were) of the disease she diagnosed, and after a while her failing strength compelled her to give it up.

CHAPTER XIX

THE MEDIUMSHIP OF LOTTIE FOWLER

As I was introduced to Lottie Fowler many years before I met Bessie Fitzgerald, I suppose the account of her mediumship should have come first; but I am writing this veracious narrative on no fixed or artificial plan, but just as it occurs to me, though not from memory, because notes were taken of every particular at the time of occurrence. In 1874 I was largely employed on the London Press, and constantly sent to report on anything novel or curious, and likely to afford matter for an interesting article. It was for such a purpose that I received an order from one of the principal news-papers in town to go and have a complimentary *séance* with an American clairvoyant newly arrived in England, Miss Lottie Fowler. Until I received my directions I had never heard the medium's name, and I knew very little of clairvoyance. She was lodging in Conduit Street, and I reached her house one morning as early as ten o'clock, and sent in a card with the name of the paper only written on it. I was readily admitted. Miss Fowler was naturally anxious to be noticed by the press and introduced to London society. I found her a stylish-looking, well-dressed woman, with a pleasant, intelligent face. Those of my readers who have only met her since sickness and misfortune made inroads on her appearance may smile at my description, but I repeat that seventeen years ago Lottie Fowler was prosperous and energetic-looking. She received me very cordially, and asked me into a little back parlour, of which, as it was summer weather, both the windows and doors were left open. Here, in the sunshine, she sat down and took my hand in hers, and began chatting of what she wished and hoped to do in London. Suddenly her eyes closed and her head fell back. She breathed hard for a few minutes, and then sat up, still with her eyes closed, and began to talk in a high key, and in broken English. This was her well-known control, "Annie," without doubt one of the best clairvoyants living. She began by explaining to me that she had been a German girl in earth life, and couldn't speak English properly, but I should understand her better when I was more familiar with her. She then commenced with my birth by the sea, described my father's personality and occupation, spoke of my mother, my brothers and sisters, my illnesses, my marriage, and my domestic life. Then she said, "Wait! now I'll go to your house, and tell you what I see there." She then repeated the names of all my children, giving a sketch of the character of each one, down to the "baby with the flower name," as she called my little Daisy. After she had really exhausted the subject of my past and present, she said, "You'll say I've read all this out of your mind, so now I'll tell you what I see in the future. You'll be married a second time." Now, at this period I was editing a fashionable magazine, and drew a large number of literary men around me. I kept open house on Tuesday evenings, and had innumerable friends, and I *may* (I don't say I *had*), but I may have sometimes speculated what my fate might be in the event of my becoming free. The *séance* I speak of took place on a Wednesday morning; and when "Annie" told me I should be married a second time, my thoughts involuntarily took to themselves wings, I suppose, for she immediately followed up her assertion by saying, "No! not to the man who broke the tumbler at your house last night. You will marry another soldier." "No, thank you," I exclaimed; "no more army men for me. I've had enough of soldiers to last me a lifetime." "Annie" looked very grave. "You *will* marry another soldier," she reiterated; "I can see him now, walking up a terrace. He is very tall and big, and has brown hair cut quite short, but so soft and shiny. At the back of his head he looks as sleek as a mole. He has a broad face, a pleasant, smiling face, and when he laughs he shows very white teeth. I see him knocking at your door. He says, 'Is Mrs. Ross-Church at home?' 'Yes, sir.' Then he goes into a room full of books. 'Florence, my wife is dead. Will you be my wife?' And you say 'Yes.' " "Annie" spoke so naturally, and I was so astonished at her knowledge of my affairs, that it never struck me till I returned home that she had called me by my name, which had been kept carefully from her. I asked her, "When will my husband die?" "I don't see his death anywhere," she answered. "But how can I marry again unless he dies?" I said. "I don't know, but I can't tell you what I don't see. I see a house all in confusion, papers are thrown about, and everything is topsy-turvy, and two people are going different ways; and, oh, there is so much trouble and so many tears! But I don't see any death anywhere."

I returned home, very much astonished at all Miss Fowler had said regarding my past and present, but very incredulous with respect to her prophecies for the future. Yet, three years afterwards, when much of what she told me had come to pass, I was travelling from Charing Cross to Fareham with Mr. Grossmith, to give our entertainment of "*Entre Nous*," when the train stopped as usual to water at Chatham. On the platform stood Colonel Lean, in uniform, talking to some friends. I had never set eyes on him till that moment; but I said at once to Mr. Grossmith, "Do you see that officer in the undress uniform? That is the man Lottie Fowler told me I should marry." Her description had been so exact that I recognized him at once. Of course, I got well laughed at, and was ready after a while to laugh at myself. Two months afterwards, however, I was engaged to recite at the Literary Institute at Chatham, where I had never set foot in my life before. Colonel Lean came to the Recital, and introduced himself to me. He became a visitor at my house in London (which, by the by, had been changed for one in a *terrace*), and two years afterwards, in June, 1879, we were married. I have so far overcome a natural scruple to make my private affairs public, in justice to Lottie Fowler. It is useless narrating anything to do with the supernatural (although I have been taught that this is a wrong term, and that nothing that exists is *above* nature, but only a continuation of it), unless one is prepared to prove that it was true. Lottie Fowler did not make a long stay in England on that occasion. She returned to America for some time, and I was Mrs. Lean before I met her again. The second visit was a remarkable one. I had been to another medium, who had made me very unhappy by some prophecies with regard to my husband's health; indeed, she said he would not live a couple of years, and I was so excited about it that my friend Miss Schonberg advised our going then and there to see Lottie Fowler, who had just arrived in England, and was staying in Vernon Place, Bloomsbury; and though it was late at night, we set off at once. The answer to our request to see Miss Fowler was that she was too tired to receive any more visitors that day. "Do ask her to see me," I urged. "I won't detain her a moment; I only want to ask her one question." Upon this, we were admitted, and found Lottie nearly asleep. "Miss Fowler," I began, "you told me five years ago that I should be married a second time. Well, I *am* married, and now they tell me I shall lose my husband." And then I told her how ill he was, and what the doctors said, and what the medium said. "You told me the truth before," I continued; "tell it me now. Will he die?" Lottie took a locket containing his hair in her hand for a minute, and then replied confidently. "They know nothing about it. He will not die—that is not yet—not for a long while." "But *when?*" I said, despairingly. "Leave that to God, child," she answered, "and be happy now." And in effect Colonel Lean recovered from his illness, and became strong and hearty again. But whence did Miss Fowler gain the confidence to assert that a man whom she had never seen, nor even heard of, should recover from a disease which the doctors pronounced to be mortal? From that time Lottie and I became fast friends, and continue so to this day. It is a remarkable thing that she would never take a sixpence from me in payment for her services, though I have sat with her scores of times, nor would she accept a present, and that when she has been sorely in need of funds. She said she had been told she should never prosper if she touched my money. She has one of the most grateful and affectionate and generous natures possible, and has half-starved herself for the sake of others who lived upon her. I have seen her under sickness, and poverty, and trouble, and I think she is one of the kindest-hearted and best women living, and I am glad of even this slight opportunity to bear testimony to her disposition. At one time she had a large and fashionable *clientèle* of sitters, who used to pay her handsomely for a *séance*, but of late years her clients have fallen off, and her fortunes have proportionately decreased. She has now returned to the Southern States of America, and says she has seen the last of England. All I can say is, that I consider her a great personal loss as a referee in all business matters as well as a prophet for the future. She also, like Bessie Fitzgerald, is a great medical diagnoser. She was largely consulted by physicians about the Court at the time of the Prince of Wales' dangerous illness, and predicted his recovery from the commencement. It was through her mediumship that the body of the late Lord Lindesay of Balcarres, which was stolen from the family vault, was eventually recovered; and the present Lord Lindesay gave her a beautiful little watch, enamelled and set in diamonds, in commemoration of the event. She predicted the riot that took place in London some years ago, and the Tay Bridge disaster; but who is so silly as to believe the prophecies of media nowadays? There has hardly been an event in my life, since I have known Lottie Fowler, that she has not prepared me for beforehand, but the majority of them are too insignificant to interest the reader. One, however, the saddest I have ever been called upon to encounter, was wonderfully foretold. In February, 1886, Lottie (or rather, "Annie") said to me, "There is a great trouble in store for you, Florris" (she always called me "Florris"); "you are passing under black clouds, and there is a coffin hanging over you. It will leave your house." This made me very uneasy. No one lived in my house but my husband and myself. I asked, "Is it my own coffin?" "No!" "Is it my husband's?" "No; it is that of a much younger person."

I questioned her very closely, but she would not tell me any more, and I tried to dismiss the idea from my mind. Still it would constantly recur, for I knew, from experience, how true her predictions were. At last I felt as if I could bear the suspense no longer, and I went to her and said, "You *must* tell me that the coffin you spoke of is not for one of my children, or the uncertainty will drive me mad." "Annie" thought a minute, and then said slowly, "No; it is not for one of your children." "Then I can bear anything else," I replied. The time went on, and in April an uncle of mine died. I rushed again to Lottie Fowler. "Is *this* the death you prophesied?" I asked her. "No," she replied; "the coffin must leave your house. But this death will be followed by another in the family," which it was within the week. The following February my next-door neighbours lost their only son. I had known the boy for years, and I was very sorry for them. As I was watching the funeral preparations from my bedroom window, I saw the coffin carried out of the hall door, which adjoined mine with only a railing between. Knowing that many prophetical media *see* the future in a series of pictures, it struck me that Lottie must have seen this coffin leaving, and mistaken the house for mine. I went to her again. This proves how the prediction had weighed all this time upon my mind. "Has not the death you spoke of taken place *now*?" I asked her. "Has not the coffin left my house?" "No," she answered; "it will be a relative, one of the family. It is much nearer now than it was." I felt uncomfortable, but I would not allow it to make me unhappy. "Annie" had said it was not one of my own children, and so long as they were spared I felt strong enough for anything.

In the July following my eldest daughter came to me in much distress. She had heard of the death of a friend, one who had been associated with her in her professional life, and the news had shocked her greatly. She had always been opposed to Spiritualism. She didn't see the good of it, and thought I believed in it a great deal more than was necessary. I had often asked her to accompany me to *séances*, or to see trance media, and she had refused. She used to say she had no one on the other side she cared to speak to. But when her young friend died, she begged me to take her to a medium to hear some news of him, and we went together to Lottie Fowler. "Annie" did not wait for any prompting, but opened the ball at once. "You've come here to ask me how you can see your friend who has just passed over," she said. "Well, he's all right. He's in this room now, and he says you will see him very soon." "To which medium shall I go?" said my daughter. "Don't go to any medium. Wait a little while, and you will see him with your own eyes." My daughter was a physical medium herself, though I had prevented her sitting for fear it should injure her health; and I believed, with her, that "Annie" meant that her friend would manifest through her own power. She turned to me and said, "Oh, Mother, I shall be awfully frightened if he appears to me at night"; and "Annie" answered, "No, you won't be frightened when you see him. You will be very pleased. Your meeting will be a source of great pleasure on both sides." My daughter had just signed a lucrative engagement, and was about to start on a provincial tour. Her next request was, "Tell me what you see for me in the future." "Annie" replied, "I cannot see it clearly. Another day I may be able to tell you more, but to-day it is all dim. Every time I try to see it a wall seems to rise behind your head and shut it out." Then she turned to me and said, "Florris, that coffin is very near you now. It hangs right over your head!" I answered carelessly, "I wish it would come and have done with it. It is eighteen months now, Annie, since you uttered that dismal prophecy!" Little did I really believe that it was to be so quickly and so terribly fulfilled. Three weeks after that *séance*, my beloved child (who was staying with me) was carried out of my house in her coffin to Kensal Green. I was so stunned by the blow, that it was not for some time after that I remembered "Annie's" prediction. When I asked her *why* she had tortured me with the suspense of coming evil for eighteen months, she said she had been told to do so by my guardian spirits, or my brain would have been injured by the suddenness of the shock. When I asked why she had denied it would be one of my children, she still maintained that she had obeyed a higher order, because to tell the truth so long beforehand would have half-killed me as indeed it would. "Annie" said she had no idea, even during that last interview, that the death she predicted was that of the girl before her. She saw her future was misty, and that the coffin was over my head, but she did not connect the two facts together. In like manner I have heard almost every event of my future through Lottie Fowler's lips, and she has never yet proved to be wrong, except in one instance of *time*. She predicted an event for a certain year and it did not take place till afterwards; and it has made "Annie" so wary, that she steadfastly refuses now to give any dates. I always warn inquirers not to place faith in any given dates. The spirits have told me they have *no time* in the spheres, but judge of it simply as the reflection of the future appears nearer, or further, from the sitter's face. Thus, something that will happen years hence appears cloudy and far off, whilst the events of next week or next month seem bright and distinct, and quite near. This is a method of judging which can only be gained by practice and must at all times be uncertain and misleading.

I have often acted as amanuensis for Lottie Fowler, for letters are constantly arriving for her from every part of the world which can only be answered under trance, and she has asked me to take down the replies as "Annie" dictated them. I have answered by this means the most searching questions from over the seas relating to health and money and lost articles whilst Lottie was fast asleep and "Annie" dictated the letters, and have received many answers thanking me for acting go-between, and saying how wonderfully correct and valuable the information "Annie" had sent them had proved to be. Of course, it would be impossible, in this paper, to tell of the constant intercourse I have had with Lottie Fowler during the last ten or twelve years, and the manner in which she has mapped out my future for me, preventing my cherishing false hopes that would never be realized, making bad bargains that would prove monetary losses, and believing in apparent friendship that was only a cloak for selfishness and treachery. I have learned many bitter lessons from her lips. I have also made a good deal of money through her means. She has told me what will happen to me between this time and the time of my death, and I feel prepared for the evil and content with the good. Lottie Fowler had very bad health for some time before she left England, and it had become quite necessary that she should go; but I think if the British public had known what a wonderful woman was in their midst, they would have made it better worth her while to stay amongst them.

CHAPTER XX

PRIVATE MEDIA

A MEDIUM whose health paid the sacrifice demanded of her for the exhibition of a power over which, at one time, she had no control, and which never brought her in anything but the thanks of her friends, is Mrs. Keningale Cook (Mabel Collins), whom I have mentioned in the "Story of my Spirit Child." There was a photographer in London, named Hudson, who had been very successful in developing spirit photographs. He would prepare to take an ordinary photograph, and on developing the plate, one or more spirit forms would be found standing by the sitter, in which forms were recognized the faces of deceased friends. Of course, the generality of people said that the plates were prepared beforehand with vague misty figures, and the imagination of the sitter did the rest. I had been for some time anxious to test Mr. Hudson's powers for myself, and one morning very early, between nine and ten o'clock, I asked Mrs. Cook, as a medium, to accompany me to his studio. He was not personally acquainted with either of us, and we went so early that we found him rather unwilling to set to work. Indeed, at first he declined. We disturbed him at breakfast and in his shirt sleeves, and he told us his studio had been freshly painted, and it was quite impossible to use it until dry. But we pressed him to take our photographs until he consented, and we ascended to the studio. It was certainly very difficult to avoid painting ourselves, and the screen placed behind was perfectly wet. We had not mentioned a word to Mr. Hudson about spirit photographs, and the first plate he took out and held up to the light, we saw him draw his coat sleeve across. When we asked him what he was doing, he turned to us and said, "Are you ladies Spiritualists?" When we answered in the affirmative, he continued, "I rubbed out the plate because I thought there was something on it, and most sitters would object. I often have to destroy three or four negatives before I get a clear picture. We begged him not to rub out any more as we were curious to see the results. He consequently developed three photographs of us, sitting side by side. The first was too indistinct to be of any use. It represented us, with a third form, merely a patch of white, lying on the ground, whilst a mass of hair was over my knee. "Florence" afterwards informed me that this was an attempt to depict herself. The second picture showed Mrs. Cook and myself as before, with "Charlie" standing behind me. I have spoken of "Charlie" (Stephen Charles Bernard Abbott) in "Curious Coincidences," and how much he was attached to me and mine. In the photograph he is represented in his cowl and monk's frock—with ropes round his waist, and his face looking down. In the third picture, an old lady in a net cap and white shawl was standing with her two hands on Mrs. Cook's shoulders. This was her grandmother, and the profile was so distinctly delineated that her father, Mr. Mortimer Collins, recognized it at once as the portrait of his mother. The old lady had been a member of the Plymouth Brethren sect, and wore the identical shawl of white silk with an embroidered border which she used to wear during her last years on earth. I have seen many other spirit photographs taken by Mr. Hudson, but I adhere to my resolution to speak only of that which I have proved by the exercise of my own senses. I have the two photographs I mention to this day, and have often wished that Mr. Hudson's removal from town had not prevented my sitting again to him in order to procure the likenesses of other friends.

Miss Caroline Pawley is a lady who advertises her willingness to obtain messages for others from the spirit world, but it is forbidden by her guides to take presents or money. I thought at first this must be a *"ruse"*. "Surely," I said to a friend who knew Miss Pawley, "I ought to take books, or flowers, or some little offering in my hand." "If you do she will return them," was the reply. "All that is necessary is to write and make an appointment, as her time is very much take up." Accordingly I did write, and Miss Pawley kindly named an early date for my visit. It was but a few months after I had lost my beloved daughter, and I longed for news of her. I arrived at Miss Pawley's residence, a neat little house in the suburbs, and was received by my hostess, a sweet, placid-faced woman, who looked the embodiment of peace and calm happiness. After we had exchanged greetings she said to me, "You have lost a daughter." "I lost one about twenty years ago—a baby of ten days old," I replied. "I don't mean her," said Miss Pawley, "I mean a young woman. I will tell you how I came to know of it. I took out my memoranda yesterday and was looking it through to see what engagements I had made for to-day, and I read the names aloud to myself. As I came to the entry, 'Mrs. Lean, 3 o'clock,' I heard a low voice say behind me, 'That is my dear, *dear* mother!' and when I turned round I saw standing at my elbow a young woman about the middle height, with blue eyes and very long brown hair, and she told me that it is *she* whom you are grieving for at present." I made no answer to this speech, for my wound was too fresh to permit me to talk of her; and Miss Pawley proceeded. "Come!" she said cheerfully, "let us get paper and pencil and see what the dear child has to say to us." She did not go under trance, but wrote rapidly for a few moments and then handed me a letter written in the following manner. I repeat (what I have said before) that I do not test the genuineness of such a manifestation by the act itself. *Anyone* might have written the letter, but no one but myself could recognize the familiar expressions and handwriting, nor detect the apparent inconsistencies that made it so convincing. It was written in two different hands on alternate lines, the first line being written by "Eva," and the next by "Florence," and so on. Now, my earthly children from their earliest days have never called me anything but "Mother," whilst "Florence," who left me before she could speak, constantly calls me "Mamma." This fact alone could never have been known to Miss Pawley. Added to which the portion written by my eldest daughter was in her own clear decided hand, whilst "Florence's" contribution was in a rather childish, or "young ladylike" scribble.

The lines ran thus. The italics are "Florence's":—

"My own beloved mother.
My dear, dear, dearest Mamma.
You must not grieve so terribly for me.
And knowing all we have taught you, you should not grieve.
Believe me, I am not unhappy.
Of course not, and she will be very happy soon.
But I suffer pain in seeing you suffer.
Dear Mamma, do try to see that it is for the best.
Florence is right. It is best! dear Mother.
And we shall all meet so soon, you know.
God bless you for all your love for me.
Good-bye, dear, dearest Mamma.
          Your own girl.
          Your loving little Florence."

I cannot comment on this letter. I only make it public in a cause that is sacred to me.

To instance another case of mediumship which is exercised for neither remuneration nor applause. I am obliged in this example to withhold the name, because to betray their identity would be to ill requite a favour which was courteously accorded me. I had heard of a family of the name of D—— who held private sittings once a week, at which the mother and brothers and sisters gone before materialized and joined the circle; and having expressed my desire, through a mutual acquaintance, to assist at their *séances*, Mr. D—— kindly sent me an invitation to one. I found he was a high-class tradesman, living in a good house in the suburbs, and that strangers were very seldom (if ever) admitted to their circle. Mr. D——explained to me before the *séance* commenced, that they regarded Spiritualism as a most sacred thing, that they sat only to have communication with their own relations, his wife and children, and that his wife never manifested except when they were alone. His earth family consisted of a young married daughter and her husband, and four or five children of different ages. He had lost, I think he told me, a grown-up son, and two little ones. William Haxby, the medium, whom I wrote of in my chapter "On Sceptics," and who had passed over since then, had been intimate with their family, and often came back to them. These explanations over, the *séance* began. The back and front parlours were divided by lace curtains only. In the back, where the young married daughter took up her position on a sofa, were a piano and an American organ. In the front parlour, which was lighted by an oil lamp, we sat about on chairs and sofas, but without any holding of hands. In a very short time the lace curtains parted and a young man's face appeared. This was the grown-up brother. "Hullo! Tom," they all exclaimed, and the younger ones went up and kissed him. He spoke a while to his father, telling what they proposed to do that evening, but saying his mother would not be able to materialize. As he was speaking, a little boy stood by his side. "Here's Harry," cried the children, and they brought their spirit brother out into the room between them. He seemed to be about five years old. His father told him to come and speak to me, and he obeyed, just like a little human child, and stood before me with his hand resting on my knee. Then a little girl joined the party, and the two children walked about the room, talking to everybody in turn. As we were occupied with them, we heard the notes of the American organ. "Here's Haxby," said Mr. D——. "Now we shall have a treat." (I must say here that Mr. Haxby was an accomplished organist on earth.) As he heard his name, he, too, came to the curtains, and showed his face with its ungainly features, and intimated that he and "Tom" would play a duet. Accordingly the two instruments pealed forth together, and the spirits really played gloriously—a third influence joining in with some stringed instrument. This *séance* was so much less wonderful than many I have written of, that I should not have included a description of it, except to prove that all media do not ply their profession in order to prey upon their fellow-creatures. The D—— family are only anxious to avoid observation. There could be no fun or benefit in deceiving each other, and yet they devote one evening in each week to holding communion with those they loved whilst on earth and feel are only hidden from them for a little while, and by a very flimsy veil.

In the house of the lady I have mentioned in "The Story of the Monk," Mrs. Uniacke of Bruges, I have witnessed marvellous phenomena. They were not pleasant manifestations, very far from it, but there was no doubt they they were genuine. Whether they proceeded from the agency of Mrs. Uniacke, my sister Blanche, or a young lady called Miss Robinson, who sat with them, or from the power of all three combined, I cannot say, but they had experienced them on several occasions before I joined them, and were eager that I should be a witness of them. We sat in Mrs. Uniacke's house, in a back drawing-room, containing a piano and several book-cases, full of books—some of them very heavy. We sat round a table in complete darkness, only we four women, with locked doors and bolted windows. Accustomed as I was to all sorts of manifestations and mediumship, I was really frightened by what occurred. The table was most violent in its movements, our chairs were dragged from under us, and heavy articles were thrown about the room. The more Mrs. Uniacke expostulated and Miss Robinson laughed, the worse the tumult became. The books were taken from the shelves and hurled at our heads, several of the blows seriously hurting us; the keys of the piano at the further end of the room were thumped and crashed upon as if they would be broken; and in the midst of it all Miss Robinson fell prone upon the floor, and commenced talking in Flemish, a language of which she had no knowledge. My sister understands it, and held a conversation with the girl; and she told us afterwards that Miss Robinson had announced herself by the name of a Fleming lately deceased in the town, and detailed many events of his life, and messages which he wished to be delivered to his family—all of which were conveyed in good and intelligible Flemish. When the young lady had recovered she resumed her place at the table, as my sister was anxious I should see another table, which they called "Mademoiselle," dance, whilst unseen hands thumped the piano. The manifestation not occurring, however, they thought it must be my presence, and ordered me away from the table. I went and stood up close against the folding doors that led into the front room, keeping my hand, with a purpose, on the handle. The noise and confusion palpably increased when the three ladies were left alone. "Mademoiselle," who stood in a corner of the room, commenced to dance about, and the notes of the piano crashed forcibly. There was something strange to me about the manifestation of the piano. It sounded as if it were played with feet instead of hands. When the tumult was at its height, I suddenly, and without warning, threw open the folding door and let the light in upon the scene, and I saw *the music-stool mounted on the keyboard* and hammering the notes down. As the light was admitted, both "Mademoiselle" and the music-stool fell with a crash to the floor, and the *séance* was over. The ladies were seated at the table, and the floor and articles of furniture were strewn with the books which had been thrown down—the bookshelves being nearly emptied—and pots of flowers. I was never at such a pandemonium before or after.

The late Sir Percy Shelley and his wife, Lady Shelley, having no children of their own, adopted a little girl, who, when about four or five years, was seriously burned about the chest and shoulders, and confined for some months to her bed. The child's cot stood in Lady Shelley's bedroom and when her adopted mother was about to say her prayers, she was accustomed to give the little girl a pencil and piece of paper to keep her quiet. One day the child asked for pen and ink instead of a pencil, and on being refused began to cry, and said, "The *man* said she must have pen and ink." As it was particularly enjoined that she must not cry for fear of reopening her wounds, Lady Shelley provided her with the desired articles, and proceeded to her devotions. When she rose from them, she saw to her surprise that the child had drawn an outline of a group of figures in the Flaxman style, representing mourners kneeling round a couch with a sick man laid upon it. She did not understand the meaning of the picture, but she was struck with amazement at the execution of it, as was everybody who saw it. From that day she gave the little girl a sheet of cardboard each morning, with pen and ink, and obtained a different design, the child always talking glibly of "the man" who helped her to draw. This went on until the drawings numbered thirty or forty, when a "glossary of symbols" was written out by this baby, who could neither write nor spell, which explained the whole matter. It was then discovered that the series of drawings represented the life of the soul on leaving the body, until it was lost "in the Infinity of God"—a likely subject to be chosen, or understood, by a child of five. I heard this story from Lady Shelley's lips, and I have seen (and well examined) the original designs. They were at one time to be published by subscription, but I believe it never came to pass. I have also seen the girl who drew them, most undoubtedly under control. She was then a young married woman and completely ignorant of anything relating to Spiritualism. I asked her if she remembered the circumstances under which she drew the outlines, and she laughed and said no. She knew she had drawn them, but she had no idea how. All she could tell me was that she had never done anything wonderful since, and she had no interest in Spiritualism whatever.

CHAPTER XXI

VARIOUS MEDIA

A VERY strong and remarkable clairvoyant is Mr. Towns, of Portobello Road. As a business adviser or foreteller of the Future, I don't think he is excelled. The inquirer after prophecy will not find a grand mansion to receive him in Portobello Road. On the contrary, this soothsayer keeps a small shop in the oil trade, and is himself only an honest, and occasionally rather rough-spoken, tradesman. He will see clients privately on any day when he is at home, though it is better to make an appointment, but he holds a circle on his premises each Tuesday evening, to which everybody is admitted, and where the contribution is anything you may be disposed to give, from coppers to gold. These meetings, which are very well attended, are always opened by Mr. Towns with prayer, after which a hymn is sung, and the *séance* commences. There is full gas on all the time, and Mr. Towns sits in the midst of the circle. He does not go under trance, but rubs his forehead for a few minutes and then turns round suddenly and addresses members of his audience, as it may seem, promiscuously, but it is just as he is impressed. He talks, as a rule, in metaphor, or allegorically, but his meaning is perfectly plain to the person he addresses. It is not only silly women, or curious inquirers, who attend Mr. Towns' circles. You may see plenty of grave, and often anxious, business men around him, waiting to hear if they shall sell out their shares, or hold on till the market rises; where they are to search for lost certificates or papers of value; or on whom they are to fix the blame of money or articles of value that have disappeared. Once in my presence a serious-looking man had kept his eye fixed on him for some time, evidently anxious to speak. Mr. Towns turned suddenly to him. "You want to know, sir," he commenced, without any preface, "where that baptismal certificate is to be found." "I do, indeed," replied the man; "it is a case of a loss of thousands if it is not forthcoming." "Let me see," said Mr. Towns, with his finger to his forehead. "Have you tried a church with a square tower without any steeple, an ugly, clumsy building, white-washed inside, standing in a village. Stop! I can see the registrar books—the village's name is——. The entry is at page 200. The name is ——. The mother's name is ——. Is that the certificate you want?" "It is, indeed," said the man; "and it is in the church at——?" "Didn't I say it was in the church at ——?" replied Mr. Towns, who does not like to be doubted or contradicted. "Go and you will find it there." And the man *did* go and did find it there. To listen to the conversations that go on between him and his clients at these meetings Mr. Towns is apparently not less successful with love affairs than with business affairs, and it is an interesting experience to attend them, if only for the sake of curiosity. But naturally, to visit him privately is to command much more of his attention. He will not, however, sit for everybody, and it is of no use attempting to deceive him.

A short time ago I received a summons to the county court, and although I *knew* I was in the right, yet law has so many loopholes that I felt nervous. The case was called for eleven o'clock on a certain Wednesday, and the evening before I joined Mr. Towns' circle. When it came to my turn to question him, I said, "Do you see where I shall be to-morrow morning?" He replied, "I can see you are called to appear in a court-house, but the case will be put off." "*Put off*," I repeated, "but it is fixed for eleven. It can't be put off." "Cases are sometimes relegated to another court," said Mr. Towns. Then I thought he had quite got out of his depth, and replied, "You are making a mistake. This is quite an ordinary business. It can't go to a higher court. But shall I gain it?" "In the afternoon," said the medium. His answers so disappointed me that I placed no confidence in them, and went to the county court on the following morning in a nervous condition. But he was perfectly correct. The case was called for eleven, but as the defendant was not forthcoming, it was passed over, and the succeeding hearings occupied so much time, that the magistrate thought mine would never come off, so he *relegated it at two o'clock to another court* to be heard before the registrar, who decided it at once in my favour, so that I *gained it in the afternoon.*

.   .   .   .

One afternoon in my "green sallet" days of Spiritualism, when every fresh experience almost made my breath stop, I turned into the Progressive Library in Southampton Row, to ask if there were any new media come to town. Mr. Burns did not know of any, but asked me if I had ever attended one of Mrs. Olive's *séances,* a series of which were being held weekly in the Library Rooms. I had not, and I bought a half-crown ticket for admission, and returned there the same evening. When I entered the *séance* room, the medium had not arrived, and I had time to take stock of the audience. It seemed a very sad and serious one. There was no whispering nor giggling going on, and it struck me they looked more like patients waiting the advent of the doctor, than people bound on an evening's amusement. And that, to my surprise, was what I afterwards found they actually were. Mrs. Olive did not keep us long waiting, and when she came in, dressed in a lilac muslin dress, with her golden hair parted plainly on her forehead, her *very* blue eyes, and a sweet, womanly smile for her circle, she looked as unlike the popular idea of a professional medium as anyone could possibly do. She sat down on a chair in the middle of the circle, and, having closed her eyes, went off to sleep. Presently she sat up and, still with her eyes closed, said in a very pleasant, but decidedly *manly,* voice, "And now, my friends, what can I do for you?"

A lady in the circle began to ask advice about her daughter. The medium held up her hand. "Stop!" she exclaimed, "you are doing *my* work. Friend, your daughter is ill, you say. Then it is *my* business to see what is the matter with her. Will you come here, young lady, and let me feel your pulse." Having done which, the medium proceeded to detail exactly the contents of the girl's stomach, and to advise her what to eat and drink for the future. Another lady then advanced with a written prescription. The medium examined her, made an alteration or two in the prescription, and told her to go on with it till further orders. My curiosity was aroused, and I whispered to my next neighbour to tell me who the control was. "Sir John Forbes, a celebrated physician," she replied. "He has almost as large a connection now as he had when alive." I was not exactly ill at the time, but I was not strong, and nothing that my family doctor prescribed for me seemed to do me any good. So wishing to test the abilities of "Sir John Forbes," I went up to the medium and knelt down by her side. "What is the matter with me, Sir John?" I began. "Don't call me by that name, little friend," he answered; "we have no titles on this side the world." "What shall I call you, then?" I said. "Doctor, plain Doctor," was the reply, but in such a kind voice. "Then tell me what is the matter with me, Doctor." "Come nearer, and I'll whisper it in your ear." He then gave me a detailed account of the manner in which I suffered, and asked what I had been taking. When I told him. "All wrong, all wrong," he said, shaking his head. "Here! give me a pencil and paper." I had a note-book in my pocket, with a metallic pencil, which I handed over to him, and he wrote a prescription in it. "Take that, and you'll be all the better, little friend," he said, as he gave it to me back again. When I had time to examine what he had written, I found to my surprise that the prescription was in abbreviated Latin, with the amount of each ingredient given in the regular medical shorthand. Mrs. Olive, a simple though

intelligent-looking woman, seemed a very unlikely person
to me to be educated up to this degree. However, I determined to obtain a better opinion than my own, so the next
time my family doctor called to see me, I said, "I have had a
prescription given me, Doctor, which I am anxious, with
your permission, to try. I wish you would glance your eye
over it and see if you approve of my taking it." At the same
time I handed him the note-book, and I saw him grow very
red as he looked at the prescription. "Anything wrong?" I
inquired. "O! dear no!" he replied in an offended tone; "you
can try your remedy, and welcome, for aught I care—only,
next time you wish to consult a new doctor, I advise you to
dismiss the old one first." "But this prescription was not
written by a doctor," I argued. At this he looked still more
offended. "It's no use trying to deceive me, Mrs. Ross-
Church! That prescription was written by no one but a
medical man." It was a long time before I could make him
really believe *who* had transcribed it, and under what circumstances. When he was convinced of the truth of my statement,
he was very much astonished, and laid all his professional
pique aside. He did more. He not only urged me to have the
prescription made up, but he confessed that his first chagrin
was due to the fact that he felt he should have thought of it
himself. "*That*," he said, pointing to one ingredient, "is the
very thing to suit your case, and it makes me feel such a fool
to think that a *woman* should think of what *I* passed over."

Nothing would make this doctor believe in Spiritualism,
though he continued to aver that only a medical man could
have prescribed the medicine; but as I saw dozens of other
cases treated at the time by Mrs. Olive, and have seen dozens
since, I know that she does it by a power not her own. For
several years after that "Sir John Forbes" used to give me
advice about my health, and when his medium married
Colonel Greck and went to live in Russia, he was so sorry
to leave his numerous patients, and they to lose him, that he

wanted to control *me* in order that I might carry on his practice, but after several attempts he gave it up as hopeless. He said my brain was too active for any spirit to magnetize; and he is not the first, nor last, who has made the same attempt, and failed. "Sir John Forbes" was not Mrs. Olive's only control. She had a charming spirit called "Sunshine," who used to come for clairvoyance and prophecy; and a very comical negro named "Hambo," who was as humorous and full of native wit and repartee, as negroes generally are, and as Mrs. Olive, who is a very gentle, quiet woman, decidedly was *not*. "Hambo" was the business adviser and director, and sometimes materialized, which the others did not. These three influences were just as opposite from one another. and from Mrs. Olive, as any creatures could possibly be. "Sir John Forbes," so dignified, courteous, and truly benevolent—such a thorough old *gentleman*; "Sunshine," a sweet, sympathetic Indian girl, full of gentle reproof for wrong and exhortations to lead a higher life; and "Hambo," humorous and witty, calling a spade a spade, and occasionally descending to coarseness, but never unkind or wicked. I knew them all over a space of years until I regarded them as old friends. Mrs. Greck is now a widow, and residing in England, and, I hear, sitting again for her friends. If so, a great benefit in the person of "Sir John Forbes" has returned for a portion of mankind.

I have kept a well-known physical medium to the last, not because I do not consider his powers to be completely genuine, but because they are of a nature that will not appeal to such as have not witnessed them. I allude to Mr. Charles Williams, with whom I have sat many times alone, and also with Mrs. Guppy Volckman. The manifestations that take place at his *séances* are always material. The much written of "John King" is his principal control, and invariably appears under his mediumship; and "Ernest" is the name of another. I have seen Charles Williams leave the cabinet under trance and wander in an aimless manner about the room, whilst both "John King" and "Ernest" were with the circle, and have heard them reprove him for rashness. I have also seen him under the same circumstances, during an afternoon *séance*, mistake the window curtains for the curtains of the cabinet, and draw them suddenly aside, letting the full light of day in upon the scene, and showing vacancy where a moment before two figures had been standing and talking.

Once when "John King" asked Colonel Lean what he should bring him, he was told *mentally* to fetch the half-hoop diamond ring from my finger and place it on that of my husband.

This half-hoop ring was worn between my wedding-ring and a heavy gold snake ring, and I was holding the hand of my neighbour all the time, and yet the ring was abstracted from between the other two and transferred to Colonel Lean's finger without my being aware of the circumstance.

CHAPTER XXII

SPIRITUALISM IN AMERICA

I. *Mrs. M. A. Williams*

I WENT to America on a professional engagement in October, 1884. Some months beforehand a very liberal offer had been made me by the Spiritualists of Great Britain to write my experiences for the English press, but I declined to do so until I could add my American notes to them. I had corresponded (as I have shown) with the *Banner of Light* in New York; and what I had heard of Spiritualism in America had made me curious to witness it. But I was determined to test it on a strictly private plan. I said to myself: "I have seen and heard pretty nearly all there is to be seen and heard on the subject in England, but, with one or two exceptions, I have never sat at any *séance* where I was not known. Now I am going to visit a strange country where, in a matter like Spiritualism, I can conceal my identity, so as to afford the media no clue to my surroundings or the names of my deceased friends." I sailed for America quite determined to pursue a strictly secret investigation, and with that end in view I never mentioned the subject to anyone.

I had a few days holiday in New York before proceeding to Boston, where my work opened, and I stayed at one of the largest hotels in the city. I landed on Sunday morning, and on Monday evening I resolved to make my first venture. Had I been a visitor in London, I should have had to search out the right sort of people, and make a dozen inquiries before I heard where the media were hiding themselves from dread of the law; but they order such things better on the other side of the Atlantic. People are allowed to hold their private opinions and their private religion there without being swooped down upon and clapped into prison for rogues and vagabonds. Whatever the views of the majority may be, upon this subject or any other (and Heaven knows I would have each man strong enough to cling to his opinion, and brave enough to acknowledge it before the world), I think it is a discredit to a civilized country to allow old laws, that were made when we were little better than savages, to remain in force at the present day. We are far too much over-ridden by a paternal Government, which has grown so blind and senile that it swallows camels while it is straining after a gnat.

There was no obstacle to my wish, however, in New York. I had but to glance down the advertisement columns of the newspapers to learn where the media lived, and on what days they held their public *séances*. It so happened that Mrs. M. A. Williams was the only one who held open house on Monday evenings for Materialization; and thither I determined to go. There is no such privacy as in a large *hotel*, where no one has the opportunity to see what his neighbour is doing. As soon, therefore, as my dinner was concluded, I put on a dark cloak, hat and veil, and walking out into the open, got into one of the cars that ran past the street where Mrs. Williams resided. Arrived at the house, I knocked at the door, and was about to inquire if there was to be any *séance* there that evening, when the attendant saved me the trouble by saying, "Upstairs, if you please, madam," and nothing more passed between us. When I had mounted the stairs, I found myself in a large room the floor of which was covered with a thick carpet, nailed all round the wainscotting. On one side were some thirty or forty cane-bottomed chairs, and directly facing them was the cabinet. This consisted of four uprights nailed over the carpet, with iron rods connecting them at the top. There was no roof to it, but curtains of a dark maroon colour were usually drawn around, but when I entered, they were flung back over the iron rods, so as to disclose the interior. There was a stuffed armchair for the use of the medium, and in front of the cabinet a narrow table with papers and pencils on it, the use of which I did not at first discover. At the third side of the room was a harmonium, so placed that the performer sat with his back both to the cabinet and the sitters. A large gas lamp, almost like a limelight, made in a square form like a lantern, was fixed against the wall, so as to throw the light upon the cabinet, but it was fitted with a sliding shade of red silk, with which it could be darkened if necessary. I was early, and only a few visitors were occupying the chairs. I asked a lady if I might sit where I chose, and on her answering "Yes," I took the chair in the front row, exactly opposite the cabinet, not forgetting that I was there in the cause of Spiritualism as well as for my own interests. The seats filled rapidly and there must have been thirty-five or forty people present, when Mrs. Williams entered the room, and nodding to those she knew, went into the cabinet. Mrs. Williams is a stout woman of middle age, with dark hair and eyes, and a fresh complexion. She was dressed in a tight-fitting gown of pale blue, with a good deal of lace about the neck and sleeves. She was accompanied by a gentleman, and I then discovered for the first time that it is usual in America to have, what they call, a "conductor" of the *séance*. The conductor sits close to the cabinet curtains, and, if any spirit is too weak to show itself, outside or to speak audibly, he conveys the message it may wish to send to its friends; and when I knew how very few precautions Americans take to prevent such outrages as occurred in England, and how many more materializations take place in an evening there than here, I saw the necessity of a conductor to protect the medium, and to regulate the order of the *séance*.

Mrs. Williams' conductor opened the proceedings with a very neat little speech. He said, "I see several strange faces here this evening, and I am very pleased to see them, and I hope they may derive both pleasure and profit from our meeting. We have only one rule for the conduct of our *séances*, that you shall behave like ladies and gentlemen. You may not credit all you see, but remember this is our religion, and the religion of many present, and as you would behave yourselves reverently and decorously, if you were in a church of another persuasion to your own, so I beg of you to behave yourselves here. And if any spirits should come for you whom you do not immediately recognize, don't wound them by denying their identity. They may have been longing for this moment to meet you again, and doing their very utmost to assume once more the likeness they wore on earth; yet some fail. Don't make their failure harder to bear by roughly repudiating all knowledge of them. The strangers who are present to-night may mistake the reason of this little table being placed in front of the cabinet, and think it is intended to keep them from too close an inspection of the spirits. No such thing! On the contrary, all will be invited in turn to come up and recognize their friends. But we make it a rule at these *séances* that no materialized spirit, who is strong enough to come beyond that table, shall be permitted to return to the cabinet. They must dematerialize in sight of the sitters, that no possible

7

suspicion may rest upon the medium. These pencils and papers are placed here in case any spirit who is unable to speak may be impressed to write instead. And now we will begin the evening with a song."

The accompanist then played "Footsteps of Angels," the audience sung it with a will, and the curtains having been drawn round Mrs. Williams, the shade was drawn across the gaslight, and the *séance* began.

I don't think it could have been more than a minute or two before we heard a voice whispering, "Father," and *three girls*, dressed in white clinging garments, appeared at the opening in the curtains. An old man with white hair left his seat and walked up to the cabinet, when they all three came out at once and hung about his neck and kissed him, and whispered to him. I almost forgot where I was. They looked so perfectly human, so joyous and girl-like, somewhere between seventeen and twenty, and they all spoke at once, so like what girls on earth would do, that it was most mystifying. The old man came back to his seat, wiping his eyes. "Are those your daughters, sir?" asked one of the sitters. "Yes! my three girls," he replied. "I lost them all before ten years old, but you see I've got them back again here."

Several other forms appeared after this—one, a little child of about three years old, who fluttered in and out of the cabinet like a butterfly, and ran laughing away from the sitters who tried to catch her. Some of the meetings that took place for the first time were very affecting. One young man of about seventeen or eighteen, who was called up to see his mother's spirit, sobbed so bitterly, it broke my heart to hear him. There was not the least doubt if *he* recognized her or no. He was so overcome, he hardly raised his eyes for the rest of the evening. One lady brought her spirit-son up to me, that I might see how perfectly he had materialized. She spoke of it as proudly as she might have done if he had passed some difficult examination. The young man was dressed in a suit of evening clothes, and he shook hands with me at his mother's bidding, with the firm grasp of a mortal. Naturally, I had seen too much in England for all this to surprise me. Still I had never assisted at a *séance* where everything appeared to be so strangely human—so little mystical, except indeed the rule of dematerializing before the sitters, which I had only seen "Katie King" do before. But here, each form, after having been warned by the conductor that its time was up, sunk down right through the carpet as though it were the most ordinary mode of egression. Some, and more especially the men, did not advance beyond the curtains; then their friends were invited to go up and speak to them, and several went inside the cabinet. There were necessarily a good many forms, familiar to the rest, of whom I knew nothing; one was an old minister under whom they had all sat, another a gentleman who had been a constant attendant at Mrs. Williams' *séances*.

Once the conductor spoke to me. "I am not aware of your name," he said (and I thought, "No! my friend, and, you won't be aware of it just yet either!"), "but a spirit here wishes you would come up to the cabinet." I advanced, expecting to see some friend, and there stood a Catholic priest with his hand extended in blessing. I knelt down and he gave me the usual benediction and then closed the curtains. "Did you know the spirit?" the conductor asked me. I shook my head; and he continued, "He was Father Hayes, a well-known priest in this city. I suppose you are a Catholic?" I told him "Yes," and went back to my seat. The conductor addressed me again. "I think Father Hayes must have come to pave the way for some of your friends," he said. "Here is a spirit who says she has come for a lady named 'Florence,' who has just crossed the sea. Do you answer to the description?" I was about to say "Yes," when the curtains parted again and my daughter "Florence" ran across the room and fell into my arms. "Mother!" she exclaimed, "I said I would come with you and look after you—didn't I?"

I looked at her. She was exactly the same in appearance as when she had come to me in England—the same luxuriant brown hair and features and figure, as I had seen under the different mediumships of Florence Cook, Arthur Colman, Charles Williams and William Eglinton; the same form which in England had been declared to be half a dozen different media dressed up to represent my daughter, stood before me there in New York, thousands of miles across the sea, and by the power of a person who did not even know who I was. If I had not been convinced before, how could I have helped being convinced then?

"Florence" appeared as delighted as I was, and kept on kissing me and talking of what had happened to me on board ship coming over, and was evidently quite *au fait* of all my proceedings. Presently she said, "There's another friend of yours here, Mother! We came over together. I'll go and fetch him." She was going back to the cabinet when the conductor stopped her. "You must not return this way, please. Any other you like," and she immediately made a kind of court curtsey and went down through the carpet. I was standing where "Florence" had left me, wondering what would happen next, when she came *up again* a few feet off from me, head first, and smiling as if she had discovered a new game. She was allowed to enter the cabinet this time, but a moment afterwards she popped her head out again, and said, "Here's your friend, Mother!" and by her side was standing William Eglinton's control, "Joey," clad in his white suit, with a white cap drawn over his head. " 'Florence' and I have come over to make new lines for you here," he said; "at least, I've come over to put her in the way of doing it, but I can't stay long, you know, because I have to go back to 'Willy'."

I really didn't care if he stayed long or not. I seemed to have procured the last proof I needed of the truth of the doctrine

I had held so long, that there is no such thing as Death, as we understand it in this world. Here were the two spiritual beings (for believing in the identity of whom I had called myself a credulous fool fifty times over, only to believe in them more deeply still) in *propria personæ* in New York, claiming me in a land of strangers, who had not yet found out who I was. I was more deeply affected than I had ever been under such circumstances before, and more deeply thankful. "Florence" made great friends with our American cousins even on her first appearance. Mrs. Williams' conductor told me he thought he had never heard anything more beautiful than the idea of the spirit-child crossing the ocean to guard its mother in a strange country, and particularly, as he could feel by her influence, what a pure and beautiful spirit she was. When I told him she had left this world at ten days old, he said that accounted for it, but he could see there was nothing earthly about her.

I was delighted with this *séance*, and hoped to sit with Mrs. Williams many times more, but fate decreed that I should leave New York sooner than I had anticipated. The perfect freedom with which it was conducted charmed me, and the spirits seemed so familiar with the sitters. There was no "Sweet Spirit, hear my prayer" business about it. No fear of being detained or handled among the spirits, and no awe, only intense tenderness on the part of their relations. It was to this cause I chiefly attributed the large number of materializations I witnessed—*forty* having taken place that evening. They spoke far more distinctly and audibly too than those I had seen in England, but I believe the dry atmosphere of the United States is far more favourable to the process of materialization. I perceived another difference. Although the female spirits were mostly clad in white, they wore dresses and not simply drapery, whilst the men were invariably attired in the clothes (or semblances of the clothes) they would have worn had they been still on earth. I left Mrs. Williams' rooms, determined to see as much as I possibly could of mediumship whilst I was in the United States.

CHAPTER XXIII

II. *Mrs. Eva Hatch*

I WAS so disappointed at being hurried off to Boston before I had seen any more of the New York media, that I took the earliest opportunity of attending a *séance* there. A few words I had heard dropped about Eva Hatch made me resolve to visit her first. She was one of the Shaker sect, and I heard her spoken of as a remarkably pure and honest woman, and most reliable medium. Her first appearance quite gave me that impression. She had a fair, placid countenance, full of sweetness and serenity, and a plump matronly figure. I went incognita, as I had done to Mrs. Williams, and mingled unnoticed with the crowd. Mrs. Hatch's cabinet was quite different from Mrs. Williams'. It was built of planks like a little cottage, and the roof was pierced with numerous round holes for ventilation, like a pepper-box. There was a door in the centre, with a window on either side, all three of which were shaded by dark curtains. The windows, I was told, were for the accommodation of those spirits who had not the power to materialize more than a face, or head and bust. Mrs. Hatch's conductor was a woman, who sat near the cabinet, as in the other case.

Mrs. Eva Hatch had not entered the cabinet five minutes before she came out again, under trance, with a very old lady with silver hair clinging to her arm, and walked round the circle. As they did so, the old lady extended her withered hand, and blessed the sitters. She came quite close to each one and was distinctly visible to all. I was told that this was the spirit of Mrs. Hatch's mother, and that it was her regular custom to come first and give her blessing to the *séance*. I had never seen the spirit of an aged person before, and it was a beautiful sight. She was the sweetest old lady, too, very small and fragile-looking, and half reclining on her daughter's bosom, but smiling serenely upon every one there. When they had made the tour of the room, Mrs. Hatch re-entered the cabinet, and did not leave it again until the sitting was concluded.

There were a great many sitters present, most of whom were old patrons of Mrs. Hatch, and so, naturally, their friends came for them first. It is surprising though, when once familiarized with materialization, how little one grows to care to see the spirits who come for one's next-door neighbour. They are like a lot of prisoners let out, one by one, to see their friends and relations. The few moments they have to spare are entirely devoted to home matters of no possible interest to the bystander. The first wonder and possible shock at seeing the supposed dead return in their old likeness to greet those they left on earth over, one listens with languid indifference, and perhaps a little impatience for one's own turn to come, to the whispered utterances of strangers. Mrs. Hatch's "cabinet spirits" or "controls," however, were very interesting. One, who called herself the "Spirit of Prayer," came and knelt down in the middle of the circle, and prayed with us. She had asked for the gas to be extinguished first, and as she prayed she became illuminated with flashes of light, in the shape of stars and crosses, until she was visible from head to foot, and we could see her features and dress as if she had been surrounded by electricity.

Two more cabinet spirits were a negro and negress, who appeared together, chanting some of their native hymns and melodies. When I saw these apparitions, I thought to myself, "Here is a good opportunity to discover trickery, if trickery there is." The pair were undoubtedly of the negro race. There was no mistaking their thick lips and noses and yellow-white eyes, nor their polished brown skins, which no charcoal can properly imitate. They were negroes without doubt; but how about the negro bouquet? Everyone who has mixed with coloured people in the East or the West knows what that is, though it is very difficult to describe, being something like warm rancid oil mingled with the fumes of charcoal, with a little worse thrown in. "Now," I thought, "if these forms are human, there will be some odour attached to them, and that I am determined to find out." I caught, therefore, at the dress of the young woman as she passed, and asked her if she would kiss me. She left her companion directly, and put her arms (which were bare) round my neck, and embraced me several times; and I can declare, on my oath, that she was as completely free from anything like the smell of a coloured woman as it was possible for her to be. She felt as fresh and sweet and pure as a little child.

Many other forms appeared and were recognized by the circle, notably a very handsome one who called herself the Empress Josephine; but as they could not add a grain's weight to my testimony I pass them over. I had begun to think that "Florence" was not going to visit me that evening, when the conductor of the *séance* asked if there was anybody in the room who answered to the name of "Bluebell." I must indulge in a little retrospect here, and tell my readers that ten years previous to the time I am writing of, I had lost my brother-in-law, Edward Church, under very painful circumstances. He had been left an orphan and in control of his fortune at a very early age, and had lived with my husband, Colonel Ross-Church, and myself. But poor "Ted" had been his own worst enemy. He had possessed a most generous heart and affectionate disposition, but these had led him into extravagances that swallowed up his fortune, and then he had taken to drinking and killed himself by it. I and my children had loved him dearly, but all our prayers and entreaties had had no avail, and in the end he had become so bad that the doctors had insisted upon our separation. Poor "Ted" had consequently died in exile, and this had been a further aggravation of our grief.

For ten years I had been trying to procure communication with him in vain, and I had quite given up expecting to see him again. Only once had I heard "Bluebell" (his pet name for me) gasped out by an entranced clairvoyant, but nothing further had come of it. Now, as I heard it for the second time, from a stranger's lips, in a foreign country, it naturally roused my expectations, but I thought it might be only a message for me from "Ted."

"Is there anyone here who recognizes the name of 'Bluebell'?" repeated the conductor. "I was once called so by a friend," I said. "Someone is asking for that name. You had better come up to the cabinet," she replied. I rose at once and did as she told me, but when I reached the curtain I encountered "Florence." "My darling child," I said, as I embraced her, "why did you ask for 'Bluebell'?" She did not answer me, except by shaking her head, placing her finger on her lips, and pointing downwards to the carpet. I did not know what to make of it. I had never known her unable to articulate before. "What is the matter, dear?" I said; "can't you speak to me to-night?" Still she shook her head, and tapped my arm with her hand, to attract my attention to the fact that she was pointing vigorously downwards. I looked down, too, when, to my astonishment, I saw rise through the carpet what looked to me like the bald head of a baby or an old man, and a little figure, *not more than three feet in height*, with Edward Church's features, but no hair on its head, came gradually into view, and looked up in my face with a pitiful, deprecating expression, as if he were afraid I should strike him. The face, however, was so unmistakably Ted's, though the figure was so ludicrously insignificant, that I could not fail to recognize him. "Why, Ted!" I exclaimed, "have you come back to see me at last?" and held out my hand. The little figure seized it, tried to convey it to his lips, burst into tears, and sank down through the carpet much more rapidly than he had come up.

I began to cry too. It was so pitiful. With her uncle's disappearance "Florence" found her tongue. "Don't cry, Mother," she said; "poor Uncle Ted is overcome at seeing you. That's why he couldn't materialize better. He was in such a terrible hurry. He'll look more like himself next time. I was trying so hard to help him, I didn't dare to use up any of the power by speaking. He'll be so much better, now he's seen you. You'll come here again, won't you?" I told her I certainly would, if I could; and, indeed, I was all anxiety to see my poor brother-in-law again. To prove how difficult it would have been to deceive me on this subject, I should like to say a little about Edward Church's personal appearance. He was a very remarkable looking man—indeed, I have never seen anyone a bit like him before or after. He was very small; not short only, but small altogether, with tiny hands and feet, and a little head. His hair and eyes were of the deepest black—the former parted in the middle, with a curl on either side, and was naturally waved. His complexion was very dark, his features delicate, and he wore a small pointed moustache. As a child he had suffered from an attack of confluent small-pox, which had deeply pitted his face, and almost eaten away the tip of his nose. Such a man was not to be easily imitated, even if anyone in Boston had ever heard of his inconsequential existence. To me, though, he had been a dear friend and brother, before the curse of Drink had seemed to change his nature, and I had always been anxious to hear how he fared in that strange country whither he had been forced to journey, like all of us, *alone*. I was very pleased then to find that business would not interfere with my second visit to Mrs. Eva Hatch, which took place two nights afterward. On this occasion "Florence" was one of the first to appear, and "Ted" came with her, rather weak and trembling on his second introduction to this mundane sphere, but no longer bald-headed or under-sized. He was his full height now, about five feet seven; his head was covered with his black, crisp hair, parted just as he used to wear it while on earth; in every particular he resembled what he used to be, even down to his clothes. I could have sworn I had seen that very suit of clothes; the little cut-away coat he always wore, with the natty tie and collar, and a dark blue velvet smoking cap upon his head, exactly like one I remembered being in his possession. "Florence" still seemed to be acting as his interpreter and guide. When I said to him, "Why! Ted, you look quite like your old self to-day," she answered, "He can't talk to you, Mamma, he is weak still, and he is so thankful to meet you again. He wants me to tell you that he has been trying to communicate with you often, but he never could manage it in England. He will be so glad when he can talk freely to you." Whilst she was speaking, "Ted" kept on looking from her to me like a deaf and dumb animal trying to understand what was going on in a manner that was truly pitiful. I stooped down and kissed his forehead. The touch seemed to break the spell that hung over him. "*Forgive*," he uttered in a choked voice. "There is nothing to forgive, dear," I replied, "except as we all have need to forgive each other. You know how we all loved you, Ted, and we loved you to the last and grieved for you deeply. You remember the children, and how fond you were of them and they of you. They often speak to this day of their poor Uncle Ted." "Eva—Ethel," he gasped out, naming my two elder children. At this juncture he seemed suddenly to fail, and became so weak that "Florence" took him back into the cabinet again. No more spirits came for me that evening, but towards the close of the *séance* "Florence" and "Ted" appeared again together and embraced me fondly. "Florence" said, "He's so happy now, Mother; he says he shall rest in peace now that he knows that you have forgiven him. And he won't come without his hair again," she added, laughing. "I hope he won't," I answered, "for he frightened me." And then they both kissed me "good night," and retreated to the cabinet, and

I looked after them longingly and wished I could go there too.

CHAPTER XXIV

III. *The Misses Berry*

No one introduced me to the Misses Berry. I saw their advertisement in the public papers and went incognita to their *séance*, as I had done to those of others. The first thing that struck me about them was the superior class of patrons whom they drew. In the ladies' cloak room, where they left their heavy wraps and umbrellas, the conversation that took place made this sufficiently evident. Helen and Gertrude Berry were pretty, unaffected, lady-like girls; and their conductor, Mr. Abrow, one of the most courteous gentlemen I have ever met. The sisters, both highly mediumistic, never sat together, but on alternate nights, but the one who did *not* sit always took a place in the audience, in order to prevent suspicion attaching to her absence. Gertrude Berry had been lately married to a Mr. Thompson, and on account of her health gave up her *séances*, soon after I made her acquaintance. She was a tall, finely-formed young woman, with golden hair and a beautiful complexion. Her sister Helen was smaller, paler and more slightly built. She had been engaged to be married to a gentleman who died shortly before the time fixed for their wedding, and his spirit, whom she called "Charley," was the principal control at her *séances*, though he never showed himself. I found the *séance* room, which was not very large, crammed with chairs which had all been engaged beforehand, so Mr. Abrow fetched one from downstairs and placed it next his own for me, which was the very position I should have chosen. I asked him afterwards how he dared admit a stranger to such close proximity, and he replied that he was a medium himself and knew who he could and who he could *not* trust at a glance. As my professional duties took me backwards and forwards to Boston, which was my central starting-point, sometimes giving me only a day's rest there, I was in the habit afterwards, when I found I should have "a night off," of wiring to Mr. Abrow to keep me a seat, so difficult was it to secure one unless it were bespoken. Altogether I sat five or six times with the Berry sisters, and wished I could have sat fifty or sixty times instead, for I never enjoyed any *séances* so *much* in my life before. The cabinet was formed of an inner room with a separate door, which had to undergo the process of being sealed up by a committee of strangers every evening. Strips of gummed paper were provided for them, on which they wrote their names before affixing them across the inside opening of the door. On the first night I inspected the cabinet also as a matter of principle, and gummed my paper with "Mrs. Richardson" written on it across the door. The cabinet contained only a sofa for Miss Helen Berry to recline upon. The floor was covered with a nailed-down carpet. The door which led into the cabinet was shaded by two dark curtains hung with rings upon a brass rod. The door of the *séance* room was situated at a right angle with that of the cabinet, both opening upon a square landing, and, to make "assurance doubly sure," the door of the *séance* room was left open, so that the eyes of the sitters at that end commanded a view, during the entire sitting, of the outside of the locked and gummed-over cabinet door. To make this fully understood, I append a diagram of the two rooms—

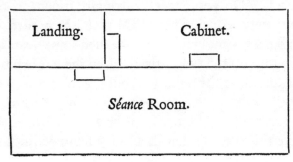

Landing.   Cabinet.

Séance Room.

By the position of these doors, it will be seen how impossible it would have been for anybody to leave or enter the cabinet without being detected by the sitters, who had their faces turned towards the *séance* room door. The first materialization that appeared that evening was a bride, dressed in her bridal costume; and a gentleman, who was occupying a chair in the front row, and holding a white flower in his hand, immediately rose, went up to her, embraced her, and whispered a few words, then gave her the white flower, which she fastened in the bosom of her dress, after which he bowed slightly to the company, and, instead of resuming his seat, left the room. Mr. Abrow then said to me, "If you like, madam, you can take that seat now," and as the scene had excited my curiosity I accepted his offer, hoping to find some one to tell me the meaning of it. I found myself next to a very sweet-looking lady, whom I afterwards knew personally as Mrs. Seymour. "Can you tell me why that gentleman left so suddenly?" I asked her in a whisper. "He seldom stays through a *séance*," she replied; "he is a business man, and has no time to spare, but he is here every night. The lady you saw him speak to is his wife. She died on her wedding day, eleven years ago, and he has never failed to meet her on every opportunity since. He brings her a white flower every time he comes. She appears always first, in order that he may be able to return to his work." This story struck me as very interesting, and I always watched for this gentleman afterwards, and never failed to see him waiting for his bride, with the white flower in his hand. "Do you expect to see any friends to-night?" I said to my new acquaintance. "O! yes!" she replied. "I have come to see my daughter 'Bell.' She died some years ago, and I am bringing up the two little children she left behind her. I never do anything for them without consulting their mother. Just now I have to change their nurse, and I have received several excellent characters of others, and I have brought them here this evening that 'Bell' may tell me which to write for. I have the pattern for the children's winter frocks, too," she continued, producing some squares of woollen cloths, "and I always like to let 'Bell' choose which she likes best." This will give my readers some idea of how much more the American spiritualists regard their departed friends as still forming part of the home circle, and interested in their domestic affairs. "Bell" soon after made her appearance, and Mrs. Seymour brought her up to me. She was a young woman of about three or four and twenty, and looked very happy and smiling. She perused the servants' characters as practically as her mother might have done, but said she would have none of them, and Mrs. Seymour was to wait till she received some more. The right one had not come yet. She also looked at the patterns, and indicated the one she liked best. Then, as she was about to retire, she whispered to her mother, and Mrs. Seymour said, to my surprise (for it must be remembered I had not disclosed my name to her), "Bell tells me she knows a daughter of yours in the spirit life, called 'Florence.' Is that the case?" I answered I had a daughter of that name; and Mrs. Seymour added "'Bell' says she will be here this evening, that she is a very pure and very elevated spirit, and they are great friends." Very shortly after this, Mr. Abrow remarked, "There is a young girl in the cabinet now, who says that if her mother's name is 'Mrs. Richardson,' she must have married for the third time since she saw her last, for she was 'Mrs. Lean' then." At this remark I laughed; and Mr. Abrow said, "Is she come for you, madam? Does the cap fit?" I was obliged to acknowledge then that I *had* given a false name in order to avoid recognition. But the mention of my married name attracted no attention to me, and was only a proof that it had not been given from any previous knowledge of Mr. Abrow's concerning myself. I was known in the United States as "Florence Marryat" only, and to this day they believe me to be still "Mrs. Ross-Church," that being the name under which my first novels were written.

So I recognized "Florence" at once in the trick that had been played me, and had risen to approach the curtain, when she came *bounding* out and ran into my arms. I don't think I had ever seen her look so charming and girlish before. She looked like an embodiment of sunshine. She was dressed in a low frock which seemed manufactured of lace and muslin, her hair fell loose down her back to her knees, and her hands were full of damask roses. This was in December, when hot-house roses were selling for a dollar a piece in Boston, and she held, perhaps, twenty. Their scent was delicious, and she kept thrusting them under my nose, saying, "Smell my roses, Mother. Don't you wish you had my garden? We have *fields* of them in the Summer Land! O! how I wish you were there." "Shan't I come soon, darling?" I said. "No! not yet," replied "Florence." "You have a lot of work to do still. But when you come, it will be all flowers for you and me." I asked her if she knew "Bell," and she said, "O! yes! We came together this evening." Then I asked her to come and speak to "Bell's" mother, and her manner changed at once. She became shy and timid, like a young girl, unused to strangers, and quite hung on my arm, as I took her up to Mrs. Seymour's side. When she had spoken a few words to her in a very low voice, she turned to me and said, "I must go now, because we have a great surprise for you this evening—a *very* great surprise." I told her I like great surprises, when they were pleasant ones, and "Florence" laughed, and went away. I found that her *début* had created such a sensation amongst the sitters—it being so unusual for a materialized spirit to appear-so strong and perfect on the first occasion of using a medium—that I felt compelled to give them a little explanation on the subject. And when I told them how I had lost her as a tiny infant of ten days old—how she had returned to me through various media in England, and given such unmistakable proofs of her *identity*—and how I, being a stranger in their country, and only landed there a few weeks, had already met her through Mrs. Williams, Mrs. Hatch and Miss Berry—they said it was one of the most wonderful and perfect instances of materialization they had ever heard of. And when one considers how perfect the chain is, from the time when "Florence" first came back to me as a child, too weak to speak, or even to understand where she was, to the years through which she had grown and became strong almost beneath my eyes, till she could *"bound"* (as I have narrated) into my arms like a human being, and talk as distinctly as (and far more sensible than) I did myself, I think my readers will acknowledge also, that hers is no common story, and that I have some reason to believe in Spiritualism.

Towards the close of the evening Mr. Abrow said, "There is a spirit here now who is very anxious to show himself, but it is the first time he has ever attempted to fully materialize, and he is not at all certain of success. He tells me there is a lady in the circle who has newly arrived in America, and that this lady years ago sang a song by his dying bed in India. If she will step up to the cabinet now and sing that song again he will try and show himself to her."

Such of my readers as have perused "The Story of John Powles," will recognize at once who this was. I did, of course, and I confess that as I rose to approach the cabinet I trembled like an aspen leaf. I had tried so often, and failed so often to see this dear old friend of mine, that to think of meeting him now was like a veritable resurrection from the dead. Think of it! We had parted in 1860, and this was 1884—twenty-four years afterwards. I had been a girl when we said "Good-bye," and he went forth on that journey which seemed then so mysterious an one to me. I was a middle-aged woman now, who had passed through so much from which *he* had been saved, that I felt more like his mother than his friend. Of all my experiences this was to me really the most solemn and interesting. I hardly expected to see more than his face, but I walked up to the cabinet and commenced to sing in a very

shaky voice the first stanza of the old song he was so fond
of:—

> "Thou art gone from my gaze like a beautiful dream,
> And I seek thee in vain by the meadow and stream;
> Oft I breathe thy dear name to the winds passing by,
> But thy sweet voice is mute to my bosom's lone sigh.
> In the stillness of night when the stars mildly shine,
> O! then oft my heart holds communion with thine,
> For I feel thou art near, and where'er I may be,
> That the Spirit of Love keeps a watch over me."

I had scarcely reached the finish of these lines when both
the curtains of the cabinet were drawn apart so sharply that
the brass rings rattled on the rod, and John Powles stood
before me. Not a face, nor a half-formed figure, nor an
apparition that was afraid to pass into the light—but *John
Powles himself*, stalwart and living, who stepped out briskly
and took me in his arms and kissed me four or five times, as a
long-parted brother might have done; and strange to say, I
didn't feel the least surprised at it, but clung to him like a
sister. For John Powles had never once kissed me during his
lifetime. Although we had lived for four years in the closest
intimacy, often under the same roof, we had never indulged
in any familiarities. I think men and women were not so
lax in their manners then as they are now; at any rate, the only
time I had ever kissed him was when he lay dead, and my husband had told me to do so. And yet it seemed quite natural on
meeting him again to kiss him and cry over him. At last I
ventured to say, "O, Powles! is this really you?" "Look at me
and see for yourself," he answered. I looked up. It was
indeed himself. He had possessed *very* blue eyes in earth life,
good features, a florid complexion, auburn hair and quite a
golden beard and moustache. The eyes and hair and features
were just the same, only his complexion was paler, and he
wore no beard. "O!" I exclaimed, "where is your beard?"
"Don't you remember I cut it off just before I left this

world?" he said; and then I recalled the fact that he had done so owing to a Government order on the subject.

And bearing on this question I may mention what seems a curious thing—that spirits almost invariably return to earth the first time *just as they left it*, as though their thoughts at the moment of parting clothed them on their return. This, however, was not John Powles' first *attempt* at materialization, although it was his first success, for it may be remembered he tried to show himself through Miss Showers, and then he *had* a beard. However, when I saw him through Miss Berry, he had none, nor did he resume it during my stay in America. When we had got over the excitement of meeting, he began to speak to me of my children, especially of the three who were born before his death, and of whom he had been very fond. He spoke of them all by name, and seemed quite interested in their prospects and affairs. But when I began to speak of other things he stopped me. "I know it all," he said, "I have been with you in spirit through all your trials, and I can never feel the slightest interest in, or affection for, those who caused them. My poor friend, you have indeed had your purgatory upon earth." "But tell me of yourself, dear Powles! Are you quite happy?" I asked him. He paused a moment and then replied, "Quite happy, waiting for you." "Surely you are not suffering still?" I said, "after all these years?" "My dear Florence," he answered, "it takes more than a few years to expiate a life of sin. But I am happier than I was, and every year the burden is lighter, and coming back to you will help me so much."

As he was speaking to me the curtain opened again, and there stood my brother-in-law, Edward Church, not looking down-spirited and miserable, as he had done at Mrs. Eva Hatch's, but bright and smiling, and dressed in evening clothes, as also I perceived, when I had time to think of it, was John Powles. I didn't know which to talk to first, but kept turning from one to the other in a dazed manner. John

Powles was telling me that *he* was preparing my house for me in the Summer Land, and would come to take me over to it when I died, when "Ted" interrupted him. "That ought to have been *my* work, Bluebell," he said, "only Powles had anticipated me." "I wish I could go back with you both at once, I am sick of this world," I replied. "Ted" threw his arms round me and strained me to his breast. "O! it is so hard to part again. How I wish I could carry you away in my arms to the Summer Land! I should have nothing left to wish for then." "You don't want to come back then, Ted?" I asked him. "*Want to come back*," he said with a shudder; "not for anything! Why, Bluebell, death is like an operation which you must inevitably undergo, but which you fear because you know so little about it. Well, with me *the operation's over*. I know the worst, and every day makes the term of punishment shorter. I am *thankful* I left the earth so soon." "You look just like your old self, Ted," I said; "the same little curls and scrubby little moustache." "Pull them," he answered gaily. "Don't go away, Bluebell, and say they were false and I was Miss Berry dressed up. Feel my biceps," he continued, throwing up his arm as men do, "and feel my heart," placing my hand above it, "feel how it is beating for my sister Bluebell."

I said to John Powles, "I hardly know you in evening costume. I never saw you in it before" (which was true, as all our acquaintance had taken place in India, where the officers are never allowed to appear in anything but uniform, especially in the evenings). "I wish," I continued "that you would come next time in uniform." "I will try," he replied, and then their time was up for that occasion, and they were obliged to go.

A comical thing occurred on my second visit to the Berrys. Of course I was all eagerness to see my brother-in-law and "Powles" again, and when I was called up to the cabinet and saw a slim, dark, young man standing there, I took him at once for "Ted," and, without looking at him, was just about to kiss him, when he drew backwards and said, "I am not 'Edward'! I am his friend 'Joseph,' to whom he has given me permission to make your acquaintance." I then perceived that "Joseph" was very different from "Ted," taller and better looking, with a Jewish cast of countenance. I stammered and apologized, and felt as awkward as if I had nearly kissed a mortal man by mistake. "Joseph" smiled as if it were of very little consequence. He said he had never met "Ted" on earth, but they were close friends in the spirit world, and "Ted" had talked so much to him of me, that he had become very anxious to see me, and speak to me. He was a very elegant-looking young man, but he did not seem to have very much to say for himself, and he gave me the impression that he had been a "masher" whilst here below, and had not quite shaken off the remembrance in the spirit world.

There was one spirit who often made her appearance at these sittings and greatly interested me. This was a mother with her infant of a few weeks old. The lady was sweet and gentle-looking, but it was the baby that so impressed me—a baby that never whined nor squalled, nor turned red in the face, and yet was made of neither wax nor wood, but was palpably living and breathing. I used always to go up to the cabinet when this spirit came, and ask her to let me feel the little baby. It was a tiny creature, with a waxen-looking face, and she always carried it enveloped in a full net veil, yet when I touched its hand the little fingers tightened round mine in baby fashion, as it tried to convey them to its mouth. I had seen several spirit children materialized before, but never such a young infant as this. The mother told me she had passed away in child-birth, and the baby had gone with her. She had been a friend of the Misses Berry, and came to them for that reason.

On Christmas Eve I happened to be in Boston, and disengaged, and as I found it was a custom of the American spiritualists to hold meetings on that anniversary for the purpose of seeing their spirit friends, I engaged a seat for the occasion. I arrived some time before the *séance* commenced, and next to me was seated a gentleman, rather roughly dressed, who was eyeing everything about him with the greatest attention. Presently he turned to me and said, rather sheepishly, "Do you believe in this sort of thing?" "I do," I replied, "and I have believed in it for the last fifteen years." "Have you ever seen anybody whom you recognized?" he continued. "Plenty," I said. Then he edged a little nearer to me, and lowered his voice. "Do you know," he commenced, "that I have ridden on horseback forty miles through the snow to-day to be present at this meeting, because my old mother sent me a message that she would meet me here! I don't believe in it, you know. I've never been at a *séance* before, and I feel as if I was making a great fool of myself now, but I couldn't neglect my poor old mother's message, whatever came of it." "Of course not," I answered, "and I hope your trouble will be rewarded." I had not much faith in my own words, though because I had seen people disappointed again and again over their first *séance*, from either the spirits of their friends being too weak to materialize, or from too many trying to draw power at once, and so neutralizing the effect on all. My bridegroom friend was all ready on that occasion with his white flowers in his hand and I ventured to address him and tell him how very beautiful I considered his wife's fidelity and his own. He seemed pleased at my notice, and began to talk quite freely about her. He told me she had returned to him before her body was buried, and had been with him ever since. "She is so really and truly *my wife*," he said, "as I received her at the altar, that I could no more marry again than I could if she were living in my house." When the *séance* commenced she appeared first as usual, and her husband brought her up to my side. "This is Miss Florence Marryat, dear," he said (for by this time I had laid aside my *incognita* with the Berrys). "You know her name, don't you?" "O! yes," she answered, as she gave me her hand," I know you quite well. I used to read your books." Her face was covered with her bridal veil, and her husband turned it back that I might see her. She was a very pretty girl of perhaps twenty—quite a gipsy, with large dark eyes and dark curling hair, and a brown complexion. "She has not altered one bit since the day we were married," said her husband, looking fondly at her, "whilst I have grown into an old man." She put up her hand and stroked his cheek. "We shall be young together some day," she said. Then he asked her if she was not going to kiss me, and she held up her face to mine like a child, and he dropped the veil over her again and led her away. The very next spirit that appeared was my rough friend's mother, and his astonishment and emotion at seeing her were very unmistakable. When first he went up to the cabinet and saw her his head drooped, and his shoulders shook with the sobs he could not repress. After a while he became calmer, and talked to her, and then I saw him also bringing her up to me. "I must bring my mother to you," he said, "that you may see she has really come back to me." I rose, and the old lady shook hands with me. She must have been, at the least, seventy years old, and was a most perfect specimen of old age. Her face was like wax, and her hair like silver; but every wrinkle was distinct, and her hands were lined with blue veins. She had lost her teeth, and mumbled somewhat in speaking, and her son said, "She is afraid you will not understand what she says; but she wants you to know that she will be quite happy if her return will make me believe in a future existence." "And will it?" I asked. He looked at his mother. "I don't understand it," he replied. "It seems too marvellous to be true; but how *can* I disbelieve it, when *here she is*?" And his words were so much the echo of my own grounds for belief, that I quite sympathized with them. "John Powles,"

and "Ted," and "Florence," all came to see me that evening;
and when I bid "Florence" "good-bye" she said, "Oh, it
isn't 'good-bye' yet, Mother! I'm coming again, before
you go." Presently something that was the very farthest
thing from my mind—that had, indeed, never entered it—
happened to me. I was told that a young lady wanted to speak
to me, and on going up to the cabinet I recognized a girl
whom *I knew by sight, but had never spoken to*—one of a large
family of children, living in the same terrace in London as
myself, and who had died of malignant scarlet fever about a
year before. "Mrs. Lean," she said, hurriedly, noting my
surprise, "don't you know me? I am May ——." "Yes, I do
recognize you, my dear child," I replied; "but what makes
you come to me?" "Minnie and Katie are so unhappy about
me," she said. "They do not understand. They think I have
gone away. They do not know what death is—that it is only
like going into the next room, and shutting the door." "And
what can I do, May?" I asked her. "Tell them you have seen
me, Mrs. Lean. Say I am alive—more alive than they are; that
if they sit for me, I will come to them and tell them so much
they know nothing of now." "But where are your sisters?" I
said. She looked puzzled. "I don't know. I can't say the
place; but you will meet them soon, and you will tell them."
"If I meet them, I certainly will tell them," I said; but I had
not the least idea at that moment where the other girls
might be. Four months later, however, when I was staying
in London, Ontario, they burst unexpectedly into my hotel
room, having driven over (I forget how many miles) to see
me play. Naturally I kept my promise; but though they cried
when "May" was alluded to, they evidently could not
believe my story of having seen her, and so, I suppose, the poor
little girl's wish remains ungratified. I think the worst purgatory in the next world must be to find how comfortably our
friends get on without us in this. As a rule, I did not take much
interest in the spirits that did not come for me; but there was

one who appeared several times with the Berrys, and seemed quite like an old friend to me. This was "John Brown," not her Majesty's "John Brown," but the hero of the song—

> "Hang John Brown on a sour apple tree,
> But his soul goes touting around.
> Glory! glory! Halleluia!
> For his soul goes touting around."

When I used to hear this song sung with much shouting and some profanity in England, I imagined (and I fancy most people did) that it was a comic song in America. But it was no such thing. It was a patriotic song, and the motive is (however comically put) to give glory to God, that, *although* they may hang "John Brown" on a sour apple tree, his soul will yet "go touting around." So, rightly or wrongly, it was explained to me. "John Brown" is a patriotic hero in America, and when he appeared, the whole room crowded round to see him. He was a short man, with a *singularly* benevolent countenance, iron grey hair, mutton-chop whiskers and deep china blue eyes. A kind of man, as he appeared to me, made for deeds cf love rather than heroism, but from all accounts he was both kind and heroic. A gentleman present on Christmas eve pushed forward eagerly to see the materialization, and called out, "Aye! that's him—that's my old friend—that's 'John Brown'—the best man that ever trod this earth." Before this evening's *séance* was concluded Mr. Abrow said, "There is a little lady in the cabinet at present who announces herself as a very high personage. She says she is the 'Princess Gertrude'." "*What* did you say, Mr. Abrow?" I exclaimed, unable to believe my own ears. " 'The Princess Gertie,' Mother," said "Florence," popping her head out of the curtains. "You've met her before in England, you know." I went up to the cabinet, the curtains divided, there stood my daughter "Florence" as usual, but holding in front of her a little child of about seven years old. I knelt down before this spirit of my own creation. She was a fragile-looking little creature, very fair and pale, with large grey eyes and brown hair lying over her forehead. She looked like a lily with her little white hands folded meekly in front of her. "Are you my little Gertie, darling?" I said. "I am the 'Princess Gertie,'" she replied, "and 'Florence' says you are my mother." "And are you glad to see me, Gertie?" I asked. She looked up at her sister, who immediately prompted her. "Say, 'Yes, Mother,' Gertie." "Yes! Mother," repeated the little one like a parrot. "Will you come to me, darling?" I said. "May I take you in my arms?" "Not this evening, Mother," whispered 'Florence,' "you couldn't. She is attached to me. We are tied together. You couldn't separate us. Next time, perhaps, the 'Princess' will be stronger, and able to talk more. I will take her back now." "But where is 'Yonnie'?" I asked, and "Florence" laughed. "Couldn't manage two of them at once," she said. "'Yonnie' shall come another day," and I returned to my seat, more mystified than usual.

I alluded to the "Princess Gertie" in my account of the mediumship of Bessie Fitzgerald, and said that my allusion would find its signification further on. At that time I had hardly believed it could be true that the infants who had been born prematurely and never breathed in this world should be living, sentient spirits to meet me in the next, and half thought some grown spirit must be tricking me for its own pleasure. But here, in this strange land, where my blighted babies had never been mentioned or thought of, to meet the "Princess Gertie" here, calling herself by her own name, and brought by her sister "Florence," set the matter beyond a doubt. It recalled to my mind how once, long before, when "Aimée" (Mr. Arthur Colman's guide), on being questioned as to her occupation in the spirit spheres, had said she was "a little nurse-maid," and that "Florence" was one too, my daughter had added, "Yes! I'm Mamma's nurse-maid. I have enough to do to look after her babies.

She just looked at me, and 'tossed' me back into the spirit world, and she's been 'tossing' babies after me ever since."

I had struck up a pleasant acquaintanceship with Mrs. Seymour, "Bell's" mother, by that time, and when I went back to my seat and told her what had occurred, she said to me, "I wish you would share the expenses of a private *séance* with me here. We can have one all to ourselves for ten dollars (two pounds), and it would be so charming to have an afternoon quite alone with our children and friends." I agreed readily, and we made arrangements with Mr. Abrow before we left that evening to have a private sitting on the afternoon following Christmas Day, when no one was to be admitted except our two selves. When we met there the *séance* room was lighted with gas as for the evening, but we preferred to close the door. Helen Berry was the medium, and Mr. Abrow only sat with us. The rows of chairs looked very empty without any sitters, but we established ourselves on those which faced the cabinet in the front row. The first thing which happened was the advent of the "Squaw," looking as malignant and vicious as ever, who crept in her dirty blanket, with her black hair hanging over her face, and deliberately took a seat at the further end of the room. Mr. Abrow was unmistakably annoyed at the occurrence. He particularly disliked the influence of this spirit, which he considered had a bad effect on the *séance*. He first asked her why she had come, and told her her "Brave" was not coming, and to go back to him. Then he tried severity, and ordered her to leave the *séance*, but it was all in vain. She kept her seat with persistent obstinacy, and showed no signs of "budging." I thought I would try what kindness would do for her, and approached her with that intention, but she looked so fierce and threatening, that Mr. Abrow begged me not to go near her, for fear she should do me some harm. So I left her alone, and she kept her seat through the whole of the *séance*, evidently with an eye upon me, and distrusting my behaviour when removed from the criticism of the public. Her presence, however, seemed to make no difference to our spirit friends. They trooped out of the cabinet one after another, until we had Mrs. Seymour's brother and her daughter "Bell," who brought little "Jimmie" (a little son who had gone home before herself) with her, and "Florence," "Ted," and "John Powles," all so happy and strong and talkative, that I told Mrs. Seymour we only wanted a tea-table to think we were holding an "At Home." Last, but not least (at all events in her own estimation) came the "Princess Gertie." Mr. Abrow tried to make friends with her, but she repulsed his advances vehemently. "I don't like you, Mr. Mans," she kept on saying, "you's nasty. I don't like any mans. They's *all* nasty." When I told her she was very rude, and Mr. Abrow was a very kind gentleman and loved little children, she still persisted she wouldn't speak "to no mans." She came quite alone on this occasion, and I took her in my arms and carried her across to Mrs. Seymour. She was a feather weight. I felt as if I had nothing in my arms. I said to Mrs. Seymour, "Please tell me what this child is like. I am so afraid of my senses deceiving me that I cannot trust myself." Mrs. Seymour looked at her and answered, "She has a broad forehead, with dark brown hair cut across it, and falling straight to her shoulders on either side. Her eyes are a greyish blue, large and heavy lidded, her nose is short, and her mouth decided for such a child."

This testimony, given by a stranger, of the apparition of a child that had never lived, was an exact description (of course in embryo) of her father, Colonel Lean, who had never set foot in America. Perhaps this is as good a proof of identity as I have given yet. Our private *séance* lasted for two hours, and although the different spirits kept on entering the cabinet at intervals to gain more power, they were all with us on and off during the entire time. The last pleasant thing I saw was my dear "Florence" making the "Princess" kiss her hand in farewell to me, and the only unpleasant one, the sight of the sulky "Squaw" creeping in after them with the evident conviction that her afternoon had been wasted.

CHAPTER XXV

IV. *The Doctor*

I WONDER if it has struck any of my readers as strange that, during all these manifestations in England and America, I had never seen the form, nor heard the voice, of my late father, Captain Marryat. Surely if these various media lived by trickery and falsehood, and wished successfully to deceive me, *some* of them would have thought of trying to represent a man so well known, and whose appearance was so familiar. Other celebrated men and women have come back and been recognized from their portraits only, but, though I have sat at numbers of *séances* given *for me* alone, and at which I have been the principal person, my father has never reappeared at any. Especially, if these manifestations are all fraud, might this have been expected in America. Captain Marryat's name is still "a household word" amongst the Americans, and his works largely read and appreciated, and wherever I appeared amongst them I was cordially welcomed on that account. When once I had acknowledged ny identity and my views on Spiritualism, every medium in Boston and New York had ample time to get up an imitation of my father for my benefit had they desired to do so. But never has he appeared to me; never have I been told that he was present. Twice only in the whole course of my experience have I received the slightest sign from him, and on those occasions he sent me a message—once through Mr. Fletcher (as I have related), and once through his grandson and my son, Frank Marryat. That time he told me he should never appear to me and I need never expect him. But since the American media knew nothing of this strictly private communication, and I had seen before I parted with them, *seventeen* of my friends and relations, none of whom (except "Florence," "Powles," and "Emily,") I had ever seen in England, it is at the least strange, considering his popularity (and granted their chicanery) that Captain Marryat was not amongst them.

As soon as I became known at the Berry's *séances* several people introduced themselves to me, and amongst others Mrs. Isabella Beecher Hooker, the sister of Mrs. Harriet Beecher Stowe and Henry Ward Beecher. She was delighted to find me so interested in Spiritualism, and anxious I should sit with a friend of her's, a great medium whose name became so rubbed out in my pencil notes, that I am not sure if it was Doctor Carter, or Carteret, and therefore I shall speak of him here as simply "the doctor." The doctor was bound to start for Washington the following afternoon, so Mrs. Hooker asked me to breakfast with her the next morning, by which time she would have found out if he could spare us an hour before he set out on his journey. When I arrived at her house I heard that he had very obligingly offered to give me a complimentary *séance* at eleven o'clock, so, as soon as we had finished breakfast, we set out for his abode. I found the doctor was quite a young man, and professed himself perfectly ignorant on the subject of Spiritualism. He said to me, "I don't know and I don't profess to know *what* or *who* it is that appears to my sitters whilst I am asleep. I know nothing of what goes on, except from hearsay. I don't know whether the forms that appear are spirits, or transformations, or materializations. You must judge of that for yourself. There is one peculiarity in my *séances*. They take place in utter darkness. When the apparitions (or whatever you choose to call them) appear, they must bring their own lights or you won't see them. I have no conductor to my *séances*. If whatever comes can't announce itself it must remain unknown. But I think you will find that, as a rule, they can shift for themselves. This is my *séance* room."

As he spoke he led us into an unfurnished bedroom; I say bedroom, because it was provided with the dressing closet fitted with pegs, usual to all bedrooms in America. This closet the doctor used as his cabinet. The door was left open, and there was no curtain hung before it. The darkness he sat in rendered that unnecessary. The bedroom was darkened by two frames, covered with black American cloth, which fitted into the windows. The doctor, having locked the bedroom door, delivered the key to me. He then requested us to throw our influence about it. As we did so we naturally examined it. It was only a large cupboard. It had no window and no door, except that which led into the room, and no furniture except a cane-bottomed chair. When he returned to the *séance* room, the doctor saw us comfortably established in two armchairs before he put up the black frames to exclude the light. The room was then pitch dark, and the doctor had to grope his way to his cabinet. Mrs. Hooker and I sat for some minutes in silent expectation. Then we heard the voice of a negress, singing "darkey" songs, and my friend told me it was that of "Rosa," the doctor's control. Presently "Rosa" was heard to be expostulating with, or encouraging some one, and faint lights, like sparks from a fire, could be seen flitting about the open door of the cabinet. Then the lights seemed to congregate together, and cluster about a tall form, draped in some misty material, standing just outside the cabinet. "Can't you tell us who you are?" asked Mrs. Hooker. "You must tell your name, you know," interposed "Rosa," whereupon a low voice said, "I am Janet E. Powles."

Now this was an extraordinary coincidence. I had seen Mrs. Powles, the mother of my friend "John Powles," only once— when she travelled from Liverpool to London to meet me on my return from India, and hear all the particulars of her son's death. But she had continued to correspond with me, and show me kindness till the day of her own death, and as she had a daughter of the same name, she always signed herself

"Janet *E*. Powles." Even had I expected to see the old lady, and published the fact in the Boston papers, that initial *E*. would have settled the question of her identity in my mind.

"Mrs. Powles," I exclaimed, "how good of you to come and see me." "Johnny has helped me to come," she replied. "He is so happy at having met you again. He has been longing for it for so many years, and I have come to thank you for making him happy." (Here was another coincidence. "John Powles" was never called anything but "Powles" by my husband and myself. But his mother had retained the childish name of "Johnny," and I could remember how it used to vex him when she used it in her letters to him. He would say to me, "If she would only call me 'John' or 'Jack,' or anything but 'Johnny'.") I replied, "I may not leave my seat to go to you. Will you not come to me?" For the doctor had requested us not to leave our seats, but to insist on the spirits approaching us. Mrs. Powles," said, "I cannot come out further into the room to-day. I am too weak. But you shall see me." The lights then appeared to travel about her face and dress till they became stationary, and she was completely revealed to view under the semblance of her earthly likeness. She smiled and said, "We were all at the Opera House on Thursday night, and rejoiced at your success. 'Johnny' was so proud of you. Many of your friends were there beside ourselves."

I then saw that, unlike the spirits at Miss Berry's, the form of "Mrs. Powles" was draped in a kind of filmy white, *over* a dark dress. All the spirits that appeared with the doctor were so clothed, and I wondered if the filmy substance had anything to do with the lights, which looked like electricity. An incident which occurred further on seemed to confirm my idea. When "Mrs. Powles" had gone, which we guessed by the extinguishing of the lights, the handsome face and form of "Harry Montagu" appeared. I had known him well in England before he took his fatal journey to America, and could never be mistaken in his sweet smile and fascinating manner. He did not come further than the door, either, but he was standing within twelve or fourteen feet of us for all that. He only said, "Good luck to you. We can't lose an interest in the old profession, you know, any more than in the old people." "I wish you'd come and help me, Harry," I answered. "Oh, I do!" he said, brightly; "several of us do. We are all links of the same chain. Half the inspiration in the world comes from those who have gone before. But I must go! I'm getting crowded out. Here's Ada waiting to see you. Good-bye!" And as his light went out, the sweet face of Adelaide Neilson appeared in his stead. She said, "You wept when you heard of my death; and yet you never knew me. How was that?" "Did I weep?" I answered, half forgetting; "if so, it must have been because I thought it so sad that a woman so young, and beautiful, and gifted as you were, should leave the world so soon." "Oh no! not sad," she answered brightly; "glorious! glorious! I would not be back again for worlds." "Have you ever seen your grave?" I asked her. She shook her head. "What are *graves* to us? Only cupboards, where you keep our cast-off clothes." "You don't ask me what the world says about you, now," I said to her. "And I don't care," she answered. "Don't *you* forget me! Good-bye!"

She was succeeded by a spirit who called herself "Charlotte Cushman,"and who spoke to me kindly about my professional life. Mrs. Hooker told me that, to the best of her knowledge, none of these spirits had ever appeared under the doctor's mediumship before. But now came out "Florence," dancing into the room—*literally dancing*, holding out in both hands the skirt of a dress, which looked as if it were made of the finest muslin or lace, and up and down which fireflies were darting with marvellous rapidity. She looked as if clothed in electricity, and infinitely well pleased with herself. "Look!" she exclaimed; "look at my dress! isn't it lovely?

8

Look at the fire! The more I shake it, the more fire comes! Oh, Mother! if you could only have a dress like this for the stage, what a *sensation* you would make!" And she shook her skirts about, till the fire seemed to set a light to every part of her drapery, and she looked as if she were in flames. I observed, "I never knew you to take so much interest in your dress before, darling." "Oh, it isn't the dress," she replied; "it's the *fire!*" And she really appeared as charmed with the novel experience as a child with a new toy.

As she left us, a dark figure advanced into the room, and ejaculated, "Ma! ma!" I recognized at once the peculiar intonation and mode of address of my step-son, Francis Lean, with whom, since he had announced his own death to me, I had had no communication, except through trance mediumship. "Is that you, my poor boy?" I said. "Come closer to me. You are not afraid of me, are you?" "O, no! Ma! of course not, only I was at the Opera House, you know, with the others, and that piece you recited, Ma—you know the one—it's all true, Ma—and I don't want you to go back to England. Stay here, Ma—stay here!" I knew perfectly well to what the lad alluded, but I would not enter upon it before a stranger. So I only said, "You forget my children, Francis— what would they say if I never went home again." This seemed to puzzle him but after a while he answered, "Then go to *them*, Ma; go to *them*." All this time he had been talking in the dark, and I only knew him by the sound of his voice. I said, "Are you not going to show yourself to me, Francis. It is such a long time since we met." "Never since you saw me at the docks. That was *me*, Ma, and at Brighton, too, only you didn't half believe it till you heard I was gone." "Tell me the truth of the accident, Francis," I asked him. "Was there foul play?" "No," he replied, "but we got quarrelling about *her* you know, and fighting, and that's how the boat upset. It was *my* fault, Ma, as much as anybody else's."

"How was it your body was never found?" "It got

dragged down in an undercurrent, Ma. It was out at Cape Horn before they offered a reward for it." Then he began to light up, and as soon as the figure was illuminated I saw that the boy was dressed in "jumpers" and "jersey" of dark woollen material, such as they wear in the merchant service in hot climates, but over it all—his head and shoulders included—was wound a quantity of flimsy white material I have before mentioned. "I can't bear this stuff. It makes me look like a girl," said "Francis," and with his hands he tore it off. Simultaneously the illumination ceased, and he was gone. I called him by name several times, but no sound came out of the darkness. It seemed as though the veiling which he disliked preserved his materialization, and that, with its protection removed, he had dissolved again.

When another dark figure came out of the cabinet, and approaching me, knelt at my feet, I supposed it to be "Francis" come back again, and laying my hand on the bent head, I asked, "Is that you again, dear?" A strange voice answered, with the words, "Forgive! forgive!" "*Forgive?*" I repeated, "What have I to forgive?" "The attempt to murder your husband in 1856. Arthur Yelverton Brooking has forgiven. He is here with me now. Will you forgive too?" "Certainly," I replied, "I have forgiven long ago. You expiated your sin upon the gallows. You could do no more."

The figure sprung into a standing position, and lit up from head to foot, when I saw the two men standing together, Arthur Yelverton Brooking and the Madras sepoy who had murdered him. I never saw anything more brilliant than the appearance of the sepoy. He was dressed completely in white, in the native costume, with a white "puggree" or turban on his head. But his "puggree" was flashing with jewels—strings of them were hung round his neck—and his sash held a magnificent jewelled dagger. You must please remember that I was not alone, but that this sight was beheld by Mrs. Hooker as well as myself (to whom it was as unexpected as to her), and that I know she would testify to it to-day. And now to explain the reason for these unlooked-for apparitions.

In 1856 my husband, then Lieutenant Ross-Church, was Adjutant of the 12th Madras Native Infantry, and Arthur Yelverton Brooking, who had for some time done duty with the 12th, was adjutant of another native corps, both of which were stationed at Madras. Lieutenant Church was not a favourite with his men, by whom he was considered a martinet, and one day when there had been a review on the island at Madras, and the two adjutants were riding home together, a sepoy of the 12th fired at Lieutenant Church's back with the intent to kill him, but unfortunately the bullet struck Lieutenant Brooking instead, who, after lingering for twelve hours, died, leaving a young wife and a baby behind him. For this offence the sepoy was tried and hung, and on his trial the whole truth of course came out. This then was the reason that the spirits of the murdered and the murderer came like friends, because the injury had never been really intended for Brooking.

When I said that I had forgiven, the sepoy became (as I have told) a blaze of light, and then knelt again and kissed the hem of my dress. As he knelt there he became covered, or heaped over, with a mass of the same filmy drapery as enveloped "Francis," and when he rose again he was standing in a cloud. He gathered an end of it, and laying it on my head he wound me and himself round and round with it, until we were bound up in a kind of cocoon. Mrs. Hooker, who watched the whole proceeding, told me afterwards that she had never seen anything like it before—that she could distinctly see the dark face and the white face close together all the time beneath the drapery, and that I was as brightly illuminated as the spirit. Of this I was not aware myself, but *his* brightness almost dazzled me.

Let me observe also that I have been in the East Indies,

and within a few yards' length of sepoys, and that I am sure I could never have been wrapt in the same cloth with a mortal one without having been made painfully aware of it in more ways than one. The spirit did not *unwind* me again, although the winding process had taken him some time. He whisked off the wrapping with one pull, and I stood alone once more. I asked him by what name I should call him, and he said, "The Spirit of Light." He then expressed a wish to magnetize something I wore, so as to be the better able to approach me. I gave him a brooch containing "John Powles'" hair, which his mother had given me after his death, and he carried it back into the cabinet with him. It was a valuable brooch of onyx and pearls, and I was hoping my eastern friend would not carry it *too* far, when I found it had been replaced and fastened at my throat without my being aware of the circumstance. "Arthur Yelverton Brooking" had disappeared before this, and neither of them came back again. These were not all the spirits that came under the doctor's mediumship during that *séance*, but only those whom I had known and recognized. Several of Mrs. Hooker's friends appeared and some of the doctor's controls, but as I have said before, they could not help my narrative, and so I omit to describe them. The *séance* lasted altogether two hours, and I was very grateful to the doctor for giving me the opportunity to study an entirely new phase of the science to me.

CHAPTER XXVI

V. *Mrs. Fay*

THERE was a young woman called "Annie Eva Fay," who came over from America to London some years ago, and appeared at the Hanover Square Rooms in an exhibition after the manner of the Davenport Brothers and Messrs. Maskelyne and Cook. She must not be confounded with the Mrs. Fay who forms the subject of this chapter, because they had nothing to do with one another.   Someone in Boston advised me *not* to go and sit at one of this Mrs. Fay's public *séances.* They were described to me as being too physical and un-refined; that the influences were of a low order, and the audiences matched them.   However, when I am studying a matter, I like to see everything I can and hear everything I can concerning it, and to form my own opinion independent of that of anybody else.   So I walked off by myself one night to Mrs. Fay's address, and sat down in a quiet corner, watching everything that occurred.   The circle certainl, numbered some members of a humble class, but I conclude we should see that everywhere if the fees were lower.   Media, like other professional people, fix their charges according to the quarter of the city in which they live.   But every member was silent and respectful, and evidently a believer.

One young man, in deep mourning, with a little girl also in black, of about five or six years old, attracted my attention at once, from his sorrowful and abstracted manner.   He had evidently come there, I thought, in the hope of seeing some-one whom he had lost.   Mrs. Fay (as she passed through the room to her cabinet) appeared a very quiet, simple-looking little woman to me, without any loudness or vulgarity about her.   Her cabinet was composed of two curtains only, made of some white material, and hung on uprights at one angle, in a corner of the room, the most transparent contrivance possible.   Anything like a bustle or confusion inside it, such as would be occasioned by dressing or "making up," would have been apparent at once to the audience outside, who were sitting by the light of an ordinary gas-burner and globe. Yet Mrs. Fay had not been seated there above a few minutes, when there ran out into the *séance* room two of the most extraordinary materializations I had ever seen, and both of them about as opposite to Mrs. Fay in appearance as any creatures could be.

One was an Irish charwoman or apple-woman (she might

have been either) with a brown, wrinkled face, a broken nose, tangled grey hair, a crushed bonnet, general dirt and disorder, and a tongue that could talk broad Irish, and call "a spade a spade" at one and the same time. "Biddy," as she was named, was accompanied by a street newspaper boy—one of those urchins who run after carriages and turn Catherine-wheels in the mud, and who talked "gutter-slang" in a style that was utterly unintelligible to the decent portion of the sitters. These two went on in a manner that was undoubtedly funny, but not at all edifying and calculated to drive any inquirer into Spiritualism out of the room, under the impression that they were evil spirits bent on our destruction. That either of them was represented by Mrs. Fay was out of the question. In the first place, she would, in that instance, have been so clever an actress and mimic, that she would have made her fortune on the stage—added to which the boy "Teddy" was much too small for her, and "Biddy" was much too large. Besides, no actress, however experienced, could have "made up" in the time. I was quite satisfied, therefore, that neither of them was the medium, even if I could not have seen her figure the while, through the thin curtains, sitting in her chair. *Why* such low, physical manifestations are permitted I am unable to say. It was no wonder they had shocked the sensibility of my friend. I felt half inclined myself when they appeared to get up and run away. However, I was very glad afterwards that I did not. They disappeared after a while, and were succeeded by a much pleasanter person, a cabinet spirit called "Gipsy," who looked as if she might have belonged to one of the gipsy tribes when on earth, she was so brown and arch and lively. Presently the young man in black was called up, and I saw him talking to a female spirit very earnestly. After a while he took her hand and led her outside the curtain, and called the little girl whom he had left on his seat by her name. The child looked up, screamed "Mamma! mamma!" and flew into the arms of the spirit, who knelt down and kissed her, and we could hear the child sobbing and saying, "Oh! Mamma, why did you go away?—why did you go away?" It was a very affecting scene—at least it seemed so to me. The instant recognition by the little girl, and her perfect unconsciousness but that her mother had returned *in propria persona*, would have been more convincing proof of the genuineness of Spiritualism to a sceptic, than fifty miracles of greater importance. When the spirit mother had to leave again the child's agony at parting was very apparent. "Take me with you," she kept on saying, and her father had actually to carry her back to her seat. When they got there they both wept in unison. Afterwards he said to me in an apologetic sort of way—he was sitting next to me—"It is the first time, you see, that Mary has seen her poor mother, but I wanted to have her testimony to her identity, and I think she gave it pretty plainly, poor child! She'll never be content to let me come alone now." I said, "I think it is a pity you brought her so young," and so I did.

"Florence" did not appear (she told me afterwards the atmosphere was so "rough" that she could not), and I began to think that no one would come for me, when a common seaman, dressed in ordinary sailor's clothes, ran out of the cabinet and began dancing a hornpipe in front of me. He danced it capitally too, and with any amount of vigorous snapping his fingers to mark the time, and when he had finished he "made a leg," as sailors call it, and stood before me. "Have you come for me, my friend?" I inquired. "Not exactly," he answered, "but I came with the Cap'en. I came to pave the way for him. The Cap'en will be here directly. We was in the *Avenger* together." (Now all the world knows that my eldest brother, Frederick Marryat, was drowned in the wreck of the *Avenger* in 1847; but as I was a little child at the time, and had no remembrance of him, I had never dreamt of seeing him again. He was a first lieutenant when he died, so I do not know why the seaman gave him brevet rank, but I repeat his words as he said them.) After a minute or two I was called up to the cabinet, and saw my brother Frederick (whom I recognized from his likeness) standing there dressed in naval uniform, but looking very stiff and unnatural. He smiled when he saw me, but did not attempt to kiss me. I said, "Why! Fred! is it really you? I thought you would have forgotten all about me." He replied, "Forgotten little Flo? Why should I? Do you think I have never seen you since that time, nor heard anything about you? I know everything—everything!" "You must know, then, that I have not spent a very happy life," I said. "Never mind," he answered, "you needed it. It has done you good!" But all he said was without any life in it, as if he spoke mechanically—perhaps because it was the first time he had materialized.

I had said "Good-bye" to him, and dropped the curtain, when I heard my name called twice, "Flo! Flo!" and turned to receive my sister "Emily" in my arms. She looked like herself exactly, but she had only time to kiss me and gasp out, "So glad, so happy to meet again," when she appeared to faint. Her eyes closed, her head fell back on my shoulder, and before I had time to realize what was going to happen, she had passed *through* the arm that supported her, and sunk down *through* the floor. The sensation of her weight was still making my arm tingle, but "Emily" was gone—*clean gone*. I was very much disappointed. I had longed to see this sister again, and speak to her confidentially; but whether it was something antagonistic in the influence of this *séance* room ("Florence" said afterwards that it *was*), or there was some other cause for it, I know not, but most certainly my friends did not seem to flourish there.

I had another horrible disappointment before I left. A voice from inside the cabinet called out, "Here are two babies who want the lady sitting under the picture." Now, there was only one picture hanging in the room, and I was sitting under it. I looked eagerly towards the cabinet, and saw issue from it the

"Princess Gertie" leading a little toddler with a flaxen poll and bare feet, and no clothing but a kind of white chemise. This was "Joan," the "Yonnie" I had so often asked to see, and I rose in the greatest expectation to receive the little pair. Just as they gained the centre of the room, however, taking very short and careful steps, like babies first set on their feet, the cabinet spirit "Gipsy" *bounced* out of the curtains, and saying decidedly, "Here! we don't want any children about," she placed her hand on the heads of my little ones, and *pressed them down* through the floor. They seemed to crumble to pieces before my eyes, and their place knew them no more. I couldn't help feeling angry. I exclaimed, "O! what did you do that for? Those were my babies, and I have been longing to see them so." "I can't help it," replied "Gipsy," "but this isn't a *séance* for children." I was so vexed that I took no more interest in the proceedings. A great number of forms appeared, thirty or forty in all, but by the time I returned to my hotel and began to jot down my notes, I could hardly remember what they were. I had been dreaming all the time of how much I should have liked to hold that little flaxen-haired "Yonnie" in my arms.

CHAPTER XXVII

VI. *Virginia Roberts*

WHEN I returned to New York, it was under exceptional circumstances. I had taken cold whilst travelling in the Western States, had had a severe attack of bronchitis and pneumonia at Chicago, was compelled to relinquish my business, and as soon as I was well enough to travel, was ordered back to New York to recuperate my health. Here I took up my abode in the Victoria Hotel, where a lady, whose acquaintance I had made on my former visit to the city, was living. As I have no permission to publish this lady's name, I must call her Mrs. S——. She had been a

Spiritualist for some time before I knew her, and she much interested me by showing me an entry in her diary, made *four years* previous to my arrival in America. It was an account of the utterances of a Mrs. Philips, a clairvoyant then resident in New York, during which she had prophesied my arrival in the city, described my personal appearance, profession, and general surroundings perfectly, and foretold my acquaintance-ship with Mrs. S——. The prophecy ended with words to the effect that our meeting would be followed by certain effects that would influence her future life, and that on the 17th of March, 1885, would commence a new era in her existence. It was at the beginning of March that we first lived under the same roof. As soon as Mrs. S—— found that I was likely to have some weeks of leisure, she became very anxious that we should visit the New York media together; for although she had so long been a believer in Spiritualism, she had not (owing to family opposition) met with much sympathy on the subject, or had the opportunity of much investigation. So we determined, as soon as I was well enough to go out in the evening, that we would attend some *séances*. As it happened, when that time came, we found the medium most accessible to be Miss Virginia Roberts, of whom neither of us knew anything but what we had learned from the public papers. However, it was necessary that I should be exposed as little as possible to the night air, and so we fixed, by chance as it were, to visit Miss Roberts first. We found her living with her mother and brother in a small house in one of the back streets of the city. She was a young girl of sixteen, very reserved and rather timid-looking, who had to be drawn out before she could be made to talk. She had only commenced sitting a few months before, and that be-cause her brother (who was also a medium) had had an illness and been obliged to give up his *séances* for a while. The *séance* room was very small, the manifestations taking place almost in the midst of the circle, and the cabinet (so-called) was the flimsiest contrivance I had ever seen. Four uprights of iron, not thicker than the rod of a muslin blind with cross-bars of the same, on which were hung thin curtains of lilac print, formed the contruction of this cabinet, which shook and swayed about each time a form left or entered it. A harmonium for accompanying the voices, and a few chairs for the audience, was all the furniture the room contained. The first evening we went to see Miss Roberts there were only two or three sitters beside ourselves. The medium seemed to be pretty nearly unknown, and I resolved, as I usually do in such cases, not to expect anything, for fear I should be disappointed.

Mrs. S——, on the contrary, was all expectation and excitement. If she had ever sat for materializations, it had been long before, and the idea was like a new one to her. After two or three forms had appeared, of no interest to us, a gentleman in full evening dress walked suddenly out of the cabinet, and said, "Kate," which was the name of Mrs. S——. He was a stout, well-formed man, of an imposing presence, with dark hair and eyes, and he wore a solitaire of diamonds of unusual brilliancy in his shirt front. I had no idea who he was; but Mrs. S—— recognized him at once as an old lover who had died whilst under a misunderstanding with her, and she was powerfully affected—more, she was terribly frightened. It seems that she wore at her throat a brooch which he had given her; but every time he approached her with the view of touching it, she shrieked so loudly, and threw herself into such a state of nervous agitation, that I thought she would have to return home again. However, on her being accommodated with a chair in the last row so that she might have the other sitters between her and the materialized spirits, she managed to calm herself. The only friend who appeared for me that evening was "John Powles"; and, to my surprise and pleasure, he appeared in the old uniform of the 12th Madras Native Infantry. This corps wore facings of fawn, with buttons bearing the word "Ava," encircled by a wreath of laurel. The mess jackets were lined with wadded fawn silk, and the waistcoats were trimmed with three lines of narrow gold braid. Their "karkee," or undress uniform, established in 1859, consisted of a tunic and trousers of a sad green cloth, with the regimental buttons and a crimson silk sash. The marching dress of all officers in the Indian service is made of white drill, with a cap cover of the same material. Their forage cloak is of dark blue cloth, and hangs to their heels. Their forage cap has a broad square peak to shelter the face and eyes. I mention these details for the benefit of those who are not acquainted with the general dress of the Indian army, and to show how difficult it would have been for Virginia Roberts, or any other medium, to have procured them, even had she known the private wish expressed by me to "John Powles" in Boston, that he would try and come to me in uniform. On this first occasion of his appearing so, he wore the usual everyday coat, buttoned up to his chin, and he made me examine the buttons to see that they bore the crest and motto of the regiment. And I may say here, that before I left New York he appeared to me in every one of the various dresses I have described above, and became quite a marked figure in the city.

When it was made known through the papers that an old friend of Florence Marryat had appeared through the mediumship of Virginia Roberts, in a uniform of thirty years before, I received numbers of private letters inquiring if it were true, and dozens of people visited Miss Roberts' *séances* for the sole purpose of seeing him. He took a great liking for Mrs. S——, and when she had conquered her first fear she became quite friendly with him, and I heard, after leaving New York, that he continued to appear for her as long as she attended those *séances*.

There was one difference in the female spirits that came through Virginia Roberts from those of other media. Those that were strong enough to leave the cabinet invariably disappeared by floating upwards through the ceiling. Their mode of doing this was most graceful. They would first clasp their hands behind their heads and lean backward; then their feet were lifted off the ground, and they were borne upward in a recumbent position. When I related this to my friend, Dr. George Lefferts (under whom I was for throat treatment to recover my voice), he declared there must be some machinery connected with the uprights that supported the cabinet, by which the forms were elevated. He had got it all so "pat" that he was able to take a pencil and demonstrate to me on paper exactly how the machinery worked, and how easy it would be to swing full-sized human bodies up to the ceiling with it. How they managed to disappear when they got there he was not quite prepared to say; but if he once saw the trick done, he would explain the whole matter to me, and expose it into the bargain. I told Dr. Lefferts, as I have told many other clever men, that I shall be the first person open to conviction when they can convince me, and I bore him off to a private *séance* with Virginia Roberts for that purpose only. He was all that was charming on the occasion. He gave me a most delightful dinner at Delmonico's first, and he tested all Miss Roberts' manifestations in the most delicate and gentlemanly manner (sceptics as a rule are neither delicate nor gentlemanly) but he could neither open my eyes to chicanery nor detect it himself. He handled and shook the frail supports of the cabinet and confessed they were much too weak to bear any such weight as he had imagined. He searched the carpeted floor and the adjoining room for hidden machinery without finding the slightest thing to rouse his suspicions, and yet he saw the female forms float upwards through the whitewashed ceiling, and came away from the *séance* room as wise as when he had entered it.

But this occurred some weeks after. I must relate first what happened after our first *séance* with Miss Roberts.

Mrs. S—— and I were well enough pleased with the result to desire to test her capabilities further, and with that intent we invited her to visit us at our hotel. Spiritualism is as much tabooed by one section of the American public as it is encouraged by the other, and so we resolved to breathe nothing of our intentions, but invite the girl to dine and spend the evening in our rooms with us just as if she were an ordinary visitor. Consequently, we dined together at the *table d'hote* before we took our way upstairs. Mrs. S—— and I had a private sitting-room, the windows of which were draped with white lace curtains only, and we had no other means to shut out the light. Consequently, when we wished to sit, all we could do was to place a chair for Virginia Roberts in the window recess, behind one of these pairs of curtains, and pin them together in front of her, which formed the airiest cabinet imaginable. We then locked the door, lowered the gas, and sat down on a sofa before the curtains.

In the space of five minutes, without the lace curtains having been in the slightest degree disturbed, "Francis Lean," my step-son, walked *through* them, and came up to my side. He was dressed in his ordinary costume of jersey and "jumpers," and had a little worsted cap upon his head. He displayed all the peculiarities of speech and manner I have noticed before; but he was much less timid, and stood by me for a long time talking of my domestic affairs, which were rather complicated, and giving me a detailed account of the accident which caused his death, and which had been always somewhat of a mystery. In doing this, he mentioned names of people hitherto unknown to me, but which I found on after inquiry to be true. He seemed quite delighted to be able to manifest so indisputably like himself, and remarked more than once, "I'm not much like a girl now, am I, Ma?"

Next, Mrs. S——'s old lover came, of whom she was still considerably alarmed, and her father, who had been a great politician and a well-known man. "Florence," too, of course, though never so lively through Miss Roberts as through other media, but still happy though pensive, and full of advice how I was to act when I reached England again. Presently a soft voice said, "Aunt Flo, don't you know me?" And I saw standing in front of me my niece and godchild, Lilian Thomas, who had died as a nun in the Convent of the "Dames Anglaises" at Bruges. She was clothed in her nun's habit, which was rather peculiar, the face being surrounded by a white cap, with a crimped border that hid all the hair, and surmounted by a white veil of some heavy woollen material which covered the head and the black serge dress. "Lilian" had died of consumption, and the death-like, waxy complexion which she had had for some time before was exactly reproduced. She had not much to say for herself; indeed, we had been completely separated since she had entered the convent, but she was undoubtedly *there*. She was succeeded by my sister "Emily," whom I have already so often described. And these apparitions, six in number, and all recognizable, were produced in the private room of Mrs. S—— and myself, and with no other person but Virginia Roberts, sixteen years old.

It was about this time that we received an invitation to attend a private *séance* in a large house in the city, occupied by Mr. and Mrs. Newman, who had Maud Lord staying with them as a visitor. Maud Lord's mediumship is a peculiar one. She places her sitters in a circle, holding hands. She then seats herself on a chair in the centre, and keeps on clapping her hands, to intimate that she has not changed her position. The *séance* is held in darkness, and the manifestations consist of "direct voices," *i.e.* voices that every one can hear, and by what they say to you, you must judge of their identity and truthfulness. I had only witnessed powers of this kind once before—through Mrs. Bassett, who is now Mrs. Herne—but as no one spoke to me through her whom I recognized, I have omitted to give any account of it.

As soon as Maud Lord's sitting was fully established I, heard her addressing various members of the company, telling them who stood beside them, and I heard them putting questions to, or holding conversations with, creatures who were invisible to me. The time went on, and I believed I was going to be left out of it, when I heard a voice close to my ear whisper, "Arthur." At the same moment Maud Lord's voice sounded in my direction, saying that the lady in the brown velvet hat had a gentleman standing near her, named "Arthur," who wished to be recognized. I was the only lady present in a brown velvet hat, yet I could not recall any deceased friend of the name of "Arthur" who might wish to communicate with me. (It is a constant occurrence at a *séance* that the mind refuses to remember a name, or a circumstance, and on returning home, perhaps the whole situation makes itself clear, and one wonders how one could have been so dull as not to perceive it.) So I said that I knew no one in the spirit world of that name, and Maud Lord replied, "Well, *he* knows *you*, at all events." A few more minutes elapsed, when I felt a touch on the third finger of my left hand, and the voice spoke again and said, "Arthur! 'Arthur's ring.' Have you quite forgotten?" This action brought the person to my memory, and I exclaimed, "Oh! Johnny Cope, is it you?"

To explain this, I must tell my readers that when I went out to India in 1854, Arthur Cope of the Lancers was a passenger by the same steamer; and when we landed in Madras, he made me a present of a diamond ring, which I wore at that *séance* as a guard. But he was never called by anything but his nickname of "Johnny," so that his real appellation had quite slipped my memory. The poor fellow died in 1856 or 1857, and I had been ungrateful enough to forget all about him, and should never have remembered his name had it not been coupled with the ring. It would have been still more remarkable, though, if Maud Lord, who had never seen me till that evening, had discovered an incident which happened thirty years before, and which I had completely forgotten.

Before I had been many days in New York, I fell ill again from exposing myself to the weather, this time with a bad throat. Mrs. S—— and I slept in the same room, and our sitting-room opened into the bedroom. She was indefatigable in her attentions and kindness to me during my illness, and kept running backwards and forwards from the bedroom to the sitting-room, both by night and day, to get me fresh poultices, which she kept hot on the steam stove.

One evening about eleven o'clock she got out of bed in her nightdress, and went into the next room for this purpose. Almost directly after she entered it, I heard a heavy fall. I called her by name, and receiving no answer, became frightened, jumped out of bed, and followed her. To my consternation, I found her stretched out, at full length, on a white bearskin rug, and quite insensible. She was a delicate woman, and I thought at first that she had fainted from fatigue; but when she showed no signs of returning consciousness, I became alarmed. I was very weak myself from my illness, and hardly able to stand, but I managed to put on a dressing-gown and summon the assistance of a lady who occupied the room next to us, and whose acquaintance we had already made. She was strong and capable, and helped me to place Mrs. S—— upon the sofa, where she lay in the same condition. After we had done all we could think of to bring her to herself without effect, the next-door lady became frightened. She said to me, "I don't like this. I think we ought to call in a doctor. Supposing she were to die without regaining consciousness." I replied, "I should say the same, excepting I begin to believe she has not fainted at all, but is in a trance; and in that case, any violent attempts to bring her to herself might injure her. Just see how quietly she breathes, and how very young she looks."

When her attention was called to this fact, the next-door

lady was astonished. Mrs. S——, who was a woman past forty, looked like a girl of sixteen. She was a very pretty woman, but with a dash of temper in her expression which spoiled it. Now with all the passions and lines smoothed out of it, she looked perfectly lovely. As she might have looked in death. But she was not dead. She was breathing. So I felt sure that the spirit had escaped for a while and left her free. I covered her up warmly on the sofa, and determined to leave her there till the trance had passed. After a while I persuaded the next-door lady to think as I did, and to go back to her own bed. As soon as she had gone, I administered my own poultice, and sat down to watch beside my friend. The time went on until seven in the morning—seven hours she had lain, without moving a limb, upon the sofa—when, without any warning, she sat up and gazed about her. I called her by name, and asked her what she wanted; but I could see at once, by her expression, that she did not know me. Presently she asked me, "Who are you?" I told her. "Are you Kate's friend?" she said. I answered, "Yes." "Do you know who *I* am?" was the next question, which, of course, I answered in the negative. Mrs. S—— thereupon gave me the name of a German gentleman which I had never heard before. An extraordinary scene then followed. Influenced by the spirit that possessed her, Mrs. S——rose and unlocked a cabinet of her own, which stood in the room, and taking thence a bundle of old letters, she selected several and read portions of them aloud to me. She then told me a history of herself and the gentleman whose spirit was speaking through her, and gave me several messages to deliver to herself the following day. It will be sufficient for me to say that this history was of so private a nature, that it was most unlikely she would have confided it to me or any one, particularly as she was a woman of a most secretive nature; but names, addresses, and even words of conversations were given, in a manner which would have left no room for doubt of their truthfulness, even if Mrs. S.——had not confirmed them to be facts afterwards. This went on for a long time, the spirit expressing the greatest animosity against Mrs. S—— all the while, and then the power seemed suddenly to be spent, and she went off to sleep again upon the sofa, waking up naturally about an hour afterwards, and very much surprised to hear what had happened to her meanwhile. When we came to consider the matter, we found that this unexpected seizure had taken place upon *the 17th of March*, the day predicted by Mrs. Philips four years previously as one on which a new era would commence for Mrs. S——. From that time she continually went into trances, and used to predict the future for herself and others; but whether she has kept it up to this day I am unable to say, as I have heard nothing from her since I left America.

That event took place on the 13th of June, 1885. We had been in the habit of spending our Sunday evenings in Miss Roberts' *séance* room, and she begged me not to miss the last opportunity. When we arrived there, we found that the accompanist who usually played the harmonium for them was unable to be present, and Miss Roberts asked if I would be his substitute. I said I would, on condition that they moved the instrument on a line with the cabinet, so that I might not lose a sight of what was going on. This was accordingly done, and I commenced to play "Thou art gone from my gaze." Almost immediately "John Powles" stepped out, dressed in uniform, and stood by the harmonium with his hand upon my shoulder. "I never was much of a singer, you know, Flo," he said to me; "but if you will sing that song with me, I'll try and go through it." And he actually did sing (after a fashion) the entire two verses of the ballad, keeping his hand on my shoulder the whole time. When we came to the line, "I seek thee in vain by the meadow and stream," he stooped down and whispered in my ear, "Not *quite* in vain, Flo, has it been?" I do not know if my English Spiritualistic friends can "cap" this story, but in America they told me it was quite a unique performance, particularly at a public *séance*, where the jarring of so many diverse influences often hinders instead of helping the manifestations.

"Powles" appeared to be especially strong on that occasion. Towards the middle of the evening a kind of whining was heard to proceed from the cabinet; and Miss Roberts, who was not entranced, said, "There's a baby coming out for Miss Marryat." At the same time the face of little "Yonnie" appeared at the opening of the curtains, but nearly level with the ground, as she was crawling out on all fours. Before she had had time to advance beyond them, "Powles" stepped over her and came amongst us. "Oh! Powles!" I exclaimed, "you used to love my little babies. Do pick up that one for me that I may see it properly." He immediately returned, took up "Yonnie," and brought her out into the circle on his arm. The contrast of the baby's white kind of nightgown with his scarlet uniform was very striking. He carried the child to each sitter that it might be thoroughly examined; and when he had returned "Yonnie" to the cabinet, he came out again on his own account. That evening I was summoned into the cabinet myself by the medium's guide, a little Italian girl, who had materialized several times for our benefit. When I entered it, I stumbled up against Miss Roberts' chair. There was barely room for me to stand beside it. She said to me, "Is that *you*, Miss Marryat?" and I replied, "Yes; didn't you send for me?" She said, "No; I didn't send, I know nothing about it!" A voice behind me said, "*I* sent for you!" and at the same moment two strong arms were clasped round my waist, and a man's face kissed me over my shoulder. I asked, "Who are you?" and he replied, "Walk out of the cabinet and you shall see." I turned round, two hands were placed upon my shoulders, and I walked back into the circle with a tall man walking behind me in that position. When I could look at him in the gaslight, I recognized my brother, Frank Marryat, who died in 1855, and whom I had never seen since. Of

course, the other spirits who were familiar with Mrs. S——
and myself came to wish me a pleasant voyage across the
Atlantic, but I have mentioned them all so often that I fear I
must already have tired out the patience of my readers. But
in order to be impressive it is so necessary to be explicit. All I
can bring forward in excuse is, that every word I have
written is the honest and unbiassed truth. Here, therefore,
ends the account of my experience in Spiritualism up to the
present moment—not, by any means, the half, nor yet *the
quarter of it*, but all I consider likely to interest the general
public. And those who have been interested in it may see
their own friends as I have done, if they will only take the
same trouble that I have done.

CHAPTER XXVIII

"WHAT GOOD DOES IT DO?"

My friends have so often asked me this question, that I think,
before I close this book, I am justified in answering it, at all
events, as far as I myself am concerned. How often have I
sat, surrounded by an interested audience, who knew me too
well to think me either a lunatic or a liar; and after I have told
them some of the most marvellous and thrilling of my
experiences, they have assailed me with these quetsions,
"But what *is* it? And what *good* does it do? *What is it?*"
There, my friends, I confess you stagger me! I can no more
tell you what it is than I can tell you what *you* are or what *I* am.
We know that, like Topsy, we "grew." We know that,
given certain conditions and favourable accessories, a child
comes into this world, and a seed sprouts through the dark
earth and becomes a flower; but though we know the cause
and see the effect, the greatest man of science, or the greatest
botanist, cannot tell you how the child is made, nor how
the plant grows. Neither can I (or any one) tell you *what*
the power is that enables a spirit to make itself apparent. I

can only say that it can do so, and refer you to the Creator of you and me and the entire universe. The commonest things the earth produces are all miracles, from the growing of a mustard seed to the expansion of a human brain. What is more wonderful than the hatching of an egg? You see it done every day. It has become so common that you regard it as an event of no consequence. You know the exact number of days the bird must sit to produce a live chicken with all its functions ready for nature's use, but you see nothing wonderful in it. All birds can do the same, and you would not waste your time in speculating on the wondrous effect of heat upon a liquid substance which turns to bone and blood and flesh and feathers.

If you were as familiar with the reappearance of those who have gone before as you are with chickens, you would see nothing supernatural in their manifesting themselves to you, and nothing more miraculous than in the birth of a child or the hatching of an egg. Why should it be? Who has fixed the abode of the spirit after death? Who can say where it dwells, or that it is not permitted to return to this world, perhaps to live in it altogether? Still, however the Almighty sends them, the fact remains that they come, and that thousands can testify to the fact. As to the theory advanced by some people that they are devils, sent to lure us to our destruction, that is an insult to the wisdom or mercy of an Omnipotent Creator. They cannot come except by His permission, just as He sends children to some people and witholds them from others. And the conversation of most of those that I have talked with is all on the side of religion, prayer, and self-sacrifice. *My* friends, at all events, have never denied the existence of a God or a Saviour. They have, on the contrary (and especially "Florence"), been very quick to rebuke me for anything I may have done that was wrong, for neglect of prayer and church-going, for speaking evil of my neighbours, or any other fault. They have continually inculcated the doctrine that religion consists in unselfish love to our fellow-creatures, and in devotion to God. I do not deny that there are frivolous and occasionally wicked spirits about us. Is it to be wondered at? For one spirit that leaves this world calculated to do good to his fellow-creatures, a hundred leave it who will do him harm. That is really the reason that the Church discourages Spiritualism. She does not disbelieve in it. She knows it to be true; but she also knows it to be dangerous. Since like attracts like, the numbers of thoughtless spirits who still dwell on earth would naturally attract the numbers of thoughtless spirits who have left it, and their influence is best dispensed with. Talk of devils. I have known many more devils in the flesh than out of it, and could name a number of acquaintances who, when once passed out of this world, I should steadfastly refuse to have any communication with. I have no doubt myself whatever as to *what* it is, or that I have seen my dear friends and children as I knew them upon earth. But *how* they come or *where* they go, I must wait until I join them to ascertain, even if I shall do it then.

The second question, however, I can more easily deal with, *What good is it?* The only wonder to me is that people who are not stone-blind to what is going on in this world can put such a question. What good is it to have one's faith in Immortality and another life confirmed in an age of free-thought, scepticism and utter callousness? When I look around me and see the young men nowadays—ay, and the young women too—who believe in no hereafter, who lie down and die, like the dumb animals who cannot be made to understand the love of the dear God who created them although they feel it, I cannot think of anything calculated to do them more good than the return of a father or a mother or a friend, who could convince them by ocular demonstration that there is a future life and happiness and misery, according to the one we have led here below.

"Oh, but," I seem to hear some readers exclaim, "we *do* believe in all that you say. We have been taught so from our youth up, and the Bible points to it in every line." You may *think* you believe it, my friends, and in a theoretical way you may; but you do not *realize* it, and the whole of your lives proves it. Death, instead of being the blessed portal to the Life Elysian, the gate of which may swing open for you any day, and admit you to eternal and unfading happiness, is a far-off misty phantom, whose approach you dread, and the sight of which in others you run away from. The majority of people avoid the very mention of death. They would not look at a corpse for anything; the sight of a coffin or a funeral or a graveyard fills them with horror; the idea of it for themselves makes them turn pale with fright. Is *this* belief in the existence of a tender Father and a blessed home waiting to receive them on the other side? Even professed Christians experience what they term a "natural" horror at the thought of death! I have known persons of fixed religious principles who had passed their lives (apparently) in prayer, and expressed their firm belief in Heaven waiting for them, fight against death with all their mortal energies, and try their utmost to baffle the disease that was sent to carry them to everlasting happiness. Is this logical? It is tantamount in my idea to the pauper in the workhouse who knows that directly the gate is open to let him through, he will pass from skilly, oakum, and solitary confinement to the King's Palace to enjoy youth, health, and prosperity evermore; and who, when he sees the gates beginning to unclose, puts his back and all his neighbours' backs against them to keep them shut as long as possible.

Death should not be a "horror" to any one; and if we knew more about it, it would cease to be so. It is the *mystery* that appals us. We see our friends die, and no word or sign comes back to tell us there *is* no death, so we picture them to ourselves mouldering in the damp earth till we nearly go mad with grief and dismay. Some people think me heartless because I never go near the graves of those whom I love best. Why should I? I might with more reason go and sit beside a pile of their cast-off garments. I could *see* them, and they would actually retain more of their identity and influence than the corpse which I could *not* see. I mourn their loss just the same, but I mourn it as I should do if they had settled for life in a far distant land, from which I could only enjoy occasional glimpses of their happiness.

And I may say emphatically that the greatest good Spiritualism does is to remove the fear of one's own death. One can never be quite certain of the changes that circumstances may bring about, nor do I like to boast overmuch. Disease and weakness may destroy the nerve I flatter myself on possessing; but I think I may say that as matters stand at present *I have no fear of death whatever*, and the only trouble I can foresee in passing through it will be to witness the distress of my friends. But when I remember all those who have gathered on the other side, and whom I firmly believe will be present to help me in my passage there, I can feel nothing but a great curiosity to pierce the mysteries as yet unrevealed to me, and a great longing for the time to come when I shall join those whom I loved so much on earth. Not to be happy at once by any manner of means. I am too sinful a mortal for that, but "to work out my salvation" in the way God sees best for me, to make my own Heaven or hell according as I have loved and succoured my fellow-creatures here below. Yet however much I may be destined to suffer, never without hope and assistance from those whom I have loved, and never without feeling that through the goodness of God each struggle or reparation brings me near to the fruition of eternal happiness. *This* is my belief, *this* is the good that the certain knowledge that we can never die has done for me, and the worst I wish for anybody is that they may share it with me.